Hugh Blair

Sermons

Volume the First

Hugh Blair

Sermons

Volume the First

ISBN/EAN: 9783337087845

Printed in Europe, USA, Canada, Australia, Japan

Cover: Foto ©Lupo / pixelio.de

More available books at **www.hansebooks.com**

HUGH BLAIR, D. D.

One of the MINISTERS of the HIGH CHURCH,

AND

PROFESSOR of RHETORIC and BELLES LETTRES in the UNIVERSITY, of EDINBURGH.

To which is prefixed, that admired Tract

ON THE

INTERNAL EVIDENCE

OF THE

CHRISTIAN RELIGION.

BY SOAME JENYNS,
Of the British Parliament.

VOLUME THE FIRST.

THE SIXTEENTH EDITION.

‹

===

LONDON, Printed:—
BALTIMORE: Re-printed, for the Rev. M. L. WEEMS,
by SAMUEL and JOHN ADAMS, Book-Printers, in
Market-street, between South and Gay-streets.

M DCC XCII.

VIEW

OF THE

INTERNAL EVIDENCE

OF THE

CHRISTIAN RELIGION.

MOST of the writers, who have undertaken to prove the divine origin of the Chriftian Religion, have had recourfe to arguments drawn from thefe three heads: the prophecies ftill extant in the Old Teftament, the miracles recorded in the New, or the internal evidence arifing from that excellence, and thofe clear marks of fupernatural interpofition, which are fo confpicuous in the religion itfelf: The two former have been fufficiently explained and enforced by the ableft pens; but the laft, which feems to carry with it the greateft degree of conviction, has never, I think, been confidered with that attention which it deferves.

I mean not here to depreciate the proofs arifing from either prophecies, or miracles: they both have or ought to have their proper weight; prophecies are permanent miracles, whofe authority is fufficiently confirmed by their completion, and are therefore folid proofs of the fupernatural origin of a religion, whofe truth they were intended to teftify; fuch are thofe to be found in various parts of the fcriptures relative to the coming of the Meffiah, the deftruction of Jerufalem, and the unexampled ftate in which the Jews have ever fince continued, all fo circumftantially defcriptive of the events, that they feem rather hiftories of paft, than predictions of future tranfactions;

and

and whoever will seriously consider the immense distance of time between some of them, and the events which they foretel, the uninterrupted chain by which they are connected for many thousand years, how exactly they correspond with those events, and how totally unapplicable they are to all others in the history of mankind; I say, whoever considers these circumstances, he will scarcely be persuaded to believe, that they can be the productions of preceding artifice, or posterior application, or can entertain the least doubt of their being derived from supernatural inspiration.

The miracles recorded in the New Testament to have been performed by Christ and his Apostles, were certainly convincing proofs of their divine commission to those who saw them; and as they were seen by such numbers, and are as well attested, as other historical facts, and above all, as they were wrought on so great and so wonderful an occasion, they must still be admitted as evidence of no inconsiderable force. To prove therefore the truth of the Christian Religion, we shall begin by shewing the internal marks of Divinity, which are stamped upon it.

What pure Christianity is, divested of all its ornaments, appendages, and corruption, I pretend not to say; but what it is not, I will venture to affirm, which is, that it is *not* the offspring of fraud or fiction: such on a superficial view, I know it must appear to every man whose thoughts have been altogether employed on other subjects; but if any one will give himself the trouble to examine it with accuracy and candour, he will plainly see that however fraud and fiction may have grown up with it, yet it never could have been grafted on the same stock, nor planted by the same hand.

To ascertain the true system, and genuine doctrines of this religion, and to remove all the rubbish, which artifice and ignorance have been heaping upon it during the long run of seventeen hundred years, would indeed be an arduous task, which I shall by no means undertake; but to shew, that it cannot possibly be derived from human wisdom, or human imposture, is a work, I think, attended with no great difficulty, and requiring no extraordinary abilities, and therefore I shall attempt that, and that alone, by stating, and then explaining the following plain, and undeniable propositions.

First, That there is now extant, a book, intitled, the New Testament.

Secondly, That from this book may be extracted a system of religion entirely new, both with regard to the object and the doctrines, not only infinitely superior to, but unlike every thing, which had ever before entered into the mind of man.

Thirdly, That from this book may likewise be collected a system of ethicks, in which every moral precept founded on reason is carried to a higher degree of purity and perfection, than in any other of the wisest philosophers of preceding ages; every moral precept founded on false principles is totally omitted, and many new precepts added peculiarly corresponding with the new objects of this religion.

Lastly, That such a system of religion and morality could not possibly have been the work of any man, or set of men; much less of those obscure, ignorant, and illiterate persons, who actually did discover, and publish it to the world; and that therefore it must undoubtedly have been effected by the interposition of divine power, that is, that it must derive its origin from God.

PROPOSITION I.

VERY little need be said, to establish my first proposition, which is singly this: that there is now extant, a book, intitled, the New Testament: that is, there is a collection of writings distinguished by that denomination, containing four historical accounts of the birth, life, actions, discourses and death of an extraordinary person named Jesus Christ, who was born in the reign of Augustus Cæsar, preached a new religion throughout the country of Judæa, and was put to a cruel and ignominious death in the reign of Tiberius. Also one other historical account of the travels, transactions, and orations of some mean and illiterate men, known by the title of his Apostles, whom he commissioned to propagate his religion after his death; which he foretold them he must suffer in confirmation of its truth. To these are added several epistles, addressed by these persons to their fellow-labourers in this work, or to the several churches or societies of christians, which they had established in the several cities through which they had passed.

It would not be difficult to prove, that these books were written soon after those extraordinary events, which are the subjects of them; as we find them quoted, and referred to by an uninterrupted succession of writers from those to the present times: nor would it be less easy to shew, that the truth of all those events, miracles only excepted, can no more be reasonably questioned, than the truth of any other facts recorded in any history whatever: as there can be no more reason to doubt, that there existed such a person as Jesus Christ, speaking, acting, and suffering in such a manner as is there described, than that there were such men as Tiberius, Herod, or Pontius Pilate, his cotemporaries; or to suspect that Peter, Paul and James, were not the authors of those epistles, to which their names are affixed, than that Cicero and Pliny did not write those which are ascribed to them. It might also be made appear, that these books having been wrote by various persons at different times, and in distant places, could not possibly have been the work of a single impostor, nor of a fraudulent combination, being all stamped with the same marks of an uniform originality in their very frame and composition.

But all these circumstances I shall pass over unobserved, as they do not fall in with the course of my argument, nor are necessary for the support of it. All that I assert is a plain fact, which cannot be denied, that such writings do now exist.

PROPOSITION II.

MY second proposition is not quite so simple, but I think, not less undeniable than the former, and is this: That from this book may be extracted a system of religion entirely new, both with regard to the object, and the doctrines, not only infinitely superior to, but totally unlike every thing which had ever before entered into the mind of man.

First then, The object of this religion is entirely new, and is this, to prepare us by a state of probation for the kingdom of heaven. This is every where professed by Christ and his Apostles to be the chief end of the christian's life; the crown for which he is to contend, the goal to which he is to run, the harvest which is to pay him for all his labours: Yet previous to their preaching, no such prize was ever hung out to mankind, nor any means prescribed for the attainment of it.

It is indeed true, that some of the philosophers of antiquity entertained notions of a future state, but mixed with much doubt and uncertainty: their legislators also endeavoured to infuse into the minds of the people a belief of rewards and punishments after death; but by this they only intended to give a sanction to their laws, and to enforce the practice of virtue for the benefit of mankind in the present life; this alone seems to have been their end, and a meritorious end it was; but Christianity not only operates more effectually to this end, but has a nobler design in view, which is by a proper education here to render us fit members of a celestial society hereafter. In all former religions

religions, the good of the present life was the *first* object; in the Christian it is but the *second*; in *those*, men were incited to promote that good by the hopes of a *future reward*; in this the practice of virtue is enjoined in order to *qualify* them for that reward. There is great difference, I apprehend, in these two plans, that is, an adhering to virtue from its present utility in expectation of future happiness; and this, living in such a manner as to qualify us for the acceptance and enjoyment of that happiness; and the conduct and dispositions of those who act on these different principles, must be no less different; on the first, the constant practice of justice, temperance, and sobriety, will be sufficient; but on the latter, we must add to these an habitual piety, faith, resignation, and contempt of the world: the first may make us very good citizens, but will never produce a tolerable christian. Hence it is that christianity insists more strongly, than any preceding institution, religious or moral, on purity of heart and a benevolent disposition; because these are absolutely necessary to its great end; but in those whose recommendations of virtue regard the present life only, and whose promised rewards in another were low and sensual, no preparatory qualifications were requisite to enable men to practise the one, or to enjoy the other; and therefore we see this object is peculiar to this religion; and with it was entirely new.

But although this object, and the principle on which it is founded were new, and perhaps undiscoverable by reason, yet when discovered, they are so consonant to it, that we cannot but readily assent to them. For the truth of this principle, that the present life is a state of probation, and education to prepare us for another, is confirmed by every thing which we see around us: It is the only key which can open to us the designs of Providence in the œconomy of human affairs, the only clue, which can guide us through that pathless wilderness, and the only plan on which this world could possibly have been formed, or on which the history of it can be comprehended or explained. It could never have been formed on a plan of happiness, because it is every where overspread with innumerable miseries; nor of misery, because it is interspersed with many enjoyments: It could not have been constituted for a scene of wisdom and virtue, because the history of mankind is little more than a detail of their follies, and wickedness: Nor of vice, because that is no plan at all, being destructive of all existence, and consequently of its own: But on this system all that we here meet with, may be easily accounted for; for this mixture of happiness and misery, of virtue and vice, necessarily results from a state of probation and education; as probation

* implies

implies trials, sufferings and a capacity of offending; and education a propriety of a chastisement for those offences.

In the next place the doctrines of this religion are equally new with the object, and contain ideas of God, and of man, of the present, and of a future life; and of the relations which all these bear to each other totally unheard of, and quite dissimilar from any which had ever been thought on, previous to its publication. No other ever drew so just a portrait of the worthlessness of this world, and all its pursuits, nor exhibited such distinct, lively and exquisite pictures of the joys of another; of the resurrection of the dead, the last judgment, and the triumphs of the righteous in that tremendous day; "when this corruptible shall put on incorruption, and this mortal shall put on immortality." * No other has ever represented the Supreme Being in the character of three persons united in one God. † No other has attempted to reconcile those seeming contradictory but both true propositions, the contingency of future events, and the foreknowledge of God, or the free-will of the creature with the overruling grace of the Creator. No other has so fully declared the necessity of wickedness and punishment, yet so effectually instructed individuals to resist the one, and to escape the other; no other has ever pretended to give any account of the depravity of man, or to point out any remedy for it; no other has ventured to declare the unpardonable nature of sin without the influence of a mediatorial interposition, and a vicarious atonement from the sufferings of a superior Being. ‡ These wonderful doctrines are all so far removed from every tract of the human imagination, that it seems equally impossible, that they should ever have been derived from the knowledge, or the artifice of man.

Some

* 1-Cor. xv. 53.

† *That there subsists some such union in the divine nature, the whole tenor of the New Testament seems to express, and it was so understood in the earliest ages: But how this union subsists we are not informed, and therefore on these questions it is not only unnecessary, but improper for us to decide.*

‡ *That Christ suffered and died as an atonement for the sins of mankind, is a doctrine so constantly and so strongly enforced through every part of the New Testament, that whoever will seriously peruse those writings, and deny that it is there, may, with as much reason and truth, after reading the works of Thucydides and Livy, assert, that in them no mention is made of any facts relative to the histories of Greece and Rome.*

Some indeed there are, who by perverting the established signification of words (which they call explaining) have ventured to expunge all these doctrines out of the scriptures, for no other reason than that they are not able to comprehend them; and argue thus:—The scriptures are the word of God; in his word no propositions contradictory to reason can have a place; these propositions are contradictory to reason, and therefore they are not there: But if these bold assertors would claim any regard, they should reverse their argument, and say,—These doctrines make a part, and a material part of the scriptures, they are contradictory to reason; no propositions contradictory to reason can be a part of the word of God, and therefore neither the scriptures, nor the pretended revelation contained in them, can be derived from him: This would be an argument worthy of rational and candid Deists, and demand a respectful attention; but when men pretend to disprove facts by reasoning, they have no right to expect an answer.

And here I cannot omit observing, that the personal character of the author of this religion is no less new, and extraordinary, than the religion itself, who " spake as never man spake,"* and lived as never man lived: For instance, he is the only founder of a religion in the history of mankind, which is totally unconnected with all human policy and government; and therefore totally unconducive to any worldly purpose whatever: All others, Mahomet, Numa, and even Moses himself, blended their religious institutions with their civil, and by them obtained dominion over their respective people; but Christ neither aimed at, nor would accept of any such power; he rejected every object, which all other men pursue, and made choice of all those which others fly from, and are afraid of: He refused power, riches, honours and pleasure, and courted poverty, ignominy, tortures, and death. Many have been the enthusiasts and impostors, who have endeavoured to impose on the world pretended revelations, and some of them from pride, obstinacy, or principle, have gone so far as to lay down their lives, rather than retract; but I defy history to shew one, who ever made his own sufferings and death a *necessary part* of his *original plan*, and essential to his mission: This Christ actually did; he *foresaw, foretold, declared*, their *necessity*, and *voluntarily* endured them. If we seriously contemplate the divine lessons, the perfect precepts, the beautiful discourses, and the consistent conduct of this wonderful person, we cannot avoid exclaiming in a tran-

B   sport

* *John* vii. 46.

sport of holy joy and grateful affection, Surely thou art the Son of God; verily thou art the Friend of sinners.

If any one can doubt of the superior excellence of this religion above all which preceded it, let him but peruse with attention those unparalleled writings in which it is transmitted to the present times, and compare them with the most celebrated productions of the Pagan world; and if he is not sensible of their superior beauty, simplicity, and originality, I will venture to pronounce, that he is as deficient in Taste as in Faith, and that he is as bad a Critic as a Christian; for in what school of ancient philosophy can he find a lesson of morality so perfect as Christ's sermon on the mount? From which of them can he collect an address to the Deity so concise, and yet so comprehensive of all that we want, and all that we could deprecate, as that short prayer, which he formed for, and recommended to his disciples? From the works of what sage of antiquity can he produce so pathetic a recommendation of benevolence to the distressed, and enforced by such assurances of a reward, as in those words of Christ? " Come, ye blessed of my Father! inherit the kingdom prepared for " you from the foundation of the world: for I was an hungred, and " ye gave me meat; I was thirsty, and ye gave me drink; I was a strang- " er, and ye took me in ; I was naked, and ye cloathed me ; I was " sick, and ye visited me ; I was in prison, and ye came unto me. " Then shall the righteous answer him, saying:—Lord, when saw we " thee an hungred, and fed thee, or thirsty, and gave thee drink ? " When saw we thee a stranger, and took thee in, or naked, and " cloathed thee ? Or when saw we thee sick and in prison, and came " unto thee ? Then shall I answer and say unto them :—Verily I say " unto you, inasmuch as you have done it to the least of these my " brethren, ye have done it unto me." * Where is there so just, and so elegant a reproof of eagerness and anxiety in worldly pursuits, closed with so forcible an exhortation to confidence in the goodness of our Creator, as in these words?—" Behold the fowls of the air; " for they sow not, neither do they reap, nor gather into barns, yet " your heavenly Father feedeth them. Are ye not much better than " they? Consider the lilies of the field, how they grow; they toil " not, neither do they spin; and yet I say unto you, that even So- " lomon in all his glory was not arrayed like one of these: where- " fore, if God so clothe the grass of the field, which to-day is, and " to-morrow is cast into the oven, shall he not much more clothe " you? O ye of little faith!" † By which of their most celebrated poets

* *Matt.* xxv. 34. † *Matt.* vi. 26, 28.

poets are the joys reserved for the righteous in a future state, so sublimely described, as by this short declaration, that they are superior to all description? " Eye hath not seen, nor ear heard, neither have " entered into the heart of man, the things which God hath pre-" pared for them that love him."* Where amidst the dark clouds of pagan philosophy can he shew us such a clear prospect of a future state, the immortality of the soul, the resurrection of the dead, and the general judgment, as in St. Paul's first epistle to the Corinthians? Or from whence can he produce such cogent exhortations to the practice of every virtue, such ardent incitements to piety and devotion, and such assistances to attain them, as those which are to be met with throughout every page of these inimitable writings? To quote all the passages in them relative to these subjects, would be almost to transcribe the whole; it is sufficient to observe, that they are every where stamped with such apparent marks of supernatural assistance, as render them indisputably superior to, and totally unlike all human compositions whatever; and this superiority and dissimilarity is still more strongly marked by one remarkable circumstance peculiar to themselves, which is, that whilst the *moral* parts, being of the most general use, are intelligible to the *meanest* capacities, the *learned* and *inquisitive* throughout all ages, perpetually find in them inexhaustible discoveries, concerning the nature, attributes, and dispensations of Providence.

To say the truth, before the appearance of Christianity there existed nothing like religion on the face of the earth; the Jewish only excepted: all other nations were immersed in the grossest idolatry, which had little or no connection with morality, except to corrupt it by the infamous examples of their imaginary deities: they all worshipped a multiplicity of gods and dæmons, whose favour they courted by impious, obscene, and ridiculous ceremonies, and whose anger they endeavoured to appease by the most abominable cruelties. For a full view of this important subject, see the excellent Dr. Leland's admirable books on REVELATION. In the politest ages of the politest nations in the world, at a time when Greece and Rome had carried the arts of oratory, poetry, history, architecture and sculpture to the highest perfection, and made no inconsiderable advances in those of mathematics, natural, and even moral philosophy, in religious knowledge they had made none at all; a strong presumption, that the noblest efforts of the mind of man unassisted by revelation were unequal to the task. Some few indeed of their philosophers

* 1 *Cor.* ii. 9.

lofophers were wife enough to reject thefe general abfurdities, and dared to attempt a loftier flight: Plato introduced many fublime ideas, of nature, and its firft caufe, and of the immortality of the foul, which being above his own and all human difcovery, he probably acquired from the books of Mofes or the converfation of fome Jewifh rabbies, which he might have met with in Egypt, where he refided, and ftudied for feveral years: From him Ariftotle, and from both Cicero and fome few others drew moft amazing ftores of philofophical fcience, and carried their refearches into divine truths as far as human genius alone could penetrate. But thefe were bright conftellations which appeared fingly in feveral centuries, and even thefe with all this knowledge were very deficient in true theology. From the vifible works of the Creation they traced the being and principal attributes of the Creator; but the relation which his being and attributes bear to man they little underftood; of piety and devotion they had fcarce any fenfe, nor could they form any mode of worfhip worthy of the purity and perfection of the divine nature: They occafionally flung out many elegant encomiums on the native beauty, and excellence of virtue: but they founded it not on the commands of God, nor connected it with a holy life, nor hung out the happinefs of heaven as its reward, or its object. They fometimes talked of virtue carrying men to heaven, and placing them amongft the gods; but by this virtue they meant only the invention of arts, or feats of arms: for with them heaven was open only to legiflators, and conquerors, the civilizers, or deftroyers of mankind. This was then the fummit of religion in the moft polifhed nations in the world; and even this was confined to a few philofophers, prodigies of genius and literature, who were little attended to, and lefs underftood by the generality of mankind in their own countries; whilft all the reft were involved in one common cloud of ignorance and fuperftition.

At this time Chriftianity broke forth from the eaft like a rifing-fun, and difpelled this univerfal darknefs, which obfcured every part of the globe, and even at this day prevails in all thofe remoter regions, to which its falutary influence has not as yet extended. From all thofe which it has reached, it has, notwithftanding its corruptions, banifhed all thofe enormities, and introduced a more rational devotion, and purer morals: It has taught men the unity, and attributes of the Supreme Being, the remiffion of fins, the refurrection of the dead, life everlafting, and the kingdom of heaven; doctrines as inconceivable to the wifeft of mankind antecedent to its appearance, as the Newtonian fyftem is at this day to the moft ignorant tribes of favages

vages in the wilds of America; doctrines which human reason never could have discovered, but which when discovered, coincide with, and are confirmed by it; and which, though beyond the reach of all the learning and penetration of Plato, Aristotle, and Cicero, are now clearly laid open to the eye of every peasant and mechanic with the Bible in his hand. These are all plain facts too glaring to be contradicted, and therefore, of these facts no man, who has eyes to read, or ears to hear, can entertain a doubt; because there are the books, and in them is this religion.

PROPOSITION III.

MY third proposition is this: that from this book called the New Testament, may be collected a system of ethics, in which every moral precept founded on reason is carried to a higher degree of purity and perfection, than in any of the ancient philosophers of preceding ages; every moral precept founded on false principles is entirely omitted, and many new precepts added, peculiarly corresponding with the new object of this religion.

By moral precepts founded on reason, I mean all those, which enforce the practice of such duties as reason informs us must improve our natures, and conduce to the happiness of mankind: such are piety to God, benevolence to men, justice, charity, temperance, and sobriety, with all those, which prohibit the commission of the contrary vices, all which debase our natures, and, by mutual injuries, introduce universal disorder, and consequently universal misery. By precepts founded on false principles, I mean those which recommend fictitious virtues productive of none of these salutary effects, and therefore, however celebrated and admired, are in fact no virtues at all; such are valour, patriotism, and friendship.

That virtues of the first kind are carried to a higher degree of purity and perfection by the christian religion than by any other, it is here unnecessary to prove, because this is a truth, which has been so frequently demonstrated by her friends, and never once denied by the most determined of her adversaries; but it will be proper to shew, that those of the latter sort are most judiciously omitted; because they have really no intrinsic merit in them, and are totally incompatible with the genius and spirit of this institution.

Valour, for instance, or active courage, is for the most part constitutional, and therefore can have no more claim to moral merit, than wit, beauty, health, strength, or any other endowment of the mind or body; and so far is it from producing any salutary effects by intro-

ducing

ducing peace, order, or happiness into society, that it is the usual perpetrator of all the violences, which from retaliated injuries distract the world with bloodshed and devastation. It is the engine by which the strong are enabled to plunder the weak, the proud to trample upon the humble, and the guilty to oppress the innocent; it is the chief instrument which Ambition employs in her unjust pursuits of wealth and power, and is therefore so much extolled by her votaries: it was indeed congenial with the religion of pagans, whose gods were for the most part made out of deceased heroes, exalted to heaven, as a reward for the mischiefs which they had perpetrated upon earth, and therefore with them this was the first of virtues, and had even engrossed that denomination to itself; but whatever merit it may have assumed among pagans, with christians it can pretend to none, and few or none are the occasions in which they are permitted to exert it: they are so far from being allowed to inflict evil, that they are forbid even to resist it; they are so far from being encouraged to revenge injuries, that one of their first duties is to forgive them; so far from being incited to destroy their enemies, that they are commanded to love them, and to serve them to the utmost of their power. If christian nations therefore were nations of christians, all war would be impossible and unknown amongst them, and valour could be neither of use or estimation, and therefore could never have a place in the catalogue of christian virtues, being irreconcileable with all its precepts. I object not to the praise and honours bestowed on the valiant, they are the least tribute which can be paid them by those who enjoy safety and affluence by the intervention of their dangers and sufferings; I assert only, that active courage can never be a christian virtue, because a christian can have nothing to do with it. Passive courage is indeed frequently, and properly inculcated by this meek and suffering religion, under the titles of patience and resignation: a real and substantial virtue this, and a direct contrast to the former; for passive courage arises from the noblest dispositions of the human mind, from a contempt of misfortunes, pain, and death, and a confidence in the protection of the Almighty; active from the meanest: from passion, vanity, and self-dependence: passive courage is derived from a zeal for truth, and a perseverance in duty; active is the offspring of pride and revenge, and the parent of cruelty and injustice: in short, passive courage is the resolution of a philosopher, active is the ferocity of a savage. Nor is this more incompatible with the precepts, than with the object of this religion, which is the attainment of the kingdom of heaven; for valour is not that sort of vio-

lence

lence, by which that kingdom is to be taken ; nor are the turbulent spirits of heroes and conquerors admiſſible into thoſe regions of peace, ſubordination and tranquility.

Patriotiſm alſo, that celebrated virtue ſo much practiſed in ancient, and ſo much profeſſed in modern times, that virtue, which ſo long preſerved the liberties of Greece, and exalted Rome to the empire of the world : this celebrated virtue, I ſay, muſt alſo be excluded ; becauſe it not only falls ſhort of, but directly counteracts, the extenſive Benevolence of this religion. A chriſtian is of no country, he is a citizen of the world ; and his neighbours and country-men are the inhabitants of the remoteſt regions, whenever their diſtreſſes demand his friendly aſſiſtance : Chriſtianity commands us to love all mankind, Patriotiſm to oppreſs all other countries to advance the imaginary proſperity of our own : Chriſtianity enjoins us to imitate the univerſal benevolence of our Creator, who pours forth his bleſſings on every nation upon earth ; Patriotiſm to copy the mean partiality of an Engliſh pariſh officer, who thinks injuſtice and cruelty meritorious, whenever they promote the intereſts of his own inconſiderable village. This has ever been a favourite virtue with mankind, becauſe it conceals ſelf-intereſt under the maſk of public ſpirit, not only from others, but even from themſelves, and gives a licenſe to inflict wrongs and injuries, not only with impunity, but with applauſe ; but it is ſo diametrically oppoſite to the great characteriſtic of this inſtitution, that it never could have been admitted into the liſt of chriſtian virtues.

Friendſhip likewiſe, although more congenial to the principles of Chriſtianity ariſing from more tender and amiable diſpoſitions, could never gain admittance amongſt her benevolent precepts for the ſame reaſon ; becauſe it is too narrow and confined, and appropriates that benevolence to a ſingle object, which is here commanded to be extended over all : Where friendſhips ariſe from ſimilarity of ſentiments, and diſintereſted affections, they are advantageous, agreeable, and innocent, but have little pretenſions to merit ; for it is juſtly obſerved, " If ye love them, which love you, what thanks have ye ? for ſinners " alſo love thoſe, that love them." * But if they are formed from alliances in parties, factions and intereſts, or from a participation of vices, the uſual parents of what are called friendſhips among mankind, they are then both miſchievous and criminal, and conſequently forbidden, but in their utmoſt purity deſerve no recommendation from this religion.

To the judicious omiſſion of theſe falſe virtues we may add that remarkable ſilence, which the Chriſtian Legiſlator every where preſerves

* Luke vi. 32.

on subjects esteemed by all others of the highest importance, civil government, national policy, and the rights of war and peace; of these he has not taken the least notice, probably for this plain reason, because it would have been impossible to have formed any explicit regulations concerning them, which must not have been inconsistent with the purity of his religion, or with the practical observance of such imperfect creatures as men ruling over, and contending with each other: For instance, had he absolutely forbid all resistance to the reigning powers, he had constituted a plan of despotism, and made men slaves; had he allowed it, he must have authorised disobedience, and made them rebels: had he in direct terms prohibited all war, he must have left his followers forever an easy prey to every infidel invader; had he permitted it, he must have licensed all that rapine and murder, with which it is unavoidably attended.

Let us now examine what are those new precepts in this religion peculiarly corresponding with the new object of it, that is preparing us for the kingdom of heaven: Of these the chief are poorness of spirit, forgiveness of injuries, and charity to all men; to these we may add repentance, faith, self-abasement, and a detachment from the world, all moral duties peculiar to this religion, and absolutely necessary to the attainment of its end.

" Blessed are the poor in spirit; for theirs is the kingdom of heaven." * By which poorness of spirit is to be understood a disposition of mind, meek, humble, submissive to power, void of ambition, patient of injuries, and free from all resentment: This was so new, and so opposite to the ideas of all Pagan moralists, that they thought this temper of mind a criminal and contemptible meanness, which must induce men to sacrifice the glory of their country, and their own honour, to a shameful pusillanimity; and such it appears to almost all who are called Christians even at this day, who not only reject it in practice, but disavow it in principle, notwithstanding this explicit declaration of their Master. We see them revenging the smallest affronts by premeditated murder, as individuals, on principles of honour; and, in their national capacities, destroying each other with fire and sword, for the low considerations of commercial interests, the balance of rival powers, or the ambition of princes: We see them with their last breath animating each other to a savage revenge, and, in the agonies of death, plunging with feeble arms their daggers into the hearts of their opponents: and, what is still worse, we hear all these barbarisms celebrated by historians, flattered by poets, applauded in theatres, approved in senates, and even sanctified in pulpits. But universal

* *Matt.* v. 3.

univerfal practice cannot alter the nature of things, nor univerfal error change the nature of truth: Pride was not made for man, but humility, meeknefs and refignation; that is, poornefs of fpirit was made for man, and properly belongs to his dependent and precarious fituation; and is the only difpofition of mind which can enable him to enjoy eafe and quiet here, and happinefs hereafter: Yet was this important precept entirely unknown until it was promulgated by him, who faid, " Suffer little children to come unto me, and forbid " them not; for of fuch is the kingdom of heaven: Verily I fay " unto you, whoever fhall not receive the kingdom of God as a little child, he fhall not enter therein." *

Another precept, equally new and no lefs excellent, is forgivenefs of injuries: " Ye have heard," fays Chrift to his difciples, " Thou " fhalt love thy neighbour, and hate thine enemy; but I fay unto " you, love your enemies; blefs them that curfe you, do good to " them that hate you, and pray for them which defpitefully ufe you, " and perfecute you." † This was a leffon fo new, and fo utterly unknown, 'till taught by his doctrines, and enforced by his example, that the wifeft moralifts of the wifeft nations and ages reprefented the defire of revenge as a mark of a noble mind, and the accomplifhment of it, as one of the chief felicities attendant on a fortunate man. But how much more magnanimous, how much more beneficial to mankind, is forgivenefs! it is more magnanimous, becaufe every generous and exalted difpofition of the human mind is requifite to the practice of it: for thefe alone can enable us to bear the wrongs and infults of wickednefs and folly with patience, and to look down on the perpetrators of them with pity, rather than indignation; thefe alone can teach us, that fuch are but a part of thofe fufferings allotted to us in this ftate of probation, and to know, that to overcome evil with good, is the moft glorious of all victories: it is the moft beneficial, becaufe this amiable conduct alone can put an end to an eternal fucceffion of injuries and retaliations; for every retaliation becomes a new injury, and requires another act of revenge for fatisfaction. But would we obferve this falutary precept, to love our enemies, and to do good to thofe who defpitefully ufe us, this obftinate benevolence would at laft conquer the moft inveterate hearts, and we fhould have no enemies to forgive. How much more exalted a character therefore is a Chriftian martyr, fuffering with refignation, and praying for the guilty, than that of a Pagan hero, breathing revenge, and deftroying the innocent! Yet noble, and ufeful as this virtue is, before the appearance of this religion it was not only unpractifed, but decried in principle as mean and ignominious, though

* *Matt.* x. 14.   † *Matt.* v. 43.

so obvious a remedy for most of the miseries of this life, and so necessary a qualification for the happiness of another.

A third precept, first noticed, and first enjoined by this institution, is charity to all men. What this is, we may best learn from this admirable description, painted in the following words: "Charity "suffereth long, and is kind; charity envieth not; charity vaunteth "not itself; is not puffed up; doth not behave itself unseemly; "doth not eagerly and contentiously seek her own; is not easily pro- "voked; thinketh no evil; rejoiceth not in iniquity, but rejoiceth "in truth; beareth all things; believeth all things; hopeth all "things; endureth all things." * Here we have an accurate delineation of this bright constellation of all virtues, which consists not, as many imagine, in the building of monasteries, endowment of hospitals, or the distribution of alms, but in such an amiable disposition of mind, as exercises itself every hour in acts of kindness, patience, complacency, and benevolence to all around us, and which alone is able to promote happiness in the present life, or render us capable of receiving it in another: and yet this is totally new, and so it is declared to be by the Author of it: "A new commandment I give "unto you, that ye love one another;—as I have loved you, that "ye love one another; by this shall all men know, that ye are my "disciples, if ye have love one to another." † This benevolent disposition is made the great characteristic of a christian, the test of his obedience, and the mark by which he is to be distinguished. This love for each other is that charity just now described, and contains all those qualities which are there attributed to it; humility, patience, meekness, and beneficence: without which we must live in perpetual discord, and consequently cannot pay obedience to this commandment by loving one another; a commandment so sublime, so rational, and so beneficial, so wisely calculated to correct the depravity, diminish the wickedness, and abate the miseries of human nature, that, did we universally comply with it, we should soon be relieved from all the inquietudes arising from our own unruly passions, anger, envy, revenge, malice and ambition, as well as from all those injuries to which we are perpetually exposed from the indulgence of the same passions in others. It would also preserve our minds in such a state of tranquility, and so prepare them for the kingdom of heaven, that we should slide out of a life of peace and love into that celestial society, by an almost imperceptible transition. Yet was this commandment entirely new, when given by him, who so entitles it, and has made it the capital duty of his religion, because the most
indispensably

* 1 Cor. xiii. 4. † John xiii. 34.

indifpenfably neceffary to the attainment of its great object, the kingdom of heaven; into which if proud, turbulent and vindictive fpirits were permitted to enter, they muft unavoidably deftroy the happinefs of that ftate by the operations of the fame paffions and vices, by which they difturb the prefent, and therefore all fuch muft be eternally excluded, not only as a punifhment, but alfo from incapacity.

Repentance by this we plainly fee, is another new moral duty ftrenuoufly infifted on by this religion, and by no other, becaufe abfolutely neceffary to the accomplifhment of its end; which is to purge and purify us from that depravity in our nature which renders us incapable of enjoying the heavenly happinefs. Hence alfo we may learn, that no repentance can remove this incapacity, but fuch as entirely changes the nature and difpofition of the offender; which in the language of Scripture is called "being born again." Mere contrition for paft crimes, nor even the pardon of them, cannot effect this, unlefs it operates to this entire converfion or new birth, as it is properly and emphatically named: for forrow can no more purify a mind corrupted by a long continuance in vicious habits, than it can reftore health to a body diftempered by a long courfe of vice and intemperance. Hence alfo every one, who is in the leaft acquainted with himfelf, may judge of the reafonablenefs of the hope that is in him, and of his fituation in a future ftate by that of his prefent. If he feels in himfelf a temper proud, turbulent, vindictive, and malevolent, and a violent attachment to the pleafures or bufinefs of the world, he may be affured that he muft be excluded from the kingdom of heaven; not only becaufe his conduct can merit no fuch reward, but becaufe, if admitted, he would find there no objects fatisfactory to his paffions, inclinations, and purfuits, and therefore could only difturb the happinefs of others without enjoying any fhare of it himfelf.

Faith is another moral duty enjoined by this inftitution, of a fpecies fo new, that the philofophers of antiquity had no word expreffive of this idea, nor any fuch idea to be expreffed; for the word *piftis* or *fides*, which we tranflate faith, was never ufed by any Pagan writer in a fenfe the leaft fimilar to that to which it is applied in the New Teftament: where in general it fignifies an humble, teachable, and candid difpofition, a truft in God, and confidence in his promifes: when applied particularly to chriftianity, it means no more than a belief of this fingle propofition, that Chrift was the Son of God; that is, in the language of thofe writings, the Meffiah, who was foretold

by

by the prophets, and expected by the Jews; who was sent by God into the world to preach righteousness, judgment, and everlasting life, and to die as an atonement for the sins of mankind. This was all that Christ required to be believed by those who were willing to become his disciples: he, who does not believe this, is not a Christian, and he who does, believes the whole that is essential to his profession, and all that is properly comprehended under the name of faith. This unfortunate word has indeed been so tortured and so misapplied, to mean every absurdity, which artifice could impose upon ignorance, that it has lost all pretensions to the title of virtue; but if brought back to the simplicity of its original signification, it well deserves that name, because it usually arises from the most amiable dispositions, and is always a direct contrast to pride, obstinacy, and self-conceit. If taken in the extensive sense of an assent to the evidence of things not seen, it comprehends the belief of the existence of a God, and a future state, and the absolute necessity of divine and social affections; and is therefore not only itself a moral virtue, but the source from whence all others must proceed; for on the belief of these all religion and morality must entirely depend. It cannot be altogether void of moral merit (as some would represent it) because it is in a degree voluntary; for daily experience shews us, that men not only pretend to, but actually do believe, and disbelieve almost any propositions, which best suit their interests, or inclinations, and unfeignedly change their sincere opinions with their situations and circumstances. For we have power over the mind's eye, as well as over the body's, to shut it against the strongest rays of truth and religion, whenever they become painful to us, and to open it again to the faint glimmerings of scepticism and infidelity when we "love darkness rather than light, because our deeds are evil."* And this, I think, sufficiently refutes all objections to the moral nature of faith, drawn from the supposition of its being quite involuntary, and necessarily dependent on the degree of evidence, which is offered to our understandings.

Self-abasement is another moral duty inculcated by this religion only; which requires us to impute even our own virtues to the grace and favour of our Creator, and to acknowledge, that we can do nothing good by our own powers, unless assisted by his over-ruling influence: This doctrine seems at first sight to infringe on our freewill, and to deprive us of all merit; but, on a closer examination, the truth of it may be demonstrated both by reason and experience.

and

* John iii. 19.

and that in fact it does not impair the one, or depreciate the other: and that it is productive of so much humility, resignation and dependance on God, that it justly claims a place amongst the most illustrious moral virtues. Yet was this duty utterly repugnant to the proud and self-sufficient principles of the ancient philosophers, as well as modern Deists, and therefore before the publication of the gospel totally unknown and uncomprehended.

Detachment from the world is another moral virtue constituted by this religion alone: so new, that even at this day few of its professors can be persuaded that it is required, or that it is any virtue at all. By this detachment from the world is not to be understood a seclusion from society, abstraction from all business, or retirement to a gloomy cloyster. Industry and labour, chearfulness and hospitality, are frequently recommended: nor is the acquisition of wealth and honours prohibited, if they can be obtained by honest means, and a moderate degree of attention and care: but such an unremitted anxiety and perpetual application as engrosses our whole time and thoughts, are forbid, because they are incompatible with the spirit of this religion, and must utterly disqualify us for the attainment of its great end. We toil on in the vain pursuits and frivolous occupations of the world, die in our harness, and then expect, if no gigantic crime stands in the way, to step immediately into the kingdom of heaven: but this is impossible; for without a previous detachment from the business of this world, we cannot be prepared for the happiness of another. Yet this could make no part of the morality of Pagans, because their virtues were altogether connected with this business, and consisted chiefly in conducting it with honour to themselves, and benefit to the public: But Christianity has a nobler object in view, which if not attended to, must be lost for ever. This object is that celestial mansion of which we should never lose sight, and to which we should be ever advancing during our journey thro' life: but this by no means precludes us from performing the business, or enjoying the amusements of travellers, provided they detain us not too long, nor lead us too far out of our way.

It cannot be denied, that the great Author of the christian institution, first and singly ventured to oppose all the chief principles of Pagan virtue, and to introduce a religion directly opposite to those erroneous, though long-established, opinions, both in its duties and in its object. The most celebrated virtues of the ancients were high spirit, intrepid courage, and implacable resentment.

Impiger,

Impiger, iracundus, inexorabilis, acer,

was the portrait of the most illustrious Hero, drawn by one of the first poets of antiquity: To all these admired qualities, those of a true Christian are an exact contrast; for this religion constantly enjoins poorness of spirit, meekness, patience, and forgiveness of injuries, "But I say unto you, that ye resist not evil; but whoever shall smite thee on the right cheek, turn to him the other also."[*] The favourite characters among the Pagans were the turbulent, ambitious, and intrepid, who through toils and dangers acquired wealth, and spent it in luxury, magnificence, and corruption; but both these are equally adverse to the Christian system, which forbids all criminal extraordinary efforts to obtain wealth, care to secure, or thought concerning the enjoyment of it. "Lay not up for yourselves treasures on earth, &c." "Take no thought, saying, what shall we eat, or what shall we drink, or wherewithal shall we be clothed? for after all these things do the Gentiles seek."[†] The chief object of the Pagans was immortal fame: for this their poets sang, their heroes fought, and their patriots died; and this was hung out by their philosophers and legislators, as the great incitement to all noble and virtuous deeds. But what says the Christian Legislator to his disciples on this subject? "Blessed are ye, when men shall revile you, and shall say all manner of evil against you falsely for my sake; rejoice, and be exceeding glad, for great is your reward in heaven."[‡] So widely different is the genius of the Pagan and Christian morality, that I will venture to affirm, that the most celebrated virtues of the former are more opposite to the spirit, and more inconsistent with the end of the latter, than even their most infamous vices; and that a Brutus wrenching vengeance out of his hands to whom alone it belongs, by murdering the oppressor of his country, or a Cato murdering himself from an impatience of controul, leaves the world more unqualified for, and more inadmissible into the kingdom of heaven, than even a Messalina, or an Heliogabalus, with all their profligacy about them.

Nothing, I believe, has so much contributed to corrupt the true spirit of the Christian institution, as that partiality which we contract from our earliest education for the manners of Pagan antiquity; whence we learn to adopt every moral idea, which is repugnant to it; to applaud false virtues, which that disavows; to be guided by laws of honour, which that abhors; to imitate characters, which that detests;

[*] *Matt.* v. 39.   [†] *Matt.* vi. 31.   [‡] *Matt.* v. 11.

detests; and to behold heroes, conquerors, and suicides with admiration, whose conduct that utterly condemns. From a coalition of these opposite principles was generated that monstrous system of cruelty and benevolence, of barbarism and civility, of rapine and justice, of fighting and devotion, of revenge and generosity, which harassed the world for several centuries with crusades, holy wars, knight-errantry, and single combats, and even still retains influence enough under the name of honour to defeat the most beneficent ends of this holy institution; but those who have imbibed such sentiments, and act on such principles, have no claim to the amiable and divine character of Christians. A man, whose ruling principle is honour, however virtuous he may be, cannot be a Christian, because he erects a standard of duty, and deliberately adheres to it, diametrically opposite to the whole tenour of that religion.

The contrast between the Christian, and all other institutions, religious or moral, previous to its appearance, is sufficiently evident, and surely the superiority of the former is as little to be disputed; unless any one shall undertake to prove, that humility, patience, forgiveness, and benevolence are less amiable, and less beneficial qualities, than pride, turbulence, revenge and malignity: that the contempt of riches is less noble, than the acquisition by fraud and villany, or the distribution of them to the poor, less commendable than avarice or profusion; or that a real immortality in the kingdom of heaven is an object less exalted, less rational, and less worthy of pursuit, than an imaginary immortality in the applause of men: that worthless tribute, which the folly of one part of mankind pays to the wickedness of the other; a tribute, which a wise man ought always to despise, because a good man can scarce ever obtain.

CONCLUSION.

IF I mistake not, I have now fully established the truth of my three propositions.

First, That there is now extant a book entitled the New-Testament.

Secondly, That from this book may be extracted a system of religion entirely new; both in its object, and its doctrines, not only superior to, but totally unlike every thing which had ever before entered into the mind of man.

Thirdly, That from this book may likewise be collected a system of ethics, in which every moral precept founded on reason is carried

to

to a higher degree of purity and perfection, than in any other of the wisest philosophers of preceding ages; every moral precept founded on false principles totally omitted, and many new precepts added, peculiarly corresponding with the new object of this religion.

Every one of these propositions, I am persuaded, is incontrovertibly true; and if true, this short, but certain conclusion must inevitably follow: That such a system of religion and morality could not possibly have been the work of any man, or set of men, much less of those obscure, ignorant and illiterate persons who actually did discover, and publish it to the world; and that therefore it must have been effected by the supernatural interposition of divine power and wisdom; that is, that it must derive its origin from God.

This argument seems to me little short of demonstration, and is indeed founded on the very same reasoning by which the material world is proved to be the work of his invisible hand. We view with admiration the heavens and the earth, and all therein contained; we contemplate with amazement the minute bodies of animals too small for perception, and the immense planetary orbs too vast for immagination: We are certain that these cannot be the works of man; and therefore we conclude with reason, that they must be the productions of an omnipotent Creator. In the same manner we see here a scheme of religion and morality unlike and superior to all ideas of the human mind, equally impossible to have been discovered by the knowledge, as invented by the artifice of man; and therefore by the very same mode of reasoning, and with the same justice, we conclude, that it must derive its origin from the same omnipotent and omniscient Being.

Nor was the propagation of this religion less extraordinary than the religion itself, or less above the reach of all human power, than the discovery of it was above that of all human understanding. It is well known, that in the course of a very few years it was spread over all the principal parts of Asia and Europe, and this by the ministry only of an inconsiderable number of the most inconsiderable persons; that at this time Paganism was in the highest repute, believed universally by the vulgar, and patronised by the great; that the wisest men of the wisest nations assisted at its sacrifices, and consulted its oracles on the most important occasions: Whether these were the tricks of the priests or of the devil, is of no consequence, as they were both equally unlikely to be converted, or overcome; the fact is certain, that on the preaching of a few fishermen, their altars were deserted, and their deities were dumb. This miracle they undoubtedly performed, whatever we may think of the rest: and this is surely

sufficient

sufficient to prove the authority of their commiffion; and to convince us, that neither their undertaking nor the execution of it could poffibly be their own.

How much this divine inftitution has been corrupted, or how foon thefe corruptions began, how far it has been difcoloured by the falfe notions of illiterate ages, or blended with fictions by pious frauds, or how early thefe notions and fictions were introduced, no learning or fagacity is now able precifely to afcertain; but furely no man, who ferioufly confiders the excellence and novelty of its doctrines, the manner in which it was at firft propagated through the world, the perfons who achieved that wonderful work, and the originality of thofe writings in which it is ftill recorded, can poffibly believe that it could ever have been the production of impofture, or chance; or that from an impofture the moft wicked and blafphemous, (for if an impofture, fuch it is,) all the religion and virtue now exifting on earth can derive their fource.

But notwithftanding what has been here urged, if any man can believe, that at a time when the literature of Greece and Rome, then in their meridian luftre, were infufficient for the tafk, the fon of a carpenter, together with twelve of the meaneft and moft illiterate mechanics, his affociates, unaffifted by any fupernatural power, fhould be able to difcover or invent a fyftem of theology the moft fublime and of ethics the moft perfect, which had efcaped the penetration and learning of Plato, Ariftotle, and Cicero; and that from this fyftem, by their own fagacity, they had excluded every falfe virtue, though univerfally admired, and admitted every true virtue, though defpifed and ridiculed by all the reft of the world: If any one can believe that thefe men could become impoftors, for no other purpofe than the propagation of truth, villains for no end but to teach honefty, and martyrs without the leaft profpect of honour or advantage; or that if all this fhould have been poffible, thefe few inconfiderable perfons fhould have been able, in the courfe of a few years, to have fpread this their religion over moft parts of the then known world, in oppofition to the interefts, pleafures, ambition, prejudices, and even reafon of mankind; to have triumphed over the power of princes, the intrigues of ftates, the force of cuftom, the blindnefs of zeal, the influence of priefts, the arguments of orators, and the philofophy of the world, without any fupernatural affiftance; if any one can believe all thefe miraculous events, contradictory to the conftant experience of the powers and difpofitions of human nature, he muft be

D poffeffed

possessed of much more faith than is necessary to make him a Christian, and remain an unbeliever from mere credulity.

But should these credulous infidels after all be in the right, and this pretended revelation be all a fable; from believing it, what harm could ensue? Would it render princes more tyrannical, or subjects more ungovernable? the rich more insolent, or the poor more disorderly? Would it make worse parents or children, husbands or wives, masters or servants, friends or neighbours? Or would it not make men more virtuous, and consequently more happy in every situation? It could not be criminal; it could not be detrimental. It could not be criminal, because it cannot be a crime to assent to such evidence, as has been able to convince the best and wisest of mankind; by which, if false, Providence must have permitted men to deceive each other, for the most beneficial ends, and which therefore it would be surely more meritorious to believe, from a disposition of faith and charity, which believeth all things, than to reject with scorn from obstinacy and self-conceit: It cannot be detrimental, because if christianity is a fable, it is a fable, the belief of which is the only principle which can retain men in a steady and uniform course of virtue, piety, and devotion, or can support them in the hour of distress, of sickness, and of death. Whatever might be the operations of true deism on the minds of pagan philosophers, that can now avail us nothing: for that light which once lightened the Gentiles, it now absorbed in the brighter illumination of the gospel; we can now form no rational system of deism, but what must be borrowed from that source, and, as far as it reaches towards perfection, must be exactly the same; and therefore if we will not accept of Christianity, we can have no religion at all. Accordingly we see, that those who fly from this, scarce ever stop at deism; but hasten on with great alacrity to a total rejection of all religious and moral principles whatever.

If I have here demonstrated the divine origin of the christian religion by an argument which cannot be confuted; no others, however plausible or numerous, founded on probabilities, doubts, and conjectures, can ever disprove it, because if it is once shewn to be true, it cannot be false. But as many arguments of this kind have bewildered some candid and ingenuous minds, I shall here bestow a few lines on those which have the most weight, in order to wipe out, or at least to diminish their perplexing influence.

But here I must previously observe, that the most unsurmountable, as well as the most usual obstacle to our belief, arises from our passions, appetites and interests; for faith being an act of the will as
much

much as of the underſtanding, we oftener diſbelieve for want of inclination, than want of evidence. The firſt ſtep towards thinking this revelation true, is our hopes that it is ſo; for whenever we wiſh with any propoſition to be true, we are not far from believing it. It is certainly for the intereſt of all good men, that its authority ſhould be well founded; and ſtill more beneficial to the bad, if ever they intend to be better: becauſe it is the only ſyſtem either of reaſon or religion which can give them any aſſurance of pardon. The puniſhment of vice is a debt due to juſtice, which cannot be remitted without compenſation: repentance can be no compenſation; it may change a wicked man's diſpoſitions, and prevent his offending for the future, but can lay no claim to pardon for what is paſt. If any one by profligacy and extravagance contracts a debt, repentance may make him wiſer, and hinder him from running into further diſtreſſes, but can never pay off his old bonds; for which he muſt be ever accountable, unleſs they are diſcharged by himſelf, or ſome other in his ſtead: this very diſcharge Chriſtianity alone holds forth on our repentance, and, if true, will certainly perform: the truth of it therefore muſt ardently be wiſhed for by all, except the wicked, who are determined neither to repent or reform. It is well worth every man's while, who either is, or intends to be virtuous, to believe Chriſtianity, if he can; becauſe he will find it the ſureſt preſervative againſt all vicious habits and their attendant evils, the beſt reſource under diſtreſſes and diſappointments, ill health and ill fortune, and the firmeſt baſis on which contemplation can reſt; and without ſome, the human mind is never perfectly at eaſe. But if any one is attached to a favourite pleaſure, or eagerly engaged in worldly purſuits incompatible with the precepts of this religion, and he believes it, he muſt either relinquiſh thoſe purſuits with uneaſineſs, or perſiſt in them with remorſe and diſſatisfaction, and therefore muſt commence unbeliever in his own defence. With ſuch I ſhall not diſpute, nor pretend to perſuade men by arguments to make themſelves miſerable: but to thoſe, who, not afraid that this religion may be true, are really affected by ſuch objections, I will offer the following anſwers, which, though ſhort, will, I doubt not, be ſufficient to ſhew them their weakneſs and futility.

In the firſt place then, ſome have been ſo bold as to ſtrike at the root of all revelation from God, by aſſerting, that it is incredible, becauſe unneceſſary, and unneceſſary, becauſe the reaſon which he has beſtowed on mankind is ſufficiently able to diſcover all the religious and moral duties which he requires of them, if they would but attend to her precepts, and be guided by her friendly admonitions.

Mankind

Mankind have undoubtedly at various times from the remotest ages received so much knowledge by divine communications, and have ever been so much inclined to impute it all to their own sufficiency that it is now difficult to determine what human reason unassisted can effect: But to form a true judgment on this subject, let us turn our eyes to those remote regions of the globe, to which this supernatural assistance has never yet extended, and we shall there see men endued with sense and reason not inferior to our own, so far from being capable of forming systems of religion and morality, that they are at this day totally unable to make a nail or a hatchet: from whence we may surely be convinced, that reason alone is so far from being sufficient to offer to mankind a perfect religion, that it has never yet been able to lead them to any degree of culture, or civilization whatever. These have uniformly flowed from that great fountain of divine communication opened in the east, in the earliest ages, and thence been gradually diffused in salubrious streams, throughout the various regions of the earth. Their rise and progress, by surveying the history of the world, may easily be traced backwards to their source; and whereever these have not as yet been able to penetrate, we there find the human species not only void of all true religious and moral sentiments, but not the least emerged from their original ignorance and barbarity; which seems a demonstration, that although human reason is capable of progression in science, yet the first foundations must be laid by supernatural instructions: for surely no other probable cause can be assigned why one part of mankind should have made such an amazing progress in religious, moral, metaphysical, and philosophical enquiries; such wonderful improvements in policy, legislation, commerce, and manufactures, while the other part, formed with the same natural capacities divided only by seas and mountains, should remain, during the same number of ages, in a state little superior to brutes, without government, without laws or letters, and even without cloaths and habitations; murdering each other to satiate their revenge, and devouring each other to appease their hunger: I say no cause can be assigned for this amazing difference, except that the first have received information from those divine communications recorded in the scriptures, and the latter have never yet been favoured with such assistance. This remarkable contrast seems an unanswerable, though perhaps a new proof of the necessity of revelation, and a solid refutation of all arguments against it, drawn from the sufficiency of human reason. And as reason in her natural state is thus incapable of making any progress in knowledge; so when furnished with materials by supernatural aid, if left to the guidance of

her

her own wild imaginations, she falls into more numerous, and more gross errors, than her own native ignorance could ever have suggested. There is then no absurdity so extravagant, which she is not ready to adopt: she has persuaded some, that there is no God; others, that there can be no future state; she has taught some, that there is no difference between vice and virtue, and that to cut a man's throat and to relieve his necessities are actions equally meritorious: she has convinced many, that they have no free-will in opposition to their own experience; some, that there can be no such thing as soul, or spirit, contrary to their own perceptions; and others, no such thing as matter or body, in contradiction to their senses. By analyzing all things she can shew, that there is nothing in any thing; by perpetual sifting she can reduce all existence to the invisible dust of scepticism; and by recurring to first principles, prove to the satisfaction of her followers, that there are no principles at all. How far such a guide is to be depended on in the important concerns of religion, and morals, I leave to the judgment of every considerate man to determine. This is certain, that human reason in its highest state of cultivation amongst the philosophers of Greece and Rome, was never able to form a religion comparable to Christianity; nor have all those sources of moral virtue, such as truth, beauty, and the fitness of things, which modern philosophers have endeavoured to substitute in its stead, ever been effectual to produce good men, and have themselves often been the productions of some of the worst.

To some speculative and refined observers, it has appeared incredible, that a wife and benevolent Creator should have constituted a world upon one plan, and a religion for it on another; that is, that he should have revealed a religion to mankind, which not only contradicts the principal passions and inclinations which he has implanted in their natures, but is incompatible with the whole œconomy of that world which he has created, and in which he has thought proper to place them. This, say they, with regard to the Christian, is apparently the case: the love of power, riches, honour and fame, are the great incitements to generous and magnanimous actions; yet by this institution are all these depreciated and discouraged. Government is essential to the nature of man, and cannot be managed without certain degrees of violence, corruption, and imposition: yet are all these strictly forbid. Nations cannot subsist without wars, nor war be carried on without rapine, desolation, and murder; yet are these prohibited under the severest threats. The nonresistance of evil must subject individuals to continual oppressions, and leave nations a defenceless
prey

prey to their enemies; yet is this recommended. Perpetual patience under insults aud injuries must every day provoke new insults and new injuries; yet is this enjoined. A neglect of all we eat and drink, and wear, must put an end to all commerce, manufactures, and industry; yet is this required. In short, were these precepts universally obeyed, the disposition of all human affairs must be entirely changed, and the business of the world, constituted as it now is, could not go on. To all this I answer, that such indeed is the christian revelation, and such it is constantly declared to be by him who gave it, as well as by those, who published it under his immediate direction: To these he says, "If ye were of the world, the world would love his own, but because ye are not of the world, but I have chosen you out of the world, therefore the world hateth you." * To the Jews he declares, " Ye are of this world; I am not of this world, † St. Paul writes to the Romans, "Be not conformed to this world;" ‡ and to the Corinthians, "We speak not the wisdom of this world." § St. James says, "Know ye not, that the friendship of the world is enmity with God? whosoever therefore will be a friend of the world is the enemy of God." ‖ This irreconcileable disagreement between christianity and the world is announced in numberless other places in the New Testament, and indeed by the whole tenour of those writings. These are plain declarations, which in spite of all the evasions of those good managers, who choose to take this world with them in their way to heaven, stand fixed and immoveable against all their arguments drawn from public benefit and pretended necessity, and must ever forbid any reconciliation between the pursuits of this world and the christian institution: But they who reject it on this account, enter not into the sublime spirit of this religion, which is not a code of precise laws designed for the well ordering society, adapted to the ends of worldly convenience, and amenable to the tribunal of human prudence; but a divine lesson of purity and perfection so far superior to the low considerations of conquest, government, and commerce, that it takes no more notice of them than of the battles of game-cocks, the policy of bees, or the industry of ants: they recollect not what is the first and principal object of this institution; that this is not, as has been often repeated, to make us happy, or even virtuous in the present life for the sake of augmenting our happiness *here*, but to conduct us through a state of dangers and sufferings, of sin and temptation, in such a manner as to qualify us for the enjoyment of happiness

* *John* xv. 19.   ‡ *John* viii. 23.
† *Rom.* xii. 2.   § *Cor.* ii. 6.   ‖ *Jam.* iv. 4.

happiness *hereafter*. All other institutions of religion and morals were made for the world, but the characteristic of this is to be against it; and therefore the merits of christian doctrines are not to be weighed in the scales of public utility, like those of moral precepts, because worldly utility is not their end. If Christ and his apostles had pretended that the religion which they preached would advance the power, wealth, and prosperity of nations, or of men, they would have deserved but little credit; but they constantly profess the contrary, and every where declare, that their religion is adverse to the world, and all its pursuits. It can therefore be no imputation on this religion, or on any of its precepts, that they tend not to an end which their author professedly disclaims: nor can it surely be deemed a defect, that it is adverse to the vain pursuits of this world; for so are reason, wisdom, and experience; they all teach us the same lesson, they all demonstrate to us every day, that these are begun on false hopes, carried on with disquietude, and end in disappointment. This professed incompatibility with the little, wretched, and iniquitous business of the world, is therefore so far from being a defect in this religion, that, was there no other proof of its divine origin, this alone, I think, would be abundantly sufficient. The great plan and benevolent design of this dispensation is plainly this; to enlighten the minds, purify the religion, and amend the morals of mankind in general, and to select the most meritorious of them to be successively transplanted into the kingdom of heaven: Which gracious offer is impartially tendered to all, who by perseverance in meekness, patience, piety, charity, and a detachment from the world, are willing to qualify themselves for this holy and happy society. Was this universally accepted, and did every man observe strictly every precept of the gospel, the face of human affairs, and the œconomy of the world, would indeed be greatly changed: but surely they would be changed for the better; and we should enjoy much more happiness, even here, than at present: For we must not forget that evils are by it forbid as well as resistance; injuries, as well as revenge; all unwillingness to diffuse the enjoyments of life, as well as solicitude to acquire them; all obstacles to ambition, as well as ambition itself; and therefore all contentions for power and interest would be at an end; and the world would go on much more happily than it now does. But this *universal acceptance* of such an offer was never expected from so depraved and imperfect a creature as man, and therefore could never have been any part of the design: For it was foreknown and foretold by him who made it, that few, very few would accept it on these terms. He says " Straight is the

gate,

gate, and narrow is the way which leadeth into life, and few there be that find it:" * Accordingly we see, that very few are prevailed on by the hopes of future happiness, to relinquish the pursuits of present pleasures or interests, and therefore these pursuits are little interrupted by the secession of so inconsiderable a number: As the natural world subsists by the struggles of the same elements, so does the moral by the contentions of the same passions, as from the beginning: The generality of mankind are actuated by the same motives, fight, scuffle, and scramble for power, riches and pleasures, with the same eagerness: all occupations and professions are exercised with the same alacrity, and there are soldiers, lawyers, statesmen, patriots, and politicians, just as if Christianity had never existed. Thus, we see this wonderful dispensation has answered all the purposes for which it was intended: It has enlightened the minds, purified the religion, and amended the morals of mankind; and, without subverting the constitution, policy or business of the world, opened a gate, though a straight one, through which all, who are wise enough to choose it, and good enough to be fit for it, may find an entrance into the kingdom of heaven.

Others have said, that if this revelation had really been from God, his infinite power and goodness could never have suffered it to have been so soon perverted from its original purity, to have continued in a state of corruption through the course of so many ages, and at last to have proved so ineffectual to the reformation of mankind. To these I answer, that all this, on examination, will be found inevitable, from the nature of all revelations communicated to so imperfect a creature as man, and from circumstances peculiar to the rise and progress of the Christian in particular: for when this was first preached to the Gentile nations, though they were not able to withstand the force of its evidence, and therefore received it; yet they could not be prevailed on to relinquish their old superstitions, and former opinions, but chose rather to incorporate them with it: By which means it was necessarily mixed with their ignorance, and their learning; by both which it was equally injured. The people defaced its worship by blending it with their idolatrous ceremonies, and the philosophers corrupted its doctrines by weaving them up with the notions of the Gnostics, Mystics, and Manichæans, the prevailing systems of those times. By degrees its irresistible excellence gained over princes, potentates, and conquerors to its interests, and it was supported by their patronage: but that patronage soon engaged it in their policies and contests, and destroyed that excellence by which it had been acquired. At length the meek and humble professors of the gospel enslaved these princes, and conquer-

* *Matt.* vii. 4. ed

ed these conquerors, their patrons, and erected for themselves such a stupendous fabric of wealth and power, as the world had never seen: they then propagated their religion by the same methods by which it had been persecuted; nations were converted by fire and sword, and the vanquished were baptised with daggers at their throats. All these events we see proceed from a chain of causes and consequences, which could not have been broken without changing the established course of things by a constant series of miracles, or a total alteration of human nature: whilst that continues as it is, the purest religion must be corrupted by a conjunction with power and riches. How far this institution has been effectual to the reformation of mankind, it is not easy now to ascertain, because the enormities which prevailed before the appearance of it are by time so far removed from our sight, that they are scarcely visible; but those of the most gigantic size still remain in the records of history, as monuments of the rest: Wars in those ages were carried on with a ferocity and cruelty unknown to the present: whole cities and nations were extirpated by fire and sword; and thousands of the vanquished were crucified and impaled for having endeavoured only to defend themselves and their country. The lives of new-born infants were then entirely at the disposal of their parents, who were at liberty to bring them up, or to expose them to perish by cold and hunger, or to be devoured by birds and beasts; and this was frequently practised without punishment, and even without censure. Gladiators were employed by hundreds to cut one another to pieces, in public theatres, for the diversion of the most polite assemblies; and though these combatants at first consisted of criminals only, by degrees men of the highest rank, and even ladies of the most illustrious families, enroled themselves in this honourable list. On many occasions human sacrifices were ordained; and at the funerals of rich and eminent persons, great numbers of their slaves were murdered as victims pleasing to their departed spirits. The most infamous obscenities were made part of their religious worship, and the most unnatural lusts publicly avowed, and celebrated by their most admired poets. At the approach of Christianity, all these horrid abominations vanished; and amongst those who first embraced it, scarce a single vice was to be found: to such an amazing degree of piety, charity, temperance, patience, and resignation, were the primitive converts exalted, that they seem literally to have been regenerated, and purified from all the imperfections of human nature; and to have pursued such a constant and uniform course of devotion, innocence, and virtue, as, in the present times, it is almost as difficult for us to conceive as to imitate. If it is asked, why should not the belief of the same religion now produce the same effects? the answer is short, because it is not believed: The most sovereign medicine can perform no cure, if the patient will not be persuaded to take it. Yet notwithstanding all impediments, it has certainly done a great deal towards diminishing the vices and correcting the dispositions of mankind; and was it universally adopted in belief and practice, would totally eradicate both sin and punishment.

Objections have likewise been raised to the divine authority of this religion from the incredibility of some of its doctrines, particularly of those concerning the Trinity, and atonement for sin by the sufferings and death of Christ; the one contradicting all the principles of human reason, and the other all our ideas of divine justice. To these objections I shall only say, that no arguments founded on principles, which we cannot comprehend, can possibly disprove a proposition already proved on principles which we do understand; and therefore that on this subject they ought not to be attended to: That three Beings should be one Being, is a proposition which certainly contradicts reason, that is, *our* reason; but it does not thence follow, that it cannot be true; for there are many propositions which contradict our reason, and yet are demonstrably true: one is the very first principle of all religion, the being of a God; for that any thing should exist without a cause, or be the cause of its own existence, are propositions equally contradictory to our reason; yet one of them must be true, or nothing could ever have existed: in like manner the over-ruling grace of the Creator, and the free-will of his creatures, his certain fore-knowledge of future events, and the uncertain contingency of those events, are to our apprehensions absolute contradictions to each other; and yet the truth of every one of these is demonstrable from Scripture, reason and experience. All these difficulties arise from our imagining, that the mode of existence of all Beings must be similar to our own; that is, that they must all exist in time, and space; and hence proceeds our embarrassment on this subject. We know that no two Beings, with whose mode of existence we are acquainted, can exist in the same point of time in the same point of space, and that therefore they cannot be one: but how far Beings, whose mode of existence bears no relation to time or space, may be united, we cannot comprehend: and therefore the possibility of such an union we cannot possitively deny. In like manner our reason informs us, that the punishment of the innocent, instead of the guilty, is diametrically opposite to justice, rectitude and all pretensions to utility;

lity; but we should also remember, that the short line of our reason cannot reach to the bottom of this question: it cannot inform us, by what means either guilt or punishment ever gained a place in the works of a Creator infinitely good and powerful, whose goodness must have induced him, and whose power must have enabled him to exclude them: It cannot assure us, that some sufferings of individuals are not necessary to the happiness and well-being of the whole: It cannot convince us, that they do not actually arise from this necessity, or that for this cause they may not be required of us, and levied like a tax for the public benefit: or that this tax may not be paid by one Being, as well as another; and therefore, if voluntarily offered, be justly accepted from the innocent instead of the guilty. Of all these circumstances we are totally ignorant; nor can our reason afford us any information, and therefore we are not able to assert, that this measure is contrary to justice, or void of utility: for unless we could first resolve that great question, whence came evil? we can decide nothing on the dispensations of Providence; because they must necessarily be connected with that undiscoverable principle; and, as we know not the root of the disease, we cannot judge of what is, or is not, a proper and effectual remedy. It is remarkable, that, notwithstanding all the seeming absurdities of this doctrine, there is one circumstance much in its favor; which is, that it has been universally adopted in all ages, as far as history can carry us back in our enquiries to the earliest times; in which we find all nations civilized and barbarous, however differing in all other religious opinions, agreeing alone in the expediency of appeasing their offended Deities by sacrifices, that is, by the vicarious sufferings of men or other animals. This notion could never have been derived from reason, because it directly contradicts it; nor from ignorance, because ignorance could never have contrived so unaccountable an expedient, nor have been uniform in all ages and countries in any opinion whatsoever; nor from the artifice of kings or priests, in order to acquire dominion over the people, because it seems not adapted to this end; and we find it implanted in the minds of the most remote savages at this day discovered, who have neither kings nor priests, artifice nor dominion, amongst them. It must therefore be derived from natural instinct, or supernatural revelation, *both* which are *equally* the operations of divine power. If it is further urged, that however true these doctrines may be, yet it must be inconsistent with the justice and goodness of the Creator, to require from his creatures the belief of propositions which contradict, or are above the reach of that reason which he has thought proper to be-

stow

flow upon them. To this I anfwer, that genuine Chriftianity requires no fuch belief: It has difcovered to us many important truths, with which we were before entirely unacquainted, and amongſt them are thefe, that three Beings are fome way united in the divine effence, and that God will accept of the fufferings of Chriſt as an atonement for the fins of mankind. Thefe, confidered as declarations of facts only, neither contradict, nor are above the reach of human reafon: The firſt is a propofition as plain, as that three equilateral lines compofe one triangle; the other is as intelligible, as that one man fhould difcharge the debts of another. In what manner this union is formed, or why God accepts thefe vicarious punifhments, or to what purpofes they may be fubfervient, it informs us not, becaufe no information could enable us to comprehend thefe myfteries, and therefore it does not require that we ſhould know or believe any thing about them. The truth of thefe doctrines muſt reſt entirely on the authority of thofe who taught them; but then we fhould reflect that thofe were the fame perfons who taught us a fyſtem of religion more fublime, and of ethics more perfect, than any which our faculties were ever able to difcover, but which, when difcovered, are exactly confonant to our reafon, and that therefore we fhould not haftily reject thofe informations which they have vouchfafed to give us, of which our reafon is not a competent judge. If an able mathematician proves to us the truth of feveral propofitions by demonftrations which we underſtand, we hefitate not on his authority to affent to others, the procefs of whofe proofs we are not able to follow: why therefore ſhould we refufe that credit to Chrift and his Apoſtles which we think reafonable to give to one another?

Many have objected to the whole fcheme of this revelation as partial, fluctuating, indeterminate, unjuft, and unworthy of an omnifcient and omnipotent Author, who cannot be fuppofed to have favoured particular perfons, countries, and times, with this divine communication, while others no lefs meritorious have been altogether excluded from its benefits; nor to have changed and counteracted his own defigns; that is, to have formed mankind able and difpofed to render themfelves miferable by their own wickednefs, and then to have contrived fo ftrange an expedient to reftore them that happinefs which they need never have been permitted to forfeit; and this to be brought about by the unneceffary interpofition of a Mediator. To all this I fhall only fay, that however unaccountable this may appear to us, who fee but as fmall a part of the Chriftian, as of the univerfal plan of creation; they are both in regard to all thefe circumftances exactly analogous

logous to each other. In all the difpenfations of Providence, with which we are acquainted, benefits are diftributed in a fimilar manner; health and ftrength, fenfe and fcience, wealth and power, are all beftowed on individuals and communities in different degrees and at different times. The whole economy of this world confifts of evils and remedies; and thefe for the moft part adminiftered by the inftrumentality of intermediate agents. God has permitted us to plunge ourfelves into poverty, diftrefs and mifery, by our own vices, and has afforded us the advice, inftructions and examples of others, to deter or extricate us from thefe calamities. He has formed us fubject to innumerable difeafes, and he has beftowed on us a variety of remedies. He has made us liable to hunger, thirft and nakednefs, and he fupplies us with food, drink and cloathing, ufually by the adminiftration of others. He has created poifons, and he has provided antidotes. He has ordained the winter's cold to cure the peftilential heats of the fummer, and the fummer's funfhine to dry up the inundations of the winter. Why the conftitution of nature is fo formed, why all the vifible difpenfations of Providence are fuch, and why fuch is the Chriftian difpenfation alfo, we know not, nor have faculties to comprehend. God might certainly have made the material world a fyftem of perfect beauty and regularity, without evils, and without remedies; and the Chriftian difpenfation a fcheme only of moral virtue productive of happinefs, without the intervention of any atonement or mediation. He might have exempted our bodies from all difeafes, and our minds from all depravity, and we fhould then have ftood in no need of medicines to reftore us to health, or expedients to reconcile us to his favour. It feems indeed to our ignorance, that this would have been more confiftent with juftice and reafon; but his infinite wifdom has decided in another manner, and formed the fyftems both of Nature and Chriftianity on other principles, and thefe fo exactly fimilar, that we have caufe to conclude that they both muft proceed from the fame fource of divine power and wifdom, however inconfiftent with our reafon they may appear. Reafon is undoubtedly our fureft guide in all matters, which lie within the narrow circle of her intelligence: On the fubject of revelation her province is only to examine into its authority, and when that is once proved, fhe has no more to do, but to acquiefce in its doctrines, and therefore is never fo ill employed, as when fhe pretends to accommodate them to her own ideas of rectitude and truth. God, fays this felf-fufficient teacher, is perfectly wife, juft and good; and what is the inference? That all his difpenfations muft be conformable to our notions of per-

fect

lect wisdom, justice and goodness: but it should first be proved, that man is as perfect, and as wise as his Creator, or this consequence will by no means follow; but rather the reverse, that is, that the dispensations of a perfect and all-wise Being must probably appear unreasonable, and perhaps unjust, to a Being imperfect and ignorant. Nor is it the least surprising, that we are not able to understand the spiritual dispensations of the Almighty, when his material works are to us no less incomprehensible, our reason can afford us no insight into those great properties of matter, gravitation, attraction, elasticity, and electricity, nor even into the essence of matter itself. Can reason teach us how the sun's luminous orb can fill a circle, whose diameter contains many millions of miles, with a constant inundation of successive rays during thousands of years, without any perceivable diminution of that body from whence they are continually poured, or any augmentation of those bodies on which they fall, and by which they are constantly absorbed? Can reason tell us how those rays, darted with a velocity a thousand times greater than that of a cannon ball, can strike the tenderest organs of the human frame without inflicting any degree of pain, or by what means this percussion only can convey the forms of distant objects to an immaterial mind? or how any union can be formed between material and immaterial essences, or how the wounds of the body can give pain to the soul, or the anxiety of the soul can emaciate and destroy the body? That all these things are so, we have visible and indisputable demonstration; but how they can be so, is to us as incomprehensible as the most abstruse mysteries of Revelation. In short, we see so small a part of the great Whole, we know so little of the relation which the present life bears to pre-existent and future states; we can conceive so little of the nature of God, and his attributes, or mode of existence; we can comprehend so little of the material, and so much less of the moral plan on which the universe is constituted, or on what principle it proceeds, that if a revelation from such a Being, on such subjects, was in every part familiar to our understandings, and consonant to our reason; we should have great cause to suspect its divine authority; and therefore, had this revelation been less incomprehensible, it would certainly have been more incredible.

But I shall not enter further into the consideration of these speculations, because the discussion of them would render this short essay too tedious and laborious a task for the perusal of them for whom it was principally intended; which are all those busy or idle persons, whose time and thoughts are wholly engrossed by the pursuits of business, or pleasure, ambition, or luxury, who know nothing of this religion,

except

except what they have accidentally picked up by defultory converfation or fuperficial reading, and have thence determined with themfelves, that a pretended revelation founded on fo ftrange and improbable a ftory, fo contradictory to reafon, fo adverfe to the world and all its occupations, fo, incredible in its doctrines, and in its precepts fo impracticable, can be nothing more than the impofition of priefcraft upon ignorant and illiterate ages, and artfully continued as an engine well adapted to awe and govern the fuperftitious vulgar. To talk to fuch about the Chriftian religion, is to converfe with the deaf concerning mufic, or with the blind on the beauties of painting: They want all ideas relative to the fubject, and therefore can never be made to comprehend it: to enable them to do this, their minds muft be formed for thefe conceptions by contemplation, retirement, and abftraction from bufinefs and diffipation, by ill health, difappointments, and diftreffes; and poffibly by divine interpofition, or by enthufiafm, which is ufually miftaken for it. Without fome of thefe preparatory aids, together with a competent degree of learning and application, it is impoffible that they can think or know, underftand or believe, any thing about it. If they profefs to believe, they deceive others; if they fancy that they believe, they deceive themfelves. I am ready to acknowledge, that thefe gentlemen, as far as their information reaches, are perfectly in the right; and if they are endued with good underftandings which have been entirely devoted to the bufinefs or amufements of the world, they can pafs no other judgment, and muft revolt from the hiftory and doctrines of this religion. "The preaching Chrift crucified was to the Jews a ftumbling-block, and to the Greeks foolifhnefs;"* and fo it muft appear to all, who, like them, judge from eftablifhed prejudices, falfe learning, and fuperficial knowledge; for thofe who are quite unable to follow the chain of its prophecy, to fee the beauty and juftnefs of its moral precepts, and to enter into the wonders of its difpenfations, can form no other idea of this revelation, but that of a confufed rhapfody of fictions and abfurdities.

If it is afked, was Chriftianity then intended only for learned divines and profound philofophers? I anfwer, No: it was at firft preached by the illiterate, and received by the ignorant; and to fuch are the practical, which are the moft neceffary parts of it, fufficiently intelligible: but the proofs of its authority undoubtedly are not, becaufe thefe muft be chiefly drawn from other parts, of a fpeculative nature, opening to our enquiries inexhauftible difcoveries concerning the nature, attributes, and difpenfations of God, which cannot be underftood

without

* Cor. i. 26.

without some learning and much attention. From these the generality of mankind must necessarily be excluded, and must therefore trust to others for the grounds of their belief, if they believe at all. And hence perhaps it is, that faith, or easiness of belief, is so frequently and so strongly recommended in the gospel; because if men require proofs, of which they themselves are incapable, and those who have no knowledge on this important subject will not place some confidence in those who have; the illiterate and unattentive must ever continue in a state of unbelief: but then all such should remember, that in all sciences, even in mathematics themselves, there are many propositions, which on a cursory view appear to the most acute understandings uninstructed in that science, to be impossible to be true, which yet on a closer examination are found to be truths capable of the strictest demonstration; and that therefore in disquisitions on which we cannot determine without much learned investigation, reason uninformed is by no means to be depended on; and from hence they ought surely to conclude, that it may be at least as possible for them to be mistaken in disbelieving this revelation, who know nothing of the matter, as for those great masters of reason and erudidition, Grotius, Bacon, Newton, Milton, Boyle, Locke, Addison, and Lyttelton, to be deceived in their belief: a belief, to which they firmly adhered after the most diligent and learned researches into the authenticity of its records, the completion of the prophecies, the sublimity of its doctrines, the purity of its precepts, and the arguments of its adversaries; a belief, which they have testified to the world by their writings, without any other motive, than their regard for truth and the benefit of mankind.

Should the few foregoing pages add but one mite to the treasures with which these learned writers have enriched the world; if they should be so fortunate as to persuade any of these minute philosophers to place some confidence in these great opinions, and to distrust their own; if they should be able to convince them, that notwithstanding all unfavourable appearances, Christianity may not be altogether artifice and error; if they should prevail on them to examine it with some attention, or, if that is too much trouble, not to reject it with out any examination at all; the purpose of this little work will be sufficiently answered. Had the arguments herein used, and the new hints here flung out, been more largely discussed, it might easily have been extended to a more considerable bulk; but then the busy would not have had leisure; nor the idle inclination to have read it. Should it ever have the honour to be admitted into such good company, they will immediately, I know, determine, that it must be the work of

some

some enthusiast or methodist, some beggar, or some madman. I shall therefore beg leave to assure them, that the author is very far removed from all these characters: that he once perhaps believed as little as themselves; but having some leisure and more curiosity, he employed them both in resolving a question which seemed to him of some importance,—Whether Christianity was really an imposture founded on an absurd, incredible and obsolete fable, as many suppose it? Or whether it is, what it pretends to be, a revelation communicated to mankind by the interposition of supernatural power? On a candid enquiry, he soon found, that the first was an absolute impossibility, and that its pretensions to the latter were founded on the most solid grounds: In the further pursuit of his examination, he perceived, at every step, new lights arising, and some of the brightest from parts of it the most obscure, but productive of the clearest proofs, because equally beyond the power of human artifice to invent, and human reason to discover. These arguments, which have convinced him of the divine origin of this religion, he has here put together in as clear and concise a manner as he was able, thinking they might have the same effect upon others, and being of opinion, that if there were a few more true Christians in the world, it would be beneficial to themselves, and by no means detrimental to the public.

End of Soame Jenyns.

THE

F

THE
CONTENTS.

SERMON I.
On the Union of Piety and Morality.

ACTS. x. 4. *Thy prayers and thine alms are come up for a memorial before God.*

SERMON II.
On the Influence of Religion upon Adverfity.

PSALM xxvii. 5. *In the time of trouble, he shall hide me in his pavilion; in the secret of his tabernacle shall he hide me; he shall set me up upon a rock.*

SERMON III.
On the Influence of Religion upon Profperity.

PSALM i. 3. *He shall be like a tree planted by the rivers of water, that bringeth forth his fruit in his season; his leaf also shall not wither, and whatsoever he doth shall prosper.*

SERMON IV.
On our imperfect Knowledge of a Future State.

I CORINTH. xiii. 12. *For now we see through a glass, darkly.*

SERMON V.
On the Death of Chrift.

JOHN xvii. 1. *Jesus lift up his eyes to heaven, and said, Father! the hour is come!—*

CONTENTS.

SERMON VI.
On Gentleness.

JAMES iii. 17. *The wisdom that is from above, is—gentle—*

SERMON VII.
On the Disorders of the Passions.

ESTHER v. 13. *Yet all this availeth me nothing, so long as I see Mordecai the Jew sitting at the King's gate.*

SERMON VIII.
On our Ignorance of Good and Evil in this Life.

ECCLESIAST. vi. 12. *Who knoweth what is good for man in this life, all the days of his vain life, which he spendeth as a shadow?*

SERMON IX.
On religious Retirement.

PSALM iv. 4. *Commune with your own heart, upon your bed, and be still.*

SERMON X.
On Devotion.

ACTS x. 2. *Cornelius—A devout man.*

SERMON XI.
On the Duties of the Young.

TITUS ii. 6. *Young men likewise exhort, to be sober-minded.*

SERMON XII.
On the Duties and Consolations of the Aged.

PROV. xvi. 31. *The hoary head is a crown of glory, if it be found in the way of righteousness.*

SERMON XIII.
On the Power of Conscience.

GENESIS xlii. 21, 22. *And they said one to another, We are verily guilty concerning our brother, in that we saw the anguish of his soul, when he besought us; and we would not hear: Therefore is this distress come upon us. And Reuben answered them, saying, Spake I not unto you, saying, Do not sin against the child; and ye would not hear? Therefore, behold also his blood is required.*

SERMON XIV.
On the Mixture of Joy and Fear in Religion.

PSALM ii. 11. *Rejoice with trembling.*

SERMON XV.
On the Motives to Constancy in Virtue.

GAL. vj. 9. *And let us not be weary in well-doing; for in due season we shall reap, if we faint not.*

SERMON XVI.
On the Importance of Order in Conduct.

1 CORINTH. xiv. 40. *Let all things be done—in order.*

SERMON XVII.
On the Government of the Heart.

PROVERBS iv. 23. *Keep thy heart with all diligence; for out of it are the issues of life.*

SERMON XVIII.
The same Subject continued.

PROVERBS iv. 23. *Keep thy heart with all diligence: for out of it are the issues of life.*

CONTENTS.

SERMON XIX.
On the Unchangeableness of the Divine Nature.

JAMES i. 17. *Every good and every perfect gift is from above, and cometh down from the Father of Lights, with whom is no variableness, neither shadow of turning.*

SERMON XX.
On the Compassion of Christ.

HEBREWS iv. 15. *We have not an high priest which cannot be touched with the feeling of our infirmities; but was in all points tempted like as we are, yet without sin.*

SERMON XXI.
On the Love of Praise.

JOHN xii. 43. *For they loved the praise of men more than the praise of God.*

SERMON I.

On the Union of PIETY and MORALITY.

ACTS x. 4.

Thy prayers and thine alms are come up for a memorial before God.

THE High and Lofty One who inhabiteth eternity, dwelleth also with him that is of humble and contrite heart. In the midst of his glory, the Almighty is not inattentive to the meanest of his subjects. Neither obscurity of station, nor imperfection of knowledge, sinks those below his regard, who worship and obey him. Every prayer which they send up from their secret retirements, is listened to by him; and every work of charity which they perform, how unknown soever to the world, attracts his notice. The text presents a signal instance of this comfortable truth. In the city of Cæsarea, there dwelt a Roman centurion, a military officer of inferior rank, a Gentile, neither by birth nor religion entitled to the privileges of the Jewish nation. But he was a devout and a benevolent man; who, according to his measure of religious knowledge, studied to perform his duty, *prayed to God always, and gave much alms to the people.* Such a character passed not unobserved by God. So highly was it honoured, that to this good centurion an Angel was sent from heaven, in order to direct him to the means of full instruction in the truth. The Angel accosts him with this salutation, *Cornelius, Thy prayers and thine alms are come up for a memorial before God.*

It is to the conjunction of *prayers and alms,* that I purpose now to direct your thoughts, as describing the respectable and amiable character of a man, as forming the honour and the blessedness of a true Christian; piety joined with charity, faith with good works, devotion with morality. These are things which God hath connected, and which it is impious in man to separate. It is only when

they

they remain united, that they can come up as a grateful *memorial before God*. I shall first endeavour to shew you, That alms without prayers, or prayers without alms, morality without devotion, or devotion without morality, are extremely defective; and then shall point out the happy effects of their mutual union.

LET us begin with considering the case of alms without prayers; that is, of good works without piety, or a proper sense of God and religion. Examples of this are not uncommon in the world. With many, Virtue is, or at least is pretended to be, a respectable and an honoured name, while Piety sounds meanly in their ears. They are men of the world, and they claim to be men of honour. They rest upon their humanity, their public spirit, their probity, and their truth They arrogate to themselves all the manly and the active virtues. But devout affections, and religious duties, they treat with contempt, as founded on shadowy speculations, and fit to employ the attention only of weak and superstitious minds. Now, in opposition to such persons, I contend, That this neglect of piety argues depravity of heart; and that it infers an irregular discharge of the duties of morality.

FIRST, it argues internal depravity; for it discovers a cold and a hard heart. If there be any impression which man is formed by nature to receive, it is a sense of religion. As soon as his mind opens to observation and reflection, he discerns innumerable marks of his dependent state. He finds himself placed, by some superiour power, in a vast world, where the wisdom and goodness of the Creator are conspicuous on every side. The magnificence, the beauty and order of nature, excite him to admire and adore. When he looks up to that omnipotent hand which operates throughout the universe, he is impressed with reverence. When he receives blessings which he cannot avoid ascribing to divine goodness, he is prompted to gratitude. The expressions of those affections, under the various forms of religious worship, are no other than native effusions of the human heart. Ignorance may mislead, and superstition may corrupt them; but their origin is derived from sentiments that are essential to man.

Cast your eyes over the whole earth. Explore the most remote quarters of the east or the west. You may discover tribes of men without policy, or laws, or cities, or any of the arts of life: But no where will you find them without some form of religion. In every region you behold the prostrate worshipper, the temple, the altar, and the offering. Wherever men have existed, they have been sensible that

some

some acknowledgment was due, on their part, to the Sovereign of the world. If, in their rudest and most ignorant state, this obligation has been felt, what additional force must it acquire by the improvements of human knowledge, but especially by the great discoveries of the Christian revelation? Whatever, either from reverence or from gratitude, can excite men to the worship of God, is by this revelation placed in such a light, as one should think were sufficient to overawe the most thoughtless, and to melt the most obdurate mind.

Canst thou, then, pretend to be a man of reason, nay, a man of virtue, and yet continue regardless of one of the first and chief dictates of human nature? Where is thy sensibility to what is right and fit, if that loud voice which calls all nations throughout the earth to religious homage, has never been heard by thee? Or, if it has been heard, by what strange and false refinements hast thou stifled those natural sentiments which it tends to awaken? Calling thyself a son, a citizen, a friend; claiming to be faithful and affectionate in these relations; hast thou no sense of what thou owest to thy first Parent; thy highest Sovereign, thy greatest Benefactor? Can it be consistent with true virtue or honour, to value thyself upon thy regard to inferiour obligations, and yet to violate that which is the most sacred and the most ancient of all? When simple instinct teaches the Tartar and the Indian, together with his alms and good works, to join his prayers to that Power whom he considers as the source of good, shall it be no reproach, in the most enlightened state of human nature, and under the purest dispensation of religion, to have extinguished the sense of gratitude to Heaven, and to slight all acknowledgment of the great and the true God? What does such conduct imply, but either an entire want, or a wilful suppression, of some of the best and most generous affections belonging to human nature?—Surely, there must be an essential defect in that heart which remains cold and insensible, where it ought to be affected most warmly. Surely, such a degree of depravity must be lodged there, as is sufficient to taint all the other springs of pretended virtue.

But besides this, I must contend, in the second place, That where religion is neglected, there can be no regular nor steady practice of the duties of morality. The character will be often inconsistent; and Virtue, placed on a basis too narrow to support it, will be always loose and tottering. For such is the propensity of our nature to vice, so numerous are the temptations to a relaxed and immoral conduct, that stronger restraints than those of mere reason are necessary to be imposed on man. The sense of right and wrong, the principle of honour, or the instinct of benevolence, are barriers too feeble to withstand the strength of passion. In the tranquil seasons of life, these natural principles may, perhaps, carry on the ordinary course of social duties with some regularity. But wait until some trying emergence come. Let the conflict of passions arise. Let the heart be either wounded by sore distress, or agitated by violent emotions; and you shall presently see, that virtue without religion is inadequate to the government of life. It is destitute of its proper guard, of its firmest support, of its chief encouragement. It will sink under the weight of misfortune; or will yield to the solicitation of guilt.

The great motives that produce constancy and firmness of action, must be of a palpable and striking kind. A divine Legislator, uttering his voice from heaven; an omniscient Witness, beholding us in all our retreats; an almighty Governour, stretching forth his arm to punish or reward, disclosing the secrets of the invisible world, informing us of perpetual rest prepared hereafter for the righteous, and of *indignation and wrath* awaiting the wicked: These are the considerations which overawe the world, which support integrity, and check guilt. They add to virtue that solemnity which should ever characterize it. To the admonitions of conscience they give the authority of a law. Co-operating with all the good dispositions of a pious man, they strengthen and insure their influence. On his alms you can have no certain dependence who thinks not of God, nor has joined prayer to his charitable deeds. But when humanity is seconded by piety, the spring from which it flows is rendered, of course, more regular and constant.—In short, withdraw religion, and you shake all the pillars of morality: In every heart you weaken the influence of virtue: And among the multitude, the bulk of mankind, you overthrow its power.

Having thus shewn that morality without devotion is both defective and unstable, I proceed to consider the other extreme, of prayers without alms, devotion without morality.

In every age the practice has prevailed, of substituting certain appearances of piety in the place of the great duties of humanity and mercy. Too many there have always been, who flatter themselves with the hope of obtaining the friendship of their Creator, though they neglect to do justice to their fellow-creatures. But such persons may be assured, that their supposed piety is altogether of a spurious kind. It is an invention of their own, unknown to reason, unknown in the
word

word of God. In scripture we are ever directed to try our faith by our works, our love of God by our love of men. We are directed to consider piety as a principle which regenerates the heart, and forms it to goodness. We are taught, that in vain we addrefs any acts of homage to Chrift, unlefs we *do the things which he faith ;* and that *love, peace, gentlenefs, goodnefs, meeknefs,* and *temp'rance,* are not only the injunctions of his law, but the native *fruits of his spirit**. If therefore, while piety seems ardent, morality shall decline, you have full reason to believe, that into that piety some corrupting ingredients have entered. And if ever your regard to morality shall totally fail; if, while you make many prayers, you give no alms; if, while you appear to be zealous for God, you are falfe or unjust to men; if you are hard or contracted in heart, severe in your cenfures, and oppreffive in your conduct; then conclude with certainty, that what you had termed piety was no more than an empty name. For as foon, according to the scripture similitude, will *bitter waters flow from a fweet fountain,* as such effects be produced by genuine piety.

What you have called by that name, refolves itfelf into one or other of three things. Either it is a hypocritical form of godlinefs, affumed in order to impofe on the world; or, which is the most favourable fuppofition, it is a tranfient impreffion of ferioufnefs, an accidental melting of the heart, which *paffes away like the morning cloud and the early dew;* or, which I am afraid is too often the cafe, it is the deliberate refuge of a deluded and fuperftitious, but, at the fame time, a corrupted mind. For all men, even the moft depraved, are subject, more or lefs, to compunctions of confcience. It has never been in their power to withdraw totally beyond the reach of that warning voice, which tells them that fomething is neceffary to be done, in order to make their peace with the Ruler of the world. But, backward at the fame time to refign the gains of difhonefty, or the pleafures of vice; averfe from fubmiffion to that facred law which enjoins righteoufnefs in its whole extent, they have often attempted to make a fort of compofition with Heaven; a compofition, which, though they dare not avow it in words, lurks in fecret at the bottom of many a heart. If God will only difpenfe with fome articles of obedience, they will repay him with abundant homage. If they fail in good practice, they will ftudy to be found in belief; and, by the number of their prayers, will atone, in fome meafure, for their deficiency in charitable deeds.

But the attempt is as vain as it is impious. From the fimpleft and plaineft principles of reafon it muft appear, that religious worfhip,

disjoined

* Luke vi. 46. *Gal.* v. 22.

disjoined from juſtice and virtue, can upon no account whatever find acceptance with the Supreme Being. *To what purpoſe is the multitude of your ſacrifices unto me? faith the Lord. Bring no more vain oblations. Incenſe is an abomination unto me. The new moons and ſabbaths, the calling of aſſemblies, I cannot away with; it is iniquity, even the ſolemn meetings*[*].——Ceaſe, fooliſh and impious man! Ceaſe to conſider the Almighty as a weak or vain-glorious being, who is to be appeaſed by thy devout proſtrations, and thy humble words; or to be gratified by the parade and oſtentation of external worſhip. What is all thy worſhip to him? *Will he eat the fleſh of thy ſacrifices, or drink the blood of offered goats?* Was worſhip required of thee, doſt thou think, upon his account, that thou mighteſt bring an increaſe to his glory and felicity by thy weak and inſignificant praiſes? Sooner mighteſt thou increaſe the ſplendour of the ſun by a lighted taper, or add to the thunder by thy voice. No: It is for the ſake of man, not of God, that worſhip and prayers are required; not that God may be rendered more glorious, but that man may be made better; that he may be confirmed in a proper ſenſe of his dependent ſtate, and acquire thoſe pious and virtuous diſpoſitions in which his higheſt improvement conſiſts.

Of all the principles in religion, one ſhould take this to be the moſt evident; and yet frequent admonitions are needed, to renew the impreſſion of it upon mankind. For what purpoſe did thy Creator place thee in this world, in the midſt of human ſociety, but that as a man among men thou mighteſt cultivate humanity; that each in his place might contribute to the general welfare; that as a ſpouſe, a brother, a ſon, or a friend, thou mighteſt act thy part with an upright and a tender heart; and thus aſpire to reſemble Him who ever conſults the good of his creatures, and whoſe *tender mercies are over all his works?* And dareſt thou, who haſt been ſacrificing unſuſpicious innocence to thy looſe pleaſures; thou who haſt been diſturbing the repoſe of ſociety by thine ambition or craft; thou, who, to increaſe thy treaſures, haſt been making the widow and the orphan weep; dareſt thou approach God with thy worſhip and thy prayers, and entertain the hope that he will look down upon thee in peace? Will the God of order and juſtice accept ſuch poor compenſation for his violated laws? Will the God of love regard the ſervices of one who is an enemy to his creatures? Shall a corrupter of the ſociety of men aſpire to the habitations of pure and bleſſed ſpirits?—Believe it, *He that faith he loveth God muſt love his brother alſo. Ceaſe to do evil: Learn to do well. Seek judgment, relieve the oppreſſed, judge the fatherleſs, plead for the widow:* And then, *draw nigh to God, and he will draw nigh to thee;* call upon him

* *Iſa.* i. 11. 14.

Piety and Morality.

him in the day of trouble, and he will anfwer thee. Thy prayers and thine alms fhall then afcend in joint memorial before the Moft High.

I HAVE now fhewn the evil of maiming and fplitting religion; of dividing afunder two things which though in theory they may be feparated, yet in practice muft always co-exift, if either of them be real, Devotion to God and Charity to men. Let us confider next the happy effects of their union.

Their union forms the confiftent, the graceful, the refpectable character of the real Chriftian, the man of true worth. If you leave either of them out of your fyftem, even though you excel in the other, you can ftand trial only in one point of view. It is only on one fide your character is fair; on the other, it will always be open to much reproach. And as you difhonour yourfelves, fo you do great injuftice to religion. For, by dividing its parts from one another, you never fail to expofe it to the cenfure of the world: And perhaps, by this fort of partial and divided goodnefs, religion has fuffered more in the efteem of mankind than by open profligacy. The unbeliever will fcoff at your piety, when he fees you negligent of moral duties. The bigot will decry all morality, when he fees you pretending to be a follower of virtue, though you be a defpifer of God. Whereas he who fears God, and is at the fame time juft and beneficent to men, exhibits religion to the world with full propriety. It fhines in his conduct with its native fplendour; and its rays throw a glory round him. His character is above reproach. It is at once amiable and venerable. Malice itfelf is afraid to attack him; and even the worft men refpect and honour him in their hearts.

This, too, is the man whofe life will be moft peaceful and happy. He who fails materially either in piety or in virtue, is always obnoxious to the anguifh of remorfe. His partial goodnefs may flatter him in the day of fuperficial obfervation; but when folitude or diftrefs awakens the powers of reflection, he fhall be made to feel, that one part of duty performed, atones not for another which is neglected. In the midft of his prayers, the remembrance of injuftice will upbraid him with hypocrify; and in the diftribution of his alms, the prayers which the poor put up for him, will make him blufh for his neglect of God. Confcience will fupply the place of the hand coming forth to write over againft him on the wall, *Thou art weighed in the balance, and art found wanting**. Whereas he who *holds both faith and a good confcience*, who attends equally to the difcharge of his duty towards

God

---

* *Dan.* v. 27.

God and towards man, enjoys, as far as human imperfection allows, the sense of fairness and consistency in conduct, of integrity and soundness of heart.

The man of mere morality, is a stranger to all the delicate and refined pleasures of devotion. In works of beneficence and mercy, he may enjoy satisfaction. But his satisfaction is destitute of that glow of affection, which enlivens the feelings of one who lifts his heart at the same time to the Father of the Universe, and considers himself as imitating God. The man again who rests solely in devotion, if that devotion open not his heart to humanity, not only remains a stranger to the pleasures of beneficence, but must often undergo the pain arising from bad passions. But when beneficence and devotion are united, they pour upon the man in whom they meet, the full pleasures of a good and pure heart. His alms connect him with men; his prayers with God. He looks without dismay on both worlds. All nature has to him a benign aspect. If engaged in active life, he is the friend of men ; and he is happy in the exertions of that friendship. If left in retirement, he walks among the works of nature, as with God. Every object is enlivened to him by the sense of the Divine presence. Every where he traces the beneficent hand of the Author of nature; and every where, with glowing heart, he hears and answers his secret voice. When he looks up to heaven, he rejoices in the thought that there dwells that God whom he serves and honours ; that Saviour in whom he trusts ; that Spirit of grace from whose inspiration his piety and his charity flow. When he looks around him on the world, he is soothed with the pleasing remembrance of good offices which he has done, or at least has studied to do, to many who dwell there. How comfortable the reflection, that him no poor man can upbraid for having withheld his due ; him no unfortunate man can reproach for having seen and despised his sorrows ; but that on his head are descending the prayers of the needy and the aged ; and that the hands of those whom his protection has supported, or his bounty has fed, are lifted up in secret to bless him!

Life, passed under the influence of such dispositions, naturally leads to a happy end. It is not enough to say, that faith and piety, joined with active virtue, constitute the requisite preparation for heaven. They in truth begin the enjoyment of heaven. In every state of our existence, they form the chief ingredients of felicity. Hence they are the great marks of Christian regeneration. They are the signature of that Holy Spirit, by which good men are said to be *sealed unto the day of redemption*. The text affords a striking proof of the estimation in which they are held by God. Amidst that infinite variety

riety of human events which pass under his eye, the prayers and the alms of Cornelius attracted his particular notice. He remarked the amiable dispositions which rose in the heart of this good man. But he saw that they were yet imperfect, while he remained unenlightened by the principles of the Christian religion. In order to remove this obstruction to his rising graces, and to bring him to the full knowledge of that God whom he sought to honour, he was favoured with a supernatural message from heaven. While the Princes of the earth were left to act by the counsels of their own wisdom; while, without interposition from above, Generals conquered or fell, according to the vicissitude of human things; to this good Centurion an angel was commissioned from the throne of God.

What can I say more or higher in praise of this blessed character, than that it is what God delights to honour? Men single out as the objects of distinction, the great, the brave, or the renowned. But he *who seeth not as man seeth*, passing by those qualities which often shine with false splendour to human observation, looks to the inward principles of action; to those principles which form the essence of a worthy character; and which, if called forth, would give birth to whatever is laudable or excellent in conduct.—Is there one, though in humble station or obscure life, who *feareth God and worketh righteousness;* whose prayers and alms, proceeding in regular unaffected tenour, bespeak the upright, the tender, the devout heart.—Those alms and prayers come up in memorial before that God who is *no respecter of persons.* The Almighty beholds him from his throne with complacency. Divine illumination is ready to instruct him. Angels minister to him. They now mark him out on earth as their future associate; and for him they make ready in paradise, *the white robes, the palms, and the sceptres* of the just.

To this honour, to this blessedness, let our hearts continually aspire; and throughout the whole of life, let those solemn and sacred words, with which I conclude, found in our ears, and be the great directory of our conduct: * *He hath shewed thee, O man, what is good; and what doth the Lord thy God require of thee, but—to do justly, and love mercy—and to walk humbly with thy God?*

SERMON

* *Micah* vi. 8.

SERMON II.

On the Influence of RELIGION upon ADVERSITY.

PSALM xxvii. 5.

In the time of trouble, he shall hide me in his pavilion; in the secret of his tabernacle shall he hide me; he shall set me upon a rock.

THE life of man has always been a very mixed state, full of uncertainty and viciffitude, of anxieties and fears. In every religious audience, there are many who fall under the denomination of the unfortunate; and the reft are ignorant how foon they may be called to join them. For the profperity of no man on earth is ftable and affured. Dark clouds may foon gather over the heads of thofe whofe fky is now moft bright. In the midft of the deceitful calm which they enjoy, the ftorm that is to overwhelm them has perhaps already begun to ferment. *If a man live many years, and rejoice in them all; yet let him remember the days of darknefs, for they fhall be many*[*].

Hence, to a thoughtful mind, no ftudy can appear more important, than how to be fuitably prepared for the misfortunes of life; fo as to contemplate them in profpect without difmay, and, if they muft befal, to bear them without dejection. Throughout every age, the wifdom of the wife, the treafures of the rich, and the power of the mighty, have been employed, either in guarding their ftate againft the approach of diftrefs, or in rendering themfelves lefs vulnerable by its attacks. Power has endeavoured to remove adverfity to a diftance. Philofophy has ftudied, when it drew nigh, to conquer it by patience; and Wealth has fought out every pleafure that can compenfate or alleviate pain.

While the wifdom of the world is thus occupied, religion has been no lefs attentive to the fame important object. It informs us in the text, of *a pavilion* which God erects to fhelter his fervants *in the time of trouble*, of a *fecret place in his tabernacle*, into which he brings them, of a *rock on which he fets them up;* and elfewhere he tells us, of a *fhield and a buckler* which he fpreads before them, *to cover them from the terrour*

[*] *Ecclef.* xi. 8.

rour by night, and the arrow that flieth by day. Now, of what nature are those instruments of defence, which God is represented as providing with such solicitous care for those who fear him? Has he reared up any bulworks, impregnable by misfortune, in order to separate the pious and virtuous from the rest of mankind, and to screen them from the common disasters of life? No: To those disasters we behold them liable no less than others. The defence which religion provides, is altogether of an internal kind. It is the heart, not the outward state, which it professes to guard. When the *time of trouble* comes, as come it must to all, it places good men under *the pavilion* of the Almighty, by affording them that security and peace which arises from the belief of divine protection. It brings them into the *secret of his tabernacle*, by opening to them sources of consolation which are hidden from others. By that strength of mind with which it endows them, *it sets them up upon a rock*, against which the tempest may violently beat, but which it cannot shake.

How far the comforts proceeding from religion merit those high titles under which they are here figuratively described, I shall in this discourse endeavour to show. I shall for this end compare together the situation of bad men, and that of the good, when both are suffering the misfortunes of life; and then make such improvement as the subject will naturally suggest.

I. RELIGION prepares the mind for encountering, with fortitude, the most severe shocks of adversity; whereas vice, by its natural influence on the temper, tends to produce dejection under the slightest trials. While worldly men enlarge their possessions, and extend their connections, they imagine that they are strengthening themselves against all the possible vicissitudes of life. They say in their hearts, *My mountain stands strong, and I shall never be moved.* But so fatal is their delusion, that, instead of strengthening, they are weakening that which only can support them when those vicissitudes come. It is their mind which must then support them; and their mind, by their sensual attachments, is corrupted and enfeebled. Addicted with intemperate fondness to the pleasures of the world, they incur two great and certain evils; they both exclude themselves from every resource except the world and they increase their sensibility to every blow which comes upon them from that quarter.

They have neither principles nor temper which can stand the assault of trouble. They have no principles which lead them to look beyond

H   the

the ordinary rotation of events; and therefore, when misfortunes involve them, the prospect must be comfortless on every side. Their crimes have difqualified them from looking up to the affiftance of any higher power than their own ability, or for relying on any better guide than their own wifdom. And as from principle they can derive no fupport, fo in a temper corrupted by profperity they find no relief. They have loft that moderation of mind which enables a wife man to accommodate himfelf to his fituation. Long fed with falfe hopes, they are exafperated and ftung by every difappointment. Luxurious and effeminate, they can bear no uneafinefs. Proud and prefumptuous, they can brook no oppofition. By nourifhing difpofitions which fo little fuit this uncertain ftate, they have infufed a double portion of bitternefs into the cup of woe; they have fharpened the edge of that fword which is lifted up to fmite them. Strangers to all the temperate fatisfactions of a good and a pure mind; ftrangers to every pleafure except what was feafoned by vice or vanity, their adverfity is to the laft degree difconfolate. Health and opulence were the two pillars on which they refted. Shake either of them, and their whole edifice of hope and comfort falls. Proftrate and forlorn, they are left on the ground; obliged to join with the man of Ephraim in his abject lamentation, *They have taken away my gods which I have made, and what have I more?* *—Such are the caufes to which we muft afcribe the broken fpirits, the peevifh temper, and impatient paffions, that fo often attend the declining age, or falling fortunes, of vicious men.

But how different is the condition of a truly good man in thofe trying fituations of life. Religion had gradually prepared his mind for all the events of this inconftant ftate. It had inftructed him in the nature of true happinefs. It had early weaned him from the undue love of the world, by difcovering to him its vanity, and by fetting higher profpects in his view. Afflictions do not attack him by furprife, and therefore do not overwhelm him. He was equipped for the ftorm, as well as the calm, in this dubious navigation of life. Under thofe conditions he knew himfelf to be brought hither, that he was not to retain always the enjoyment of what he loved: And therefore he is not overcome by difappointment, when that which is mortal dies; when that which is mutable begins to change; and when that which he knew to be tranfient paffes away.

All the principles which religion teaches, and all the habits which it forms, are favourable to ftrength of mind. It will be found, that whatever purifies, fortifies alfo the heart. In the courfe of living
righteoufly,

* *Judges,* xviii. 24.

righteoufly, foberly, and godly, a good man acquires a fteady and well-governed fpirit. Trained, by Divine grace, to enjoy with moderation the advantages of the world, neither lifted up by fuccefs, nor enervated with fenfuality, he meets the changes in his lot without unmanly dejection. He is inured to temperance and reftraint. He has learned firmnefs and felf-command. He is accuftomed to look up to that Supreme Providence, which difpofes of human affairs, not with reverence only, but with truft and hope.

The time of profperity was to him not merely a feafon of barren joy, but productive of much ufeful improvement. He had cultivated his mind. He had ftored it with ufeful knowledge, with good principles, and virtuous difpofitions. Thefe refources remain entire, when the days of trouble come. They remain with him in ficknefs, as in health; in poverty as in the midft of riches; in his dark and folitary hours, no lefs than when furrounded with friends and gay fociety. From the glare of profperity he can, without dejection, withdraw into the fhade. Excluded from feveral advantages of the world, he may be obliged to retreat into a narrower circle; but within that circle he will find many comforts left. His chief pleafures were always of the calm, innocent, and temperate kind; and over thefe, the changes of the world have the leaft power. His mind is a kingdom to him; and he can ftill enjoy it. The world did not beftow upon him all his enjoyments; and therefore it is not in the power of the world by its moft cruel attacks, to carry them all away.

II. The diftreffes of life are alleviated to good men, by reflections on their paft conduct; while, by fuch reflections, they are highly aggravated to the bad. During the gay and active periods of life, finners elude, in fome meafure, the force of confcience. Carried round in the whirl of affairs and pleafures; intent on contrivance, or eager in purfuit; amufed by hope, or elated by enjoyment; they are fheltered, by that crowd of trifles which furrounds them, from ferious thought. But confcience is too great a power to remain always fuppreffed. There is in every man's life, a period when he fhall be made to ftand forth as a real object to his own view: And when that period comes, wo to him who is galled by the fight! In the dark and folitary hour of diftrefs, with a mind hurt and fore from fome recent wound of fortune, how fhall he bear to have his character, for the firft time, difclofed to him in that humiliating light under which guilt will neceffarily prefent it? Then, the recollection of the paft becomes dreadful. It exhibits to him a life thrown away on vanities and follies, or confumed in fla-
gitioufnefs

gitioufnefs and fin; no ftation properly fupported; no material duties fulfilled. Crimes which once had been eafily palliated, rife before him in their native deformity. The fenfe of guilt mixes itfelf with all that has befallen him. He beholds, or thinks that he beholds, the hand of the God whom he hath offended, openly ftretched out againft him.—At a feafon when a man ftands moft in need of fupport, how intolerable is the weight of this additional load, aggravating the depreffion of difeafe, difappointment, or old age! How miferable his ftate, who is condemned to endure at once the pangs of guilt, and the vexations of calamity! *The fpirit of a man may fuftain his infirmities; but a wounded fpirit, who can bear?*

Whereas, he who is bleffed with a clear confcience, enjoys, in the worft conjunctures of human life, a peace, a dignity, an elevation of mind peculiar to virtue. The teftimony of a good confcience is indeed to be always diftinguifhed from that prefumptuous boaft of innocence, which every good Chriftian totally difclaims. The better he is, he will be the more humble, and fenfible of his failings. But though he acknowledge that he can claim nothing from God upon the footing of defert, yet he can truft in his merciful acceptance through Jefus Chrift, according to the terms of the gofpel. He can hope that his *prayers and his alms have come up in memorial before God.* The piety and virtue of his former life were as feeds fown in his profperous ftate, of which he reaps the fruits in the feafon of adverfity. The riches, the pleafures, and the friends of the world, may have made *wings to themfelves, and flown away.* But the improvement which he made of thofe advantages while they lafted, the temperate fpirit with which he enjoyed them, the beneficent actions which he performed, and the good example which he fet to others, remain behind. By the memory of thefe, he enjoys his profperity a fecond time in reflection; and perhaps this fecond and reflected enjoyment is not inferior to the firft. It arrives at a more critical and needful time. It affords him the high fatisfaction of having extracted lafting pleafure from that which is fhort; and of having fixed that which by its nature was changing.— " If my race be now about to end, I have this comfort, that it has not " been run in vain. *I have fought the good fight: I have kept the faith.* " My mind has no load. Futurity has no terrours. I have endeavoured " to do my duty, and to make my peace with God. I leave the reft " to Heaven." Thefe are the reflections which *to the upright make light arife in darknefs;* reflections which cheer the lonely houfe of virtuous poverty, and attend the confcientious fufferer into prifon or exile; which footh the complaints of grief, lighten the preffure of old age,

and

and furnish to the bed of sickness, a cordial of more grateful relish, and more sovereign virtue, than any which the world can afford.

Look abroad into life, and you will find the general sense of mankind bearing witness to this important truth, that mind is superior to fortune; that what one feels within, is of much greater importance than all that befals him without. Let a man be brought into some such severe and trying situation, as fixes the attention of the public on his behaviour. The first question which we put concerning him, is not, What does he suffer? but How does he bear it? Has he a quiet mind? or, Does he appear to be unhappy within? If we judge him to be composed and firm, resigned to Providence, and supported by conscious integrity, his character rises, and his misery lessens in our view. We esteem and admire, rather than pity him. Recollect what holy men have endured for the sake of conscience, and with what cheerfulness they have suffered. On the other hand, when conscience has concurred with outward misfortunes in distressing the guilty, think of the dreadful consequences which have ensued. How often, upon a reverse of fortune, after abused prosperity, have they madly hurried themselves over that precipice from which there is no return; and, in what nature most abhors, the voluntary extinction of life, have sought relief from that torment of reflection, which was become too great for them to bear?

Never then allow yourselves to imagine, that misfortunes alone form the chief misery of man. None but the guilty are completely miserable. The misgiving and distrust, the accusations and approaches of their minds, the sense of having drawn down upon their heads the evils which they suffer, and the terrifying expectation of more and worse evils to come; these are the essential ingredients of human misery. They not only whet the edge, but they envenom the darts of affliction, and add poison to the wound. Whereas, when misfortunes assail a good man, they carry no such fatal auxiliaries in their train. They may ruffle the surface of his soul; but there is a strength within, which resists their further impression. The constitution of his mind is sound. The world can inflict upon it no wounds, but what admit of cure.

III. Ill men, in the time of trouble, can look up to no protector; while good men commit themselves, with trust and hope, to the care of Heaven. The human mind, naturally feeble, is made to feel all its weakness by the pressure of adversity. Dejected with evils which overpower its strength, it relies no longer on itself. It calls every where around a wishing, exploring eye, for some shelter to screen, some power to uphold it; and if, when abandoned by the world, it can find nothing to which it may fly in the room of the world, its state is truly forlorn. Now, whither should the ungodly, in this situation, turn for aid? After having contended with the storms of adverse fortune till their spirits are exhausted, gladly would they retreat at last to the sanctuary of religion. But that sanctuary is shut against them; nay, it is environed with terrours. They behold there, not a Protector to whom they can fly, but a Judge whom they dread; and in those moments when they need his friendship the most, they are reduced to deprecate his wrath. If he once *called when they refused, and stretched out his hands when they would not regard*, how much reason have they to fear that he will leave them now to *eat the fruit of their own ways, and to be filled with their own devices*, that he *will laugh at their calamity, and mock when their fear cometh?*

But of all the thoughts which can enter into the mind, in the season of distress, the belief of an interest in his favour who rules the world is the most soothing. Every form of religion has afforded to virtuous men some degree of this consolation. But it was reserved for the Christian revelation, to carry it to its highest point. For it is the direct scope of that revelation, to accomodate itself to the circumstances of man, under two main views; as guilty in the sight of God, and as struggling with the evils of the world. Under the former, it discovers to him a Mediator and an atonement; under the latter, it promises him the Spirit of grace and consolation. It is a system of complete relief, extended from our spiritual to our temporal distresses. The same hand which holds out forgiveness to the penitent, and assistance to the frail, dispenses comfort and hope to the afflicted.

It deserves your particular notice, in this view, that there is no character which God more frequently assumes to himself in the sacred writings, than that of the Patron of the distressed. Compassion is that attribute of his nature which he has chosen to place in the greatest variety of lights, on purpose that he might accommodate his majesty to our weakness, and provide a cordial for human griefs. He is the hearer of all prayers; but with particular attention he is represented as listening to the *cry of the poor*, and *regarding the prayer of the destitute*. All his creatures he governs with justice and wisdom; but he takes to himself, in a special manner, the charge of *executing judgment for the oppressed*, of *protecting the stranger*, of *delivering him who hath no helper from the hand of the spoiler*. *For the oppression of the poor, and for the sighing of the needy, will I arise, saith the Lord, to set him in safety* *from him that puffeth at him.* He is the Father of the fatherless, and the Judge of the widow, in his holy habitation. He raiseth them up that are bowed down. He dwelleth with the contrite. He healeth the broken in heart. For he knoweth our frame; he remembereth that we are dust.* If the wisdom of his providence saw it necessary to place so many of his creatures in an afflicted state, that state, however, he commiserates. He disdains not to point out himself as the refuge of the virtuous and pious; and to invite them, amidst all their troubles, to pour out their hearts before him. Those circumstances which estrange others from them, interest him the more in their situation. The neglect or scorn of the world exposes them not to any contempt in his sight. No obscurity conceals them from his notice; and though they should be forgotten by every friend on earth, they are remembered by the God of heaven. That sigh heaved from the afflicted bosom, which is heard by no human ear, is listened to by him; and that tear is remarked, which falls unnoticed or despised by the world.

Such views of the Supreme Being impart the most sensible consolation to every pious heart. They present his administration under an aspect so mild and benign, as in a great measure to disperse the gloom which hangs over human life. A good man acts with a vigour, and suffers with a patience more than human, when he believes himself countenanced by the Almighty. Injured or oppressed by the world, he looks up to a Judge who will vindicate his cause; he appeals to a Witness who knows his integrity; he commits himself to a Friend who will never forsake him. When tired with the vexations of life, devotion opens to him its quiet retreat, where the tumults of the world are hushed, and its cares are lost in happy oblivion; where *the wicked cease from troubling, and the weary are at rest.* There his mind regains its serenity; the agitation of passion is calmed; and a softening balm is infused into the wounds of the spirit. Disclosing to an invisible Friend those secret griefs which he has no encouragement to make known to the world, his heart is lightened. He does not feel himself solitary or forsaken. He believes God to be present with him, and the Holy Ghost to be the inspirer of his consolations. From that *secret place of the divine tabernacle,* into which the Text represents him as admitted, he hears this voice issue, *Call upon me in the day of trouble, and I will answer thee. Fear not; for I am with thee. Be not dismayed; for I am thy God.* And as he hears a voice which speaks to none but the pure in heart, so he beholds a hand which sinners cannot see. He beholds the hand of Providence
conducting

* *Psalms* ix. 8.—cii. 17.—cxlvi. 7.—lxviii. 5.—cxlvii. 3.—ciii. 14, &c.

conducting all the hidden springs and movements of the universe; and with a secret, but unerring operation, directing every event towards the happiness of the righteous. Those afflictions which appear to others the messengers of the wrath of Heaven, appear to him the ministers of sanctification and wisdom. Where they discern nothing but the horrours of the tempest which surrounds them, his more enlightened eye beholds the angel who rides in the whirlwind, and directs the storm. Hence a *peace keeping the mind and heart,* which is no where to be found but under the *pavilion of the Almighty.*

IV. GOOD men are comforted under their troubles by the hope of Heaven; while bad men are not only deprived of this hope, but distressed with fears arising from a future state. The soul of man can never divest itself wholly of anxiety about its fate hereafter. There are hours when even to the prosperous, in the midst of their pleasures, eternity is an awful thought. But much more when those pleasures, one after another, begin to withdraw; when life alters its forms, and becomes dark and cheerless; when its changes warn the most inconsiderate, that what is so mutable will soon pass entirely away; then with pungent earnestness comes home that question to the heart. Into what world are we next to go?—How miserable the man, who, under the distractions of calamity, hangs doubtful about an event which so nearly concerns him; who, in the midst of doubts and anxieties, approaching to that awful boundary which separates this world from the next, shudders at the dark prospect before him; wishing to exist after death, and yet afraid of that existence; catching at every feeble hope which superstition can afford him, and trembling, in the same moment, from reflection upon his crimes!

But blessed be God who hath *brought life and immortality to light;* who hath not only brought them to light, but secured them to good men; and by the death and resurrection of Jesus Christ, hath *begotten them unto the lively hope of an inheritance incorruptible, undefiled, and that fadeth not away.* Justly is this hope styled in scripture, the *anchor of the soul, both sure and stedfast.* For what an anchor is to a ship in a dark night, on an unknown coast, and amidst a boisterous ocean, that is this hope to the soul when distracted by the confusions of the world. In danger, it gives security; amidst general fluctuation, it affords one fixed point of rest. It is indeed the most eminent of all the advantages which religion now confers. For, consider the mighty power of hope over the human mind. It is the universal comforter. It is the spring of all human activity. Upon futurity, men are constantly

suspended

suspended. Animated by the prospect of some distant good, they toil and suffer through the whole course of life; and it is not so much what they are at present, as what they hope to be in some after-time, that enlivens their motions, fixes attention, and stimulates industry. Now, if, in the common affairs of life, such is the energy of hope, even when its object is neither very considerable, nor very certain; what effects may it not be expected to produce, when it rests upon an object so splendid as a life of immortal felicity? Were this hope entertained with that full persuasion which Christian faith demands, it would, in truth, not merely alleviate, but totally annihilate, all human miseries. It would banish discontent, extinguish grief, and suspend the very feeling of pain.

But allowing for the mixture of human frailty; admitting those abatements which our imperfection makes upon the effect of every religious principle, still you will find, that, in proportion to the degree in which the hope of heaven operates upon good men, they will be tranquil under sufferings; nay, they will be happy, in comparison of those who enjoy no such relief. What indeed, in the course of human affairs, is sufficient to distress, far less to overwhelm, the mind of that man who can look down on all human things from an elevation so much above them? He is only a passenger through this world. He is travelling to a happier country. How disagreeable soever the occurrences of his journey may be, yet at every stage of that journey, he receives the assurance that he is drawing nearer and nearer to the period of rest and felicity.—Endure, and thou shalt overcome. Persevere, and thou shalt be successful. The time of trial hastens to a close. Thy mansion is prepared above; thy rest remaineth among the people of God. The disorders which vice has introduced into the works of God, are about to terminate; and all tears are soon to be wiped away from the eyes of the just.—The firm assurance of this happy conclusion to the vexations and the vanities of life, works a greater effect on the sincere illiterate Christian, than all the refinements of philosophy can work on the most learned Infidel. These may gratify the mind that is at ease; may sooth the heart when slightly discomposed; but when it is sore and deeply torn, when bereaved of its best and most beloved comforts, the only consolations that can then find access, arise from the hope of a better world, where those comforts shall be again restored, and all the virtuous shall be assembled, in the presence of him who made them. Such hopes banish that despair which overwhelms, and leave only that tender melancholy which softens the heart, and often renders the whole character more gentle and amiable.

Of this nature are the resources which religion provides for good men. By its previous discipline, it trains them to fortitude; by the reflections of a good conscience it sooths, by the sense of Divine favour it supports them; and when every comfort fails them on earth, it cheers them with the hope of heaven. Distinguishing his servants with such advantages, God is justly said to erect *his pavilion* over them in the evil time. He not only *spreads a tent for them in the wilderness*, but he transforms in some measure the state of nature around them. To use the beautiful language of ancient prophecy; *In the desart, the thirsty land, where no water is, he openeth springs. Instead of the thorn, he maketh the fir tree to come up; instead of the briar, the myrtle to spring. In the midst of the habitations of dragons, he maketh green pastures rise, and still waters flow around his people.*

The improvement to be made of these truths is as obvious as it is important. Let us study so to conduct our lives, that we may be qualified for deriving such consolations from religion. To their reality, and their importance, all mankind bear witness: For no sooner are they overtaken by distress, than to religion they fly. This, throughout every age, has been the universal shelter which the young and the old, the high and the low, the giddy and the serious, have sought to gain, as soon as they found that rest could be no where else procured for the weary head, or the aching heart. But amidst those multitudes that crowd to religion for relief, how few are entitled to approach that sacred source of comfort! On what feeble props do their hopes and pretensions rest! How much superstition mingles with that religion to which men are driven by distress and fear!—You must first apply to it as the guide of life, before you can have recourse to it as the refuge of sorrow. You must submit to its legislative authority, and experience its renewing influence, before you can look for its consolatory effect. You must secure the testimony of a good conscience, and peace with God through Jesus Christ; otherwise, *when the floods shall come, and the rains descend, and the winds blow,* the house which you had proposed for your retreat, shall prove the *house founded on the sand,* not *on the rock.*

There are two plans, and there are but two, on which any man can propose to conduct himself through the dangers and distresses of human life. The one is the plan of worldly wisdom; the other, that of determined adherence to conscience. He who acts upon the former, lays principle aside, and trusts his defence to his art and ability. He avails himself of every advantage which his knowledge of the world

world suggests. He attends to nothing but what he considers as his interest; and, unconfined by conscience, pursues it by every course which promises him success. This plan, though too often adopted, will be found, on trial, ineffectual and deceitful. For human ability is an unequal match for the violent and unforeseen vicissitudes of the world. When these torrents rise in their might, they sweep away in a moment the banks which worldly wisdom had reared for defence, and overwhelm alike the crafty and the artless. In the mean time, persons of this character condemn themselves to live a most unquiet life. They pass their days in perpetual anxiety, listening to every motion; startled by every alarm; changing their measures on every new occurrence; and when distress breaks in over all their defences, they are left under it, hopeless and disconsolate.

The plan, which, in opposition to this, religion recommends, as both more honourable in itself, and more effectual for security, is, at all hazards, to do your duty, and to leave the consequences to God. Let him who would act upon this plan, adopt for the rule of his conduct that maxim of the Psalmists, *Trust in the Lord, and do good*[*]. To firm integrity, let him join a humble reliance on God. Let his adherence to duty encourage his religious trust. Let his religious trust inspire him with fortitude in the performance of his duty. Let him know no path but the straight and direct one. In the most critical moments of action, let him ask no further questions, than, What is the right, the fit, the worthy part? How, as a man, and as a Christian, it becomes him to act? Having received the decision of conscience, let him *commit his way unto the Lord*. Let him, without trepidation or wavering, proceed in discharging his duty; resolved, that though the world may make him unfortunate, it shall never make him base; and confiding, that in what God and his conscience require him to act or suffer, God and a good conscience will support him.—Such principles as these, are the best preparation for the vicissitudes of the human lot. They are the shield of inward peace. He who thinks and acts thus, shall be exposed to no wounds but what religion can cure. He may feel the blows of adversity; but he shall not know the wounds of the heart.

S·E R M O N

[*] *Psalm* xxxvii. 3.

SERMON III.

On the Influence of RELIGION upon PROSPERITY.

PSALM i. 3.

He shall be like a tree planted by the rivers of water, that bringeth forth his fruit in his season; his leaf also shall not wither, and whatsoever he doth shall prosper.

THE happy influence of religion upon human life, in the time of adversity, has been considered in the preceding discourse. Concerning this the sentiments of men are more generally agreed, than with respect to some other prerogatives which religion claims. They very readily assign to it the office of a Comforter. But as long as their state is prosperous, they are apt to account it an unnecessary guest, perhaps an unwelcome intruder. Let us not be thus unjust to religion, nor confine its importance to one period only in the life of man. It was never intended to be merely the nurse of sickness, and the staff of old age. I purpose now to shew you, that it is no less essential to the enjoyment of prosperity, than to the comfort of adversity; that prosperity is prosperous, if we may be allowed the expression to a good man only; and that to every other person, it will prove, notwithstanding its fair appearance, a barren and joyless state.

The Psalmist, in the Text, by an image taken from one of the most beautiful objects in nature, describes a man who flourishes in full prosperity. But to whom is the discription limited? To him, as the preceding verses inform us, *that walketh not in the council of the ungodly, nor standeth in the way of sinners, nor sitteth in the seat of the scornful, but hath his delight in the law of God.* He only is *like the tree planted by the rivers of water;* whilst the ungodly, as he adds, *are not so;* but how prosperous soever they may appear to the world, are, in truth, but like *the chaff which the wind driveth away.* In confirmation of this doctrine, I shall lay before you some of those circumstances which distinguish the prosperity of the good man beyond that of the sinner; and shall conclude, with pointing out the dangers and miseries into which the latter is apt to be betrayed by his favourable situation in the world.

I. PIETY,

I. PIETY, and gratitude to God, contribute in a high degree to enliven prosperity. Gratitude is a pleasing emotion. The sense of being distinguished by the kindness of another, gladdens the heart, warms it with reciprocal affection, and gives to any possession, which is agreeable in itself, a double relish, from its being the gift of a friend. Favours conferred by men, I acknowledge, may prove burdensome. For human virtue is never perfect; and sometimes unreasonable expectations on the one side, sometimes a mortifying sense of dependence on the other, corrode in secret the pleasure of benefits, and convert the obligations of friendship into grounds of jealousy. But nothing of this kind can affect the intercourse of gratitude with heaven. Its favours are wholly disinterested; and with a gratitude the most cordial and unsuspicious, a good man looks up to that Almighty Benefactor, who aims at no end but the happiness of those whom he blesses, and who desires no return from them but a devout and thankful heart. While others can trace their prosperity to no higher source than a concurrence of worldly causes, and, often, of mean or trifling incidents, which occasionally favoured their designs; with what superior satisfaction does the servant of God remark the hand of that gracious Power which hath raised him up, which hath happily conducted him through the various steps of life, and crowned him with the most favourable distinction beyond his equals?

Let us farther consider, that not only gratitude for the past, but a cheering sense of God's favour at the present, enter into the pious emotion. They are only the virtuous, who in their prosperous days hear this voice addressed to them, *Go thy way, eat thy bread with joy, and drink thy wine with a merry heart; for God now accepteth thy works**. He who is the Author of their prosperity, gives them a title to enjoy, with complacency, his own gift. While bad men snatch the pleasures of the world as by stealth, without countenance from God the proprietor of the world; the righteous sit openly down to the feast of life, under the smile of approving heaven. No guilty fears damp their joys. The blessing of God rests upon all that they possess; his protection surrounds them; and hence, *in the habitations of the righteous, is found the voice of rejoicing and salvation.* A lustre unknown to others, invests, in their sight, the whole face of nature. Their piety reflects a sunshine from heaven upon the prosperity of the world; unites in one point of view, the smiling aspect, both of the powers above, and of the objects below. Not only have they

as

* *Eccles.* ix. 7.

as full a relish as others, of the innocent pleasures of life, but, moreover, in these they hold communion with God. In all that is good or fair, they trace his hand. From the beauties of nature, from the improvements of art, from the enjoyments of social life, they raise their affection to the source of all the happiness which surrounds them; and thus widen the sphere of their pleasures, by adding intellectual, and spiritual, to earthly joys.

For illustration of what I have said on this head, remark that cheerful enjoyment of a prosperous state which King David had, when he wrote the twenty-third Psalm; and compare the highest pleasures of the riotous sinner, with the happy and satisfied spirit which breathes throughout that Psalm.—In the midst of the splendour of royalty, with what amiable simplicity of gratitude does he look up to the Lord as *his Shepherd*; happier in ascribing all his success to divine favour, than to the policy of his councils, or to the force of his arms! How many instances of divine goodness arose before him, in pleasing remembrance, when with such relish he speaks of the *green pastures and still waters b side which God had led him;* of *his cup which he hath made to overflow;* and of *the table which he hath prepared for him in presence of his enemies!* With what perfect tranquillity does he look forward to the time of his passing through *the valley of the shadow of death!* unappalled by that spectre, whose most distant appearance blasts the prosperity of sinners! He fears no evil, as long as *the rod and the staff* of his Divine Shepherd are with him; and, through all the unknown periods of this and of future existence, commits himself to his guidance, with secure and triumphant hope. *Surely goodness and mercy shall follow me all the days of my life; and I will dwell in the house of the Lord for ever.*—What a purified, sentimental enjoyment of prosperity is here exhibited! How different from the gross relish of worldly pleasures, which belongs to those who behold only the terrestrial side of things; who raise their views to no higher objects than the succession of human contingencies, and the weak efforts of human ability; who have no protector or patron in the heavens, to enliven their prosperity, or to warm their hearts with gratitude and trust.

II. RELIGION affords to good men peculiar security in the enjoyment of their prosperity. One of the first reflections which must strike every thinking man, after his situation in the world has become agreeable, is, that the continuance of such a situation is most uncertain. From a variety of causes, he lies open to change. On many sides he sees that he may be pierced; and the wider his comforts

forts extend, the broader is the mark which he spreads to the arrows of misfortune. Hence many a secret alarm to the reflecting mind; and to those who reject all such alarms, the real danger increases, in proportion to their improvident security.

By worldly assistance it is vain to think of providing any effectual defence, seeing the world's mutability is the very cause of our terrour. It is from a higher principle, from a power superiour to the world, that relief must be sought, amidst such disquietudes of the heart. He who in his prosperity can look up to One who is witness to his moderation, humanity, and charity; he who can appeal to Heaven, that he has not been elated by pride, nor overcome by pleasure, but has studied to employ its gifts to the honour of the Giver; this man, if there be any truth in religion, if there be any benignity or goodness in the administration of the universe, has just cause for encouragement and hope. Not that an interest in the Divine grace will perpetuate to a good man, more than to others, a life of unruffled prosperity. Change and alteration form the very essence of the world. But let the world change around him at pleasure, he has ground to hope that it shall not be able to make him unhappy. Whatever may vary, God's providence is still the same; and his love to the righteous remains unaltered. If it shall be the Divine will to remove one comfort, he trusts that some other shall be given. Whatever is given, whatever is taken away, he confides that, in the last result, all *shall work for his good.*

Hence he is not disturbed, like bad men, by the instability of the world. Dangers, which overcome others, shake not his more steady mind. He enjoys the pleasures of life pure and unallayed, because he enjoys them, as long as they last, without anxious terrours. They are not his all, his only good. He welcomes them when they arrive; and when they pass away, he can eye them, as they depart, without agony or despair. His prosperity strikes a deeper and firmer root than that of the ungodly. And for this reason he is compared, in the Text, to a *tree planted by the rivers of water;* a tree, whose branches the tempest may indeed bend, but whose roots it cannot touch; a tree, which may occasionally be stripped of its leaves and blossoms but which still maintains its place, and in due season flourishes anew. Whereas the sinner in his prosperity, according to the allusion in the book of Job, resembles *the rush that groweth up in the mire**; a slender reed, that may flourish green for a while by the side of the brook, as long as it is cherished by the sun, and fanned by the breeze; till the first bitter blast breaks

Job viii. 11.

breaks its feeble stem, roots it out from its bed, and lays it in the dust. Lo! such is the prosperity of *them that forget God; and thus their hope shall perish.*

III. Religion forms good men to the most proper temper for the enjoyment of prosperity. A little reflection may satisfy us, that mere possession, even granting it to be secure, does not constitute enjoyment. Give a man all that is in the power of the world to the bestow; surround him with riches; crown him with honours; invest him, if you will, with absolute dominion; but leave him at the same time under some secret oppression or heaviness of heart; you bestow indeed the materials of enjoyment, but you deprive him of ability to extract it. You set a feast before him, but he wants the power of tasting it. Hence prosperity is so often an equivocal word, denoting merely affluence of possession, but unjustly applied to the miserable possessor.

We all know the effects which any indisposition of the body, even though slight, produces on external prosperity. Visit the gayest and most fortunate man on earth, only with sleepless nights; disorder any single organ of the senses; corrode but one of his smallest nerves; and you shall presently see all his gaiety vanish; and you shall hear him complain that he is a miserable creature, and express his envy of the peasant and the cottager.—And can you believe, that a disease in the soul is less fatal to enjoyment than a disease in the animal frame; or that a sound mind is not as essential as a sound body, to the prosperity of man?—Let us rate sensual gratifications as high as we please, we shall be made to feel that the seat of enjoyment is in the soul. The corrupted temper, and the guilty passions of the bad, frustrate the effect of every advantage which the world confers on them. The world may call them men of pleasure; but of all men they are the greatest foes to pleasure. From their eagerness to grasp, they strangle and destroy it. None but the temperate, the regular, and the virtuous, know how to enjoy prosperity. They bring to its comforts the manly relish of a sound uncorrupted mind. They stop at the proper point, before enjoyment degenerates into disgust and pleasure is converted into pain. They are strangers to those complaints which flow from spleen, caprice, and all the fantastical distresses of a vitiated mind. While riotous indulgence enervates both the body and the mind, purity and virtue heighten all the powers of human fruition. Moderate and simple pleasures relish high with the temperate; in the midst of his studied refinements, the voluptuary languishes.

Wherever

Wherever guilt mingles with prosperity, a certain gloom and heaviness enter along with it. Vicious intrigues never fail to entangle and embarrass those who engage in them. But innocence confers ease and freedom on the mind; leaves it open to every pleasing sensation; gives a lightness to the spirits, similar to the native gaiety of youth and health; ill imitated, and ill supplied, by that forced levity of the vicious, which arises not from the health, but from the drunkenness of the mind.

Feeble are all pleasures in which the heart has no part. The selfish gratifications of the bad, are both narrow in their circle, and short in their duration. But prosperity is redoubled to a good man, by his generous use of it. It is reflected back upon him from every one whom he makes happy. In the intercourse of domestic affection, in the attachment of friends, the gratitude of dependents, the esteem and good will of all who know him, he sees blessings multiplied round him, on every side. *When the ear heard me, then it blessed me, and when the eye saw me; it gave witness to me: Because I delivered the poor that cried, the fatherless, and him that had none to help him. The blessing of him that was ready to perish came upon me, and I caused the widow's heart to sing with joy. I was eyes to the blind, and feet was I to the lame: I was a father to the poor; and the cause which I knew not, I searched out*.*—Thus, while the righteous *flourisheth like a tree planted by the rivers of water, he bringeth forth* also *his fruit in his season:* And that fruit, to pursue the allusion of the Text, he brings forth, not for himself alone. He flourishes, not like a tree in some solitary desart, which scatters its blossoms to the wind, and communicates neither fruit nor shade to any living thing; but like a tree in the midst of an inhabited country, which to some affords friendly shelter, to others, fruit; which is not only admired by all for its beauty, but blessed by the traveller for the shade, and by the hungry for the sustenance it hath given.

IV. RELIGION heightens the prosperity of good men, by the prospect which it affords them of greater happiness to come in another world. I shewed, in the foregoing discourse, the mighty effect of the hope of Heaven, in relieving the mind under the troubles of life. And sure, if this hope be able to support the falling, it cannot but improve the flourishing state of man; if it can dispel the thickest gloom of adversity, it must needs enliven prosperity, by the additional lustre which it throws upon it. What is present, is never sufficient

* *Job* xxix. 11—17.

to give us full satisfaction. To the present we must always join some agreeable anticipations of futurity, in order to complete our pleasure. What an accession then must the prosperity of the righteous man receive, when, borne with a smooth and gentle gale along the current of life, and looking round on all the blessings of his state, he can consider these as no more than an introduction to higher scenes which are hereafter to open; he can view his present life, as only the porch through which he is to pass into the palace of bliss; and his present joys, as but a feeble stream, dispensed for his occasional refreshment, until he arrive at that river of life, which flows at God's right hand!—Such prospects purify the mind, at the same time that they gladden it. They prevent the good man from setting too high a value on his present possessions; and thereby assist him in maintaining, amidst the temptations of worldly pleasure, that command of himself which is so essential to the wise and temperate enjoyment of prosperity.

It is the fate of all human pleasures, by continuance, to fade; of most of them, to cloy. Hence, in the most prosperous state, there are frequent intervals of langour, and even of dejection. There are vacuities in the happiest life, which it is not in the power of the world to fill up. What relief so adapted to those vacant or dejected periods, as the pleasing hopes which arise from immortality? How barren and imperfect that prosperity, which can have recourse to no such subsidiary comfort, in order to animate the stagnation of vulgar life, and to supply the insufficiency of worldly pleasures!

Worldly prosperity declines with declining life. In youth its relish was brisk and poignant. It becomes more sober as life advances; and flattens as life descends. He, who lately overflowed with cheerful spirits and high hopes, begins to look back with heaviness on the days of former years. He thinks of his old companions who are gone; and reviews past scenes, more agreeable than any which are likely to return. The activity of pursuit is weakened. The gaiety of amusement is fled. The gratifications of sense languish. When his accustomed pleasures, one after another, thus steal treacherously away, what can he, who is an utter stranger to religion, and to the hope of Heaven, substitute in their place?—But even in that drooping period, the promises and hopes of religion support the spirits of a good man till the latest hour. *His leaf,* it is said in the Text, *shall not wither.* It shall not be in the power of time to blast his prosperity: But old age shall receive him into a quiet retreat, where, if lively sensations fail, gentle pleasures remain to sooth him. That hope of immortality, which formerly improved his other enjoyments,

joyments, now in a great meafure fupplies their abfence. Its importance rifes, in proportion as its object draws near. He is not forfaken by the world, but retires from it with dignity; reviewing with a calm mind, the part which he has acted, and trufting to the promife of God for an approaching reward. Such fentiments and expectations fhed a pleafing tranquility over the old age of the righteous man. They make the evening of his days go down unclouded; and allow the ftream of life, though fallen low, to run clear to the laft drop.

Thus I have fhewn, I hope, with full evidence, what material ingredients religion and a good confcience are in the profperity of life. Separated from them, profperity, how fair foever it may feem to the world, is infipid, nay frequently noxious to the poffeffor: United with them, it rifes into a real bleffing beftowed by God upon man. *God giveth to a man that is good in his fight, wifdom, and knowledge, and joy; but to the finner he giveth fore travail, to gather, and to heap up, that he may give to him that is good before God*.

Allow me now to conclude the fubject, with reprefenting to the profperous men of the world, thofe crimes and miferies into which the abufe of their condition is likely to betray them, and calling upon them to beware of the dangers with which they are threatened.

It is unfortunate for mankind, that thofe fituations which favour pleafure, are too generally adverfe to virtue. Virtue requires internal government and difcipline; profperity relaxes the mind and inflames the paffions. Virtue is fupported by a regard to what is future; profperity attaches us wholly to what is prefent. The characteriftics of virtue, are modefty and humility; the moft common attendents of profperity, are pride and prefumption. One fhould think, that profperity would prove the ftrongeft incitement to remember and to honour that God who beftows it. Yet fuch is the perverfenefs of human nature, that it proves much oftener the motive to impiety. The changes of the world call the attention of men to an Invifible Power. But a train of events proceeding according to their wifh, leads them to nothing beyond what they fee. The Supreme Giver is concealed from view by his own gifts. This inftance of fuccefs they afcribe to a fortunate concurrence of worldly caufes; that acquifition, to their own fkill and induftry; unmindful of Him, who from the beginning arranged that feries of caufes, and who placed them in circumftances where their induftry could operate with fuccefs. From forgetting God, they too often proceed to defpife him. All that

* *Ecclef.* ii. 26.

that is light or giddy in their minds, is set in motion by the gale of prosperity. Arrogance and self-sufficiency are lifted up; and their state is considered, as secured by their own strength. Hence that *pride of countenance*, through which the wicked, in their prosperity, as David observes, *refuse to seek after God*. They are described *as speaking loftily, and setting their mouth against the Heavens. They take the timbrel and harp, and rejoice at the sound of the organ; and they say unto God, Depart from us, for we desire not the knowledge of thy ways. What is the almighty that we should serve him? Or, what profit should we have, if we pray unto him?*

They say unto God, Depart from us.—What an impious voice! Could we have believed it possible, that worldly pleasures should so far intoxicate any human heart? Wretched and infatuated men! Have you ever examined on what your confidence rests?—You have said in your hearts, *You shall never be moved;* you fancy yourselves placed on a *mountain which standeth strong*. Awake from those flattering dreams, and behold how every thing totters around you! You stand on the edge of a precipice; and the ground is sliding away below your feet. In your health, life, possessions, connections, pleasures, principles of destruction work. The mine advances in secret, which saps the foundations, while you revel on the surface. No mighty effort, no long preparation of events, is needed to overturn your prosperity. By slow degrees it rose. Long time, much labour, and the concurrence of many assisting causes, were necessary to rear it up; but one slight incident can entirely overthrow it. Suspicions are infused into the patron or the prince on whom you depend; and your disgrace ensues. Exercise, or amusement, kindles a fever in the veins of those whom you loved; and you are robbed of your comforts and hopes. A few grains of sand lodge themselves within you; and the rest of your life is disease and misery. Ten thousand contingencies ever float on the current of life, the smallest of which, if it meet your frail bark in the passing, is sufficient to dash it in pieces.—Is this a place, is this a time, to swell with fancied security, to riot in unlawful pleasure, and, by your disregard of moral and religious duties, to brave the government of the Almighty? He hath stamped every possession of man with this inscription, *Rejoice with trembling.* Throughout every age, he hath pointed his peculiar displeasure against the confidence of presumption, and the arrogance of prosperity. He hath pronounced, that *whosoever exalteth himself shall be abased.* And shall neither the admonitions which you receive from the visible inconstancy of the world, nor the declarations of the Divine displeasure

Religion upon Prosperity. 77

sure be sufficient to check your thoughtless career? Know that, by your impiety you multiply the dangers which already threaten you on every side; you accelerate the speed with which the changes of the world advance to your destruction. The Almighty touches with his rod that edifice of dust, on which you stand, and boast of your strength; and, at that instant, it crumbles to nothing.

As men, then, bethink yourselves of human instability. As Christians, reverence the awful government of God. Insure your prosperity, by consecrating it to religion and virtue. Be humble in your elevation; be moderate in your views; be submissive to him who hath raised and distinguished you. Forget not that on his providence you are as dependent, and to the obedience of his laws as much bound, as the meanest of your fellow-creatures. Disgrace not your station, by that grossness of sensuality, that levity of dissipation, or that insolence of rank, which bespeak a little mind. Let the affability of your behaviour show that you remember the natural equality of men. Let your moderation in pleasure, your command of passion, and your steady regard to the great duties of life, show that you possess a mind worthy of your fortune. Establish your character on the basis of esteem; not on the flattery of dependents, or the praise of sycophants, but on the respect of the wise and the good. Let innocence preside over your enjoyments. Let usefulness and beneficence, not ostentation and vanity, direct the train of your pursuits. Let *your alms, together with your prayers, come up in memorial before God*. So shall your prosperity, under the blessing of Heaven, be *as the shining light, which shineth more and more unto the perfect day*. So shall it resemble those celestial fires which glow above, with beneficent, with regular and permanent lustre; and not prove that *mirth of fools*, which by Solomon is compared to *the crackling of thorns under a pot*, a glittering and fervent blaze, but speedily extinct.

On the whole, let this be our conclusion, that both in prosperity and in adversity, religion is the safest guide of human life. Conducted by its light, we reap the pleasures, and at the same time escape the dangers of a prosperous state. Sheltered under its protection, we stand the shock of adversity with most intrepidity, and suffer least from the violence of the storm. *He that desireth life, and loveth many days that he may see good, let him keep his tongue from evil, and his lips from guile. Let him depart from evil and do good. Let him seek peace with God, and pursue it.* Then, in his adversity, *God shall hide him in his pavilion*. In his prosperity, *he shall flourish like a tree planted by the rivers of water. The ungodly are not so; but are like the chaff, light and vile, which the wind driveth away.*

SERMON

SERMON IV.

On our Imperfect KNOWLEDGE of a FUTURE STATE.

1 COR. xiii. 12.

For now we see through a glass, darkly.—

THE Apostle here describes the imperfection of our knowledge, with relation to spiritual and eternal objects. He employs two metaphors to represent more strongly the disadvantages under which we lie: One, that we see those objects *through a glass*, that is, through the intervention of a medium which obscures their glory; the other, that we see them *in a riddle* or enigma, which our translators have rendered by seeing them *darkly;* that is, the truth in part discovered, in part concealed, and placed beyond our comprehension.

This description, however just and true, cannot fail to occasion some perplexity to an enquiring mind. For it may seem strange, that so much darkness should be left upon those celestial objects, towards which we are at the same time commanded to aspire. We are strangers in the universe of God. Confined to that spot on which we dwell, we are permitted to know nothing of what is transacting in the regions above us and around us. By much labour, we acquire a superficial acquaintance with a few sensible objects which we find in our present habitation; but we enter, and we depart, under a total ignorance of the nature and laws of the spiritual world. One subject in particular, when our thoughts proceed in this train, must often recur upon the mind with peculiar anxiety; that is, the immortality of the soul, and the future state of man. Exposed as we are at present, to such variety of afflictions, and subjected to so much disappointment in all our pursuits of happiness, Why, it may be said, has our gracious Creator denied us the consolation of a full discovery of our future existence, if indeed such an existence be prepared for us?—Reason, it is true, suggests many arguments in behalf of immortality: Revelation gives full assurance of it. Yet even that Gospel, which is said to have *brought life and immortality to light,* allows us to *see only through a glass, glafs, darkly. It doth not yet appear what we fhall be.* Our knowledge of a future world is very imperfect; our ideas of it are faint and confufed. It is not difplayed in fuch a manner, as to make an impreffion fuited to the importance of the object. The faith even of the beft men, is much inferior, both in clearnefs and in force, to the evidence of fenfe; and proves on many occafions infufficient to counterbalance the temptations of the prefent world. Happy moments indeed there fometimes are in the lives of pious men, when, fequeftered from worldly cares, and borne up on the wings of divine contemplation, they rife to a near and tranfporting view of immortal glory. But fuch efforts of the mind are rare, and cannot be long fupported. When the fpirit of meditation fubfides, this lively fenfe of a future ftate decays; and though the general belief of it remain, yet even good men, when they return to the ordinary bufinefs and cares of life, feem to rejoin the multitude, and to re-affume the fame hopes, and fears, and interefts, which influence the reft of the world.

From fuch reflections, a confiderable difficulty refpecting this important fubject, either arifes, or feems to arife. Was fuch an obfcure and imperfect difcovery of another life worthy to proceed from God? Does it not afford fome ground, either to tax his goodnefs, or to fufpect the evidence of its coming from him? —This is the point which we are now to confider; and let us confider it with that clofe attention which the fubject merits. Let us enquire whether we have any reafon either to complain of Providence, or to object to the evidence of a future ftate, becaufe that evidence is not of a more fenfible and ftriking nature. Let us attempt humbly, to trace the reafons, why, though permitted to know and to fee fomewhat of the eternal world, we are neverthelefs permitted only to *know in part, and to fee through a glafs, darkly.*

It plainly appears to be the plan of the deity, in all his difpenfations, to mix light with darknefs, evidence with uncertainty. Whatever the reafons of this procedure be, the fact is undeniable. He is defcribed in the Old Teftament *as a God that hideth himfelf*[*]. *Clouds and darknefs* are faid to *furround him. His way is in the fea, and his path in the great waters; his footfteps are not known.* Both the works and the ways of God are full of myftery. In the ordinary courfe of his government, innumerable events occur which perplex us to the utmoft. There is a certain limit to all our enquiries of religion, beyond which if we attempt to proceed, we are loft in a maze of inextricable difficulties. Even that revelation which affords fuch material inftructi-

[*] *Ifa.* xlv. 15.

on to man, concerning his duty and his happiness, leaves many doubts unresolved. Why it was not given sooner; why not to all men; why there should be so many things in it *hard to be understood*, are difficulties not inconsiderable, in the midst of that incontestible evidence by which it is supported. If, then, the future state of man be not placed in so full and clear a light as we desire, this is no more than what the analogy of all religion, both natural and revealed, gave us reason to expect.

But such a solution of the difficulty will be thought imperfect. It may, perhaps, not give much satisfaction, to shew, that all religion abounds with difficulties of a like nature. Our situation, it will be said, is so much the more to be lamented, that not on one side only we are confined in our enquiries, but on all hands environed with mysterious obscurity.—Let us then, if so much dissatisfied with our condition, give scope for once to Fancy, and consider how the plan of Providence might be rectified to our wish. Let us call upon the Sceptick, and desire him to say, what measure of information would afford him entire satisfaction.

This, he will tell us, requires not any long or deep deliberation. He desires only to have his view enlarged beyond the limits of this corporeal state. Instead of resting upon evidence which requires discussion, which must be supported by much reasoning, and which, after all, he alleges yields very imperfect information, he demands the everlasting mansions to be so displayed, if in truth such mansions there be, as to place faith on a level with the evidence of sense. What noble and happy effects, he exclaims, would instantly follow, if man thus beheld his present and his future existence at once before him! He would then become worthy of his rank in the creation. Instead of being the sport, as now of degrading passions and childish attachments, he would act solely on the principles of immortality. His pursuit of virtue would be steady; his life would be undisturbed and happy. Superiour to the attacks of distress, and to the solicitations of pleasure, he would advance, by a regular process, towards those divine rewards and honours which were continually present to his view.—Thus Fancy, with as much ease and confidence as if it were a perfect judge of creation, erects a new world to itself, and exults with admiration of its own work. But let us pause, and suspend this admiration, till we coolly examine the consequences that would follow from this supposed reformation of the universe.

CONSIDER the nature and circumstances of man. Introduced into the world in an indigent condition, he is supported at first by
the

the care of others; and, as soon as he begins to act for himself, finds labour and industry to be neceffary for fustaining his life, and supplying his wants. Mutual defence and interest give rife to fociety; and fociety, when formed, requires distinctions of property, diverfity of conditions, fubordination of ranks, and a multiplicity of occupations, in order to advance the general good. The fervices of the poor, and the protection of the rich, become reciprocally neceffary. The governours, and the governed, must co-operate for general fafety. Various arts must be studied; some respecting the cultivation of the mind, others the care of the body; some to ward off the evils, and some to provide the conveniencies of life. In a word, by the destination of his Creator, and the neceffities of his nature, man commences, at once, an active, not merely a contemplative being. Religion assumes him as such. It suppofes him employed in this world, as on a busy stage. It regulates, but does not abolish, the enterprifes and cares of ordinary life. It addreffes itself to the various ranks in fociety to the rich and the poor, to the magistrate and the subject. It rebukes the slothful; directs the diligent how to labour; and requires every man to *do his own businefs*.

Suppose, now, that veil to be withdrawn which conceals another world from our view. Let all obscurity vanish; let us no longer *fee darkly, as through a glafs;* but let every man enjoy that intuitive preception of divine and eternal objects which the Sceptick was fuppofed to desire. The immediate effect of such a discovery would be, to annihilate in our eye all human objects, and to produce a total stagnation in the affairs of the world. Were the celestial glory exposed to our admiring view; did the angelic harmony found in our enraptured ears; what earthly concerns could have the power of engaging our attention for a single moment? All the studies and pursuits, the arts and labours, which now employ the activity of man, which support the order, or promote the happinefs of fociety, would lie neglected and abandoned. Those defires and fears, those hopes and interests, by which we are at prefent stimulated, would cease to operate. Human life would prefent no objects sufficient to roufe the mind, to kindle the spirit of enterprife, or to urge the hand of industry. If the mere fense of duty engaged a good man to take some part in the businefs of the world, the task, when submitted to, would prove distasteful. Even the preservation of life would be slighted, if he were not bound to it by the authority of God. Impatient of his confinement within this tabernacle of dust, languishing for the happy day of his tranflation to thofe glorious regions which were difplayed to his fight, he would fojourn on earth as a melancholy exile. Whatever Providence has prepared for the entertainment of man, would be viewed with contempt. Whatever is now attractive in fociety, would appear infipid. In a word, he would be no longer a fit inhabitant of this world, nor be qualified for thofe exertions which are allotted to him in his prefent fphere of being. But, all his faculties being fublimated above the meafure of humanity, he would be in the condition of a being of fuperiour order, who, obliged to refide among men, would regard their purfuits with fcorn, as dreams, trifles, and puerile amufements of a day.

But to this reafoning it may perhaps be replied, That fuch confequences as I have now ftated, fuppofing them to follow, deferve not much regard.—For what though the prefent arrangement of human affairs were entirely changed, by a clearer view, and a ftronger impreffion of our future ftate ; would not fuch a change prove the higheft bleffing to man ? Is not his attachment to worldly objects the great fource both of his mifery and his guilt ? Employed in perpetual contemplation of heavenly objects, and in preparation for the enjoyment of them, would he not become more virtuous, and of courfe more happy, than the nature of his prefent employments and attachments permits him to be ?—Allowing for a moment, the confequence to be fuch, this much is yielded, that, upon the fuppofition which was made, man would not be the creature which he now is, nor human life the ftate which we now behold. How far the change would contribute to his welfare, comes to be confidered.

If there be any principle fully afcertained by religion, it is, That this life was intended for a ftate of trial and improvement to man. His preparation for a better world required a gradual purification, carried on by fteps of progreffive difcipline. The fituation, therefore, here affigned him, was fuch as to anfwer this defign, by calling forth all his active powers, by giving full fcope to his moral difpofitions, and bringing to light his whole character. Hence it became proper, that difficulty and temptation fhould arife in the courfe of his duty. Ample rewards were promifed to virtue ; but thefe rewards were left, as yet, in obfcurity and diftant profpect. The impreffions of fenfe, were fo balanced againft the difcoveries of immortality, as to allow a conflict between faith and fenfe, between confcience and defire, between prefent pleafure and future good. In this conflict, the fouls of good men are tried, improved, and ftrengthened. In this field, their honours are reaped. Here are formed the capital virtues of fortitude,

titude, temperance, and self-denial; moderation in prosperity, patience in adversity, submission to the will of God, and charity and forgivness to men, amidst the various competitions of worldly interest.

Such is the plan of Divine wisdom for man's improvement. But put the case, that the plan devised by human wisdom were to take place, and that the rewards of the just were to be more fully displayed to view; the exercise of all those graces which I have mentioned, would be entirely superseded. Their very names would be unknown. Every temptation being withdrawn, every worldly attachment being subdued by the overpowering discoveries of eternity, no trial of sincerity, no discrimination of characters, would remain; no opportunity would be afforded for those active exertions, which are the means of purifying and perfecting the good. On the competition between time and eternity, depends the chief exercise of human virtue. The obscurity which at present hangs over eternal objects, preserves the competition. Remove that obscurity, and you remove human virtue from its place. You overthrow that whole system of discipline, by which imperfect creatures are, in this life, gradually trained up for a more perfect state.

This, then, is the conclusion to which at last we arrive: That the full display which was demanded, of the heavenly glory, would be so far from improving the human soul, that it would abolish those virtues and duties which are the great instruments of its improvement. It would be unsuitable to the character of man in every view, either as an active being, or a moral agent. It would disqualify him for taking part in the affairs of the world; for relishing the pleasures, or for discharging the duties of life: In a word, it would entirely defeat the purpose of his being placed on this earth. And the question, Why the Almighty has been pleased to leave a spiritual world, and the future existence of man, under so much obscurity, resolves in the end into this, Why there should be such a creature as man in the universe of God?—Such is the issue of the improvements proposed to be made on the plans of Providence. They add to the discoveries of the superiour wisdom of God, and of the presumption and folly of man.

From what has been said it now appears, That no reasonable objection to the belief of a future state arises, from the imperfect discoveries of it which we enjoy; from the difficulties that are mingled with its evidence; from our *seeing as through a glass, darkly*, and being left to *walk by faith and not by sight*. It cannot be otherwise, it ought not to be otherwise in our present state. The evidence which is afforded, is sufficient for the conviction of a candid mind, sufficient for a rational ground of conduct; though not so striking as to withdraw our attention from the present world, or altogether to overcome the impression of sensible objects. In such evidence it becomes us to acquiesce, without indulging either doubts or complaints, on account of our not receiving all the satisfaction which we fondly desire, but which our present immaturity of being excludes. For, upon the supposition of immortality, this life is no other than the childhood of existence; and the measures of our knowledge must be proportioned to such a state. To the successive stages of human life, from infancy to old age, belong certain peculiar attachments, certain cares, desires, and interests; which open not abruptly, but by gradual advances on the mind, as it becomes fit to receive them, and is prepared for acting the part to which, in their order, they pertain. Hence, in the education of a child, no one thinks of inspiring him all at once with the knowledge, the sentiments, and views of a man, and with contempt for the exercises and amusements of childhood. On the contrary, employments suited to his age are allowed to occupy him. By these his powers are gradually unfolded; and advantage is taken of his youthful pursuits, to improve and strengthen his mind; till, step by step, he is led on to higher prospects, and prepared for a larger and more important scene of action.

This analogy, which so happily illustrates the present conduct of the Deity, towards man, deserves attention the more, as it is the very illustration used by the Apostle, when treating of this subject in the context. *Now*, says he, *we know in part—but when that which is perfect is come, that which is in part shall be done away. When I was a child, I spoke as a child, I understood as a child, I thought as a child; but when I became a man, I put away childish things. For now we see through a glass, darkly: but then, face to face: Now I know in part; but then I shall know even as I am known.* Under the care of the Almighty, our education is now going on, from a mortal to an immortal state. As much light is let in upon us, as we can bear without injury. When the objects become too splendid and dazzling for our sight, the curtain is drawn. Exercised in such a field of action, as suits the strength of our unripened powers, we are, at the same time, by proper prospects and hopes, prompted to aspire towards the manhood of our nature, the time when *childish things shall be put away*. But still, betwixt those future prospects, and the impression of present objects, such an accurate proportion is established, as on the one hand shall not produce a total contempt of earthly things, while we aspire to those that are heavenly; and on the other, shall not encourage such a degree of attachment to our present state, as would render us unworthy of future advancement. In a word, the whole course of things is so ordered, that we neither, by an irregular and precipitate education, become men too soon; nor by a fond and trifling indulgence, be suffered to continue children for ever.

Let these reflections not only remove the doubts which may arise from our obscure knowledge of immortality, but likewise produce the highest admiration of the wisdom of our Creator. The structure of the natural world affords innumerable instances of profound design, which no attentive spectator can survey without wonder. In the moral world, where the workmanship is of much finer and more delicate contexture, subjects of still greater admiration open to view. But admiration must rise to its highest point, when those parts of the moral constitution, which at first were reputed blemishes, which carried the appearance of objections, either to the wisdom or the goodness of Providence, are discovered, on more accurate inspection, to be adjusted with the most exquisite propriety. We have now seen that the darkness of man's condition is no less essential to his well-being, than the light which he enjoys. His internal powers, and his external situation, appear to be exactly fitted to each other. Those complaints which we are apt to make, of our limited capacity and narrow views, of our inability to penetrate farther into the future destination of man, are found, from the foregoing observations, to be just as unreasonable, as the childish complaints of our not being formed with a microscopic eye, nor furnished with an eagle's wing; that is, of not being endowed with powers which would subvert the nature, and counteract the laws, of our present state.

In order to do justice to the subject, I must observe, that the same reasoning which has been now employed with respect to our knowledge of immortality, is equally applicable to many other branches of intellectual knowledge. Thus, why we are permitted to know so little of the nature of that Eternal Being who rules the universe; why the manner in which he operates on the natural and moral world, is wholly concealed; why we are kept in such ignorance, with respect to the extent of his works, to the nature and agency of spiritual beings, and even with respect to the union between our own soul and body: To all these, and several other enquiries of the same kind, which often employ the solicitous researches of speculative men, the answer is the same that was given to the interesting question which makes the subject of our discourse. The degree of knowledge desired, would prove incompatible with the design and with the proper business of this life. It would raise us to a sphere too exalted; would reveal objects too great and striking for our present faculties; would excite feelings too strong for us to bear; in a word, would unfit us for thinking or acting like human creatures. It is therefore reserved for a more advanced period of our nature; and the hand of Infinite wisdom hath in mercy drawn a veil over scenes which would overpower the sight of mortals.

One instance, in particular, of Divine wisdom, is so illustrious, and corresponds so remarkably with our present subject, that I cannot pass it over without notice; that is, the concealment under which Providence has placed the future events of our life on earth. The desire of penetrating into this unknown region, has ever been one of the most anxious passions of men. It has often seized the wise as well as the credulous, and given rise to many vain and impious superstitions throughout the whole earth. Burning with curiosity at the approach of some critical event, and impatient under the perplexity of conjecture and doubt, How cruel is Providence, we are apt to exclaim, in denying to man the power of foresight, and in limiting him to the knowledge of the present moment! Were he permitted to look forward into the course of destiny, how much more suitably would he be prepared for the various turns and changes in his life! With what moderation would he enjoy his prosperity under the foreknowledge of an approaching reverse! And with what eagerness he prompted to improve the flying hours, by seeing the inevitable term draw nigh which was to finish his course!

But while Fancy indulges such vain desires and criminal complaints, this coveted foreknowledge must clearly appear to the eye of Reason, to be the most fatal gift which the Almighty could bestow. If, in this present mixed state, all the successive scenes of distress through which we are to pass, were laid before us in one view, perpetual sadness would overcast our life. Hardly would any transient gleams of intervening joy be able to force their way through the cloud. Faint would be the relish of pleasures of which we foresaw the close: Insupportable the burden of afflictions, under which we were oppressed by a load not only of present, but of anticipated sorrow. Friends would begin their union, with lamenting the day which was to dissolve it; and, with weeping eye, the parent would every moment behold the child whom he knew that he was to lose. In short, as soon as that mysterious veil, which now covers futurity, was lifted up, all

the

the gaiety of life would difappear, its flattering hopes, its pleafing illufions, would vanifh; and nothing but its vanity and fadnefs remain. The forefight of the hour of death would continually interrupt the courfe of human affairs; and the overwhelming profpect of the future, inftead of exciting men to proper activity, would render them immovable with confternation and difmay.——How much more friendly to man is that mixture of knowledge and ignorance which is allotted him in this ftate. Ignorant of the events which are to befal us, and of the precife term which is to conclude our life, by this ignorance our enjoyment of prefent objects is favoured; and knowing that death is certain, and that human affairs are full of change, by this knowledge our attachment to thofe objects is moderated. Precifely in the fame manner, as, by the mixture of evidence and obfcurity which remains on the profpect of a future ftate, a proper balance is preferved betwixt our love of this life, and our defire of a better.

The longer that our thoughts dwell on this fubject, the more we muft be convinced, that in nothing the Divine wifdom is more admirable, than in proportioning knowledge to the neceffities of man. Inftead of lamenting our condition, that we are permitted only to *fee as through a glafs, darkly,* we have reafon to blefs our Creator, no lefs for what he hath concealed, than for what he hath allowed us to know. He is *wonderful in council, as he is excellent in working. He is wife in heart, and his thoughts are deep. How unfearchable are the riches of the wifdom of the knowledge of God.*

From the whole view which we have taken of the fubject, this important inftruction arifes, That the great defign of all the knowledge, and in particular of the religious knowledge which God hath afforded us, is, to fit us for difcharging the duties of life. No ufelefs difcoveries are made to us in religion: No difcoveries even of ufeful truths, beyond the precife degree of information, which is fubfervient to right conduct. To this great end all our information points. In this centre all the lines of knowledge meet. *Life and immortality are brought to light in the gofpel;* yet not fo difplayed as to gratify the curiofity of the world with an aftonifhing fpectacle; but only fo far made known, as to affift and fupport us in the practice of our duty. If the difcovery were more imperfect, it would excite no defire of immortality; if it were more full and ftriking, it would render us carelefs of life. On the firft fuppofition, no fufficient motive to virtue would appear; on the fecond, no proper trial of it would remain. In the one cafe, we fhould think and act like men who *have their portion only in this world;* in the other cafe, like men who have no concern with this world at all. Whereas now, by the wife conftitutio.1

tution of Heaven, we are placed in the moſt favourable ſituation for acting, with propriety, our allotted part here; and for riſing, in due courſe, to higher honour and happineſs hereafter.

Let us then ſecond the kind intentions of Providence, and act upon the plan which it hath pointed out. Checking our inquiſitive ſolicitude about what the Almighty hath concealed, let us diligently improve what he hath made known. Inhabitants of the earth, we are at the ſame time candidates for Heaven. Looking upon theſe as only different views of one conſiſtent character, let us carry on our preparation for Heaven, not by abſtracting ourſelves from the concerns of this world, but by fulfilling the duties and offices of every ſtation in life. Living *ſoberly, righteouſly, and godly in the preſent world,* let us *look for that bleſſed hope, and the glorious appearing of the great God, and our Saviour Jeſus Chriſt.*

Before I conclude, it may be proper to obſerve, That the reaſonings in this diſcourſe give no ground to apprehend any danger of our being too much influenced by the belief of a future ſtate. I have ſhewn the hurtful effects which would follow from too bright and full a diſcovery of the glory of that ſtate; and in ſhowing this, I have juſtified the decree of Providence, which permits no ſuch diſcovery. But as our nature is at preſent conſtituted, attached by ſo many ſtrong connections to the world of ſenſe, and enjoying a communication ſo feeble and diſtant with the world of ſpirits, we need fear no danger from cultivating intercourſe with the latter as much as poſſible. On the contrary, from that intercourſe the chief ſecurity of our virtue is to be ſought. The bias of our nature leans ſo much towards ſenſe, that from this ſide the peril is to be dreaded, and on this ſide the defence is to be provided.

Let us then *walk by faith*. Let us ſtrengthen this principle of action to the utmoſt of our power. Let us implore the Divine grace to ſtrengthen it within us more and more: That we may thence derive an antidote againſt that ſubtile poiſon, which inceſſant commerce with the objects of ſenſe diffuſes through our ſouls; that we may hence acquire purity and dignity of manners ſuited to our divine hopes; and, undefiled by the pleaſures of the world, unſhaken by its terrours, may preſerve to the end one conſtant tenor of integrity. Till at laſt, having under the conduct of Chriſtian faith, happily finiſhed the period of diſcipline, we enter on that ſtate, where a far nobler ſcene ſhall open; where eternal objects ſhall ſhine in their native ſplendour; where, this twilight of mortal life being paſt, the *Sun of righteouſneſs* ſhall riſe; and *that which is perfect being come, that which is in part ſhall be done away.*

SERMON

SERMON V.

On the DEATH of CHRIST.

Preached at the Celebration of the Sacrament of the Lord's Supper.

JOHN, xvii. 1.

Jesus lift up his eyes to heaven, and said, Father! the hour is come.—

THESE were the words of our blessed Lord on a memorable occasion. The feast of the passover drew nigh, at which he knew that he was to suffer. The night was arrived wherein he was to be delivered into the hands of his enemies. He had spent the evening in conference with his disciples; like a dying father in the midst of his family, mingling consolations with his last instructions. When he had ended his discourse to them, he *lifted up his eyes to heaven,* and, with the words which I have now read, began that solemn prayer of intercession for the church, which closed his ministry. Immediately after, he went forth with his disciples into the garden of Gethsemane, and surrendered himself to those who came to apprehend him.

Such was the situation of our Lord at the time of his pronouncing these words. He saw his mission on the point of being accomplished. He had the prospect full before him, of all that he was about to suffer.—*Father! the hour is come.*—What hour? An hour the most critical, the most pregnant with great events, since hours had begun to be numbered, since time had begun to run. It was the hour in which the Son of God was to terminate the labours of his important life, by a death still more important and illustrious; the hour of atoning, by his sufferings, for the guilt of mankind; the hour of accomplishing prophecies, types, and symbols, which had been carried on through a series of ages; the hour of concluding the old, and of introducing to the world the new dispensation of religion; the hour of his triumphing over the world, and death and hell; the hour of his erecting that spiritual kingdom which is to last for ever. Such is the hour, such are the events, which you are to commemorate in the sacrament of our Lord's Supper. I shall attempt to set them before you as proper subjects, at this time, of your devout meditation. To display them in their genuine majesty, is beyond the ability of man.

I. This was the hour in which Christ was glorified by his sufferings. The whole of his life had discovered much real greatness, under a mean appearance. Through the cloud of his humiliation, his native lustre often broke forth; but never did it shine so bright, as in this last, this trying hour. It was indeed the hour of distress, and of blood. He knew it to be such; and when he uttered the words of the Text, he had before his eyes, the executioner and the cross, the scourge, the nails, and the spear. But by prospects of this nature his soul was not to be overcome. It is distress which ennobles every great character; and distress was to glorify the Son of God. He was now to teach all mankind, by his example, how to suffer and to die. He was to stand forth before his enemies, as the faithful witness of the truth; justifying by his behaviour the character which he assumed, and sealing with his blood the doctrine which he taught.

What magnanimity in all his words and actions on this great occasion! The court of Herod, the judgment-hall of Pilate, the hill of Calvary, were so many theatres prepared for his displaying all the virtues of a constant and patient mind. When led forth to suffer, the first voice which we hear from him, is a generous lamentation over the fate of his unfortunate, though guilty, country; and to the last moment of his life, we behold him in possession of the same gentle and benevolent spirit. No upbraiding, no complaining expression escaped from his lips, during the long and painful approaches of a cruel death. He betrayed no symptom of a weak or a vulgar, of a discomposed or impatient mind. With the utmost attention of filial tenderness, he committed his aged mother to the care of his beloved disciple *. With all the dignity of a Sovereign, he conferred pardon on a penitent fellow-sufferer. With a greatness of mind beyond example, he spent his last moments in apologies and prayers for those who were shedding his blood.

I. By wonders in heaven, and wonders on earth, was this hour distinguished. All nature seemed to feel it; and the dead and the living bore witness to its importance. The veil of the temple was *rent in twain.*

* *See John*, xix. 26, 27.

twain. The earth shook. There was darkness over all the land. The graves were opened, and *many who slept, arose and went into the Holy City*. Nor were these the only prodigies of this awful hour. The most hardened hearts were subdued and changed. The judge who, in order to gratify the multitude, passed sentence against him, publickly attested his innocence. The Roman centurion, who presided at the execution, *glorified God*, and acknowledged the sufferer to be more than man. *After he saw the things which had passed, he said Certainly this was a righteous person ; truly, this was the Son of God* The Jewish malefactor who was crucified with him, addressed him as a King, and implored his favour. Even the crowd of insensible spectators, who had come forth as to a common spectacle, and who began with clamours and insults, *returned home, smiting their breasts*. Look back on the heroes, the philosophers, the legislators of old. View them in their last moments. Recall every circumstance which distinguished their departure from the world. Where can you find such an assemblage of high virtues, and of great events, as concurred at the death of Christ ? Where, so many testimonies given to the dignity of the dying person, by earth, and by heaven ?

II. THIS was the hour in which Christ atoned for the sins of mankind, and accomplished our eternal redemption. It was the hour when that great sacrifice was offered up, the efficacy of which reaches back to the first transgression of man, and extends forward to the end of time ; the hour when, from the cross, as from an high altar, the blood was flowing, which washed away the guilt of the nations.

This awful dispensation of the Almighty contains mysteries which are beyond the discovery of man. It is one of those things into which *the angels desire to look*. What has been revealed to us is, That the death of Christ was the interposition of Heaven for preventing the ruin of human kind. We know, that under the government of God, misery is the natural consequence of guilt. After rational creatures had, by their criminal conduct, introduced disorder into the Divine kingdom, there was no ground to believe, that by their penitence and prayers alone they could prevent the destruction which threatened them. The prevalence of propitiatory sacrifices throughout the earth, proclaims it to be the general sense of mankind, that mere repentance was not of sufficient avail to expiate sin, or to stop its penal effects. By the constant allusions which are carried on in the New Testament to the sacrifices under the Law, as pre-signifying a

great

great atonement made by Christ; and by the strong expressions which are used in describing the effects of his death, the sacred writers show, as plainly as language allows, that there was an efficacy in his sufferings, far beyond that of mere example and instruction. The nature and extent of that efficacy we are unable, as yet, fully to trace. Part we are capable of beholding; and the wisdom of what we behold, we have reason to adore. We discern in this plan of redemption, the evil of sin strongly exhibited; and the justice of the Divine government awfully exemplified, in Christ suffering for sinners. But let us not imagine, that our present discoveries unfold the whole influence of the death of Christ. It is connected with causes into which we cannot penetrate. It produces consequences too extensive for us to explore. *God's thoughts are not as our thoughts.* In all things we see only in part; and here, if any where, we see also *as through a glass, darkly.*

This, however, is fully manifest, that redemption is one of the most, glorious works of the Almighty. If the hour of the creation of the world was great and illustrious; that hour, when, from the dark and formless mass, this fair system of nature arose at the Divine command; when *the morning stars sang together, and all the sons of God shouted for joy;* no less illustrious is the hour of the restoration of the world, the hour when, from condemnation and misery, it emerged into happiness and peace. With less external majesty it was attended, but is, on that account, the more wonderful, that under an appearance so simple, such great events were covered.

III. In this hour the long series of prophecies, visions, types, and figures, was accomplished. This was the centre in which they all met: This the point towards which they had tended and verged, throughout the course of so many generations. You behold the Law and the Prophets standing, if we may speak so, at the foot of the cross, and doing homage. You behold Moses and Aaron bearing the ark of the covenant; David and Elijah presenting the oracle of testimony. You behold all the priests and sacrifices, all the rights and ordinances, all the types and symbols, assembled together to receive their consummation. Without the death of Christ, the worship and ceremonies of the Law would have remained a pompous, but unmeaning institution. In the hour when he was crucified, *the book with the seven seals* was opened. Every rite assumed its significancy; every prediction met its event; every symbol displayed its correspondence.

The dark, and seemingly ambiguous method of conveying important

tant discoveries under figures and emblems, was not peculiar to the sacred books. The spirit of God, in pre-signifying the death of Christ, adopted that plan, according to which the whole knowledge of those early ages was propagated through the world. Under the veil of mysterious allusion, all wisdom was then concealed. From the sensible world, images were every-where borrowed, to describe things unseen. More was understood to be meant, than was openly expressed. By enigmatical rites, the Priest communicated his doctrines; by parables and allegories, the Philosopher instructed his disciples; even the Legislator, by figurative sayings, commanded the reverence of the people. Agreeably to this prevailing mode of instruction, the whole dispensation of the Old Testament was so conducted, as to be the shadow and the figure of a spiritual system. Every remarkable event, every distinguished personage, under the Law, is interpreted in the New Testament, as bearing some reference to the hour of which we treat. If Isaac was laid upon the altar as an innocent victim; if David was driven from his throne by the wicked, and restored by the hand of God; if the brazen serpent was lifted up to heal the people; if the rock was smitten by Moses, to furnish drink in the wilderness; all were types of Christ, and alluded to his death.

In predicting the same event the language of ancient prophecy was magnificent, but seemingly contradictory: For it foretold a Messiah, who was to be at once a sufferer and a conqueror. *The Star was to come out of Jacob, and the Branch to spring from the stem of Jesse. The Angel of the Covenant, the Desire of all Nations, was to come suddenly to his temple;* and to him was to be *the gathering of the people.* Yet at the same time, he was to be *despised and rejected of men;* he was to be taken *from prison and from judgement,* and to be *led as a lamb to the slaughter.* Though he was *a man of sorrows and acquainted with grief,* yet *the Gentiles were to come to his light, and Kings to the brightness of his rising.* In the hour when Christ died, those prophetical riddles were solved; those seeming contradictions were reconciled. The obscurity of oracles, and the ambiguity of types, vanished. The *sun of righteousness* rose; and, together with the dawn of religion, those shadows passed away.

IV. THIS was the hour of the abolition of the Law, and the introduction of the Gospel; the hour of terminating the old, and of beginning the new dispensation of religious knowledge and worship throughout the earth. Viewed in this light, it forms the most august æra which is to be found in the history of mankind. When Christ was suffering on the cross, we are informed by one of the Evangelists, gelifts, that he faid, *I thirst;* and that they filled a fpunge with vinegar, and put it to his mouth. *After he had tasted the vinegar, knowing that all things were now accomplished, and the scriptures fulfilled, he said, It is finished* *; that is, This offered draught of vinegar was the laft circumftance predicted by an ancient Prophet † that remained to be fulfilled. The vifion and the prophecy are now fealed: The Mofaic difpenfation is clofed. *And he bowed his head, and gave up the ghost.*

It is finished.—When he uttered thefe words, he changed the ftate of the univerfe. At that moment the Law ceafed, and the Gofpel commenced. This was the ever-memorable point of time which feparated the old and the new world from each other. On one fide of the point of feparation, you behold the Law, with its priefts, its facrifices, and its rites, retiring from fight. On the other fide, you behold the Gofpel, with its fimple and venerable inftitutions, coming forward into view. Significantly was the veil of the temple rent in this hour; for the glory then departed from between the cherubims. The legal High Prieft delivered up his Urim and Thummim, his breaftplate, his robes, and his incenfe: And CHRIST ftood forth as the great High Prieft of all fucceeding generations. By that one facrifice, which he now offered, he abolifhed facrifices for ever. Altars on which the fire had blazed for ages, were now to fmoke no more. Victims were no more to bleed. *Not with the blood of bulls and goats, but with his own blood, he now entered into the Holy Place, there to appear in the presence of God for us.*

This was the hour of affociation and union to all the worfhippers of God. When Chrift faid, *It is finished,* he threw down the wall of partition which had fo long divided the Gentile from the Jew. He gathered into one, all the faithful, out of every kindred and people. He proclaimed the hour to be come, when the knowledge of the true God fhould be no longer confined to one nation, nor his worfhip to one temple; but over all the earth, the worfhippers of the Father fhould *serve him in spirit and in truth.* From that hour they who dwelt in the *uttermost ends of the earth, strangers to the covenant of promise,* began to be *brought nigh* In that hour, the light of the Gofpel dawned from far on the Britifh iflands.

During a long courfe of ages, Providence feemed to be occupied in preparing the world for this revolution. The whole Jewifh œconomy was intended to ufher it in. The knowledge of God was preferved

* *John,* xix. 28, 29, 30. † *Pfalm,* lxiv. 21.

ed unextinguished in one corner of the world, that thence, in due time, might issue forth the light which was to overspread the earth. Successive revelations gradually enlarged the views of men beyond the narrow bounds of Judæa, to a more extensive kingdom of God. Signs and miracles awakened their expectation, and directed their eyes towards this great event. Whether God descended on the flaming mountain, or spoke by the Prophet's voice; whether he scattered his chosen people into captivity, or re-assembled them in their own land; he was still carrying on a progressive plan, which was accomplished at the death of Christ.

Not only in the territories of Israel, but over all the earth, the great dispensations of Providence respected the approach of this important hour. If empires rose or fell; if war divided, or peace united the nations; if learning civilized their manners, or philosophy enlarged their views; all was, by the secret decree of Heaven, made to ripen the word for that *fulness of time*, when Christ was to publish the whole counsel of God. The Persian, the Macedonian, the Roman conqueror, entered upon the stage each at his predicted period; and, *though he meant not so, neither did his heart think so*, ministered to this hour. The revolutions of power, and the succession of monarchies, were so arranged by Providence, as to facilitate the progress of the Gospel through the habitable world, after the day had arrived, *when the stone which was cut out of the mountain without hands, should become a great mountain, and fill the earth* *. This was the day which *Abraham saw afar off, and was glad*. This was the day which *many Prophets and Kings, and righteous men desired to see, but could not ;* the day for which *the earnest expectation of the creature*, long oppressed with ignorance, and bewildered in superstition, might be justly said *to wait*.

V. THIS was the hour of Christ's triumph over all the powers of darkness; the hour in which he overthrew dominions and thrones, *led captivity captive, and gave gifts unto men.* The contest which the kingdom of darkness had long maintained against the kingdom of light, was now brought to its crisis. The period was come, when *the seed of the woman should bruise the head of the serpent.* For many ages, the most gross superstition had filled the earth. *The glory of the uncorruptible God was* every-where, except in the land of Judæa, *changed into images made like to corruptible man, and to birds, and beasts, and creeping things.* The world, which the Almighty created for himself, seemed to

* *Dan.* ii. 34, 35.

to have become a temple of idols. Even to vices and paſſions altars were raiſed; and, what was entitled Religion, was in effect a diſcipline of impurity. In the midſt of this univerſal darkneſs, Satan had erected his throne; and the learned and poliſhed, as well as the ſavage nations, bowed down before him. But at the hour when Chriſt appeared on the croſs, the ſignal of his defeat was given. His kingdom ſuddenly departed from him; the reign of idolatry paſſed away: He was *beheld to fall like lightning from Heaven.* In that hour, the foundation of every Pagan temple ſhook. The ſtatue of every falſe God tottered on its baſe. The Prieſt fled from his falling ſhrine, the Heathen oracles became dumb for ever.

As on the croſs Chriſt triumphed over Satan, ſo he overcame his auxiliary the world. Long had it aſſailed him with its temptations and diſcouragements. In this hour of ſevere trial, he ſurmounted them all. Formerly he had deſpiſed the pleaſures of the world. He now baffled its terrors. Hence he is juſtly ſaid to have *crucified the world.* By his ſufferings he ennobled diſtreſs; and he darkened the luſtre of the pomp and vanities of life. He diſcovered to his followers the path which leads, through affliction, to glory and to victory; and he imparted to them the ſame ſpirit which enabled him to overcome. *My kingdom is not of this world. In this world ye ſhall have tribulation; but be of good cheer; I have overcome the world* *.

Death alſo, the laſt foe of man, was the victim of this hour. The formidable appearance of the ſpectre remained; but his dart was taken away. For, in the hour when Chriſt expiated guilt, he diſarmed death, by ſecuring the reſurrection of the juſt. When he ſaid to his penitent fellow-ſufferer, *To-day thou ſhalt be with me in paradiſe,* he announced to all his followers the certainty of heavenly bliſs. He declared *the cherubims* to be diſmiſſed, and the *flaming ſword* to be ſheathed, which had been appointed at the fall, *to keep from man the way of the tree of life* †. Faint, before this period, had been the hope, indiſtinct the proſpect, which even good men enjoyed of the heavenly kingdom. *Life and immortality were now brought to light.* From the hill of Calvary, the firſt clear and certain view was given to the world of the everlaſting manſions. Since that hour, they have been the perpetual conſolation of believers in Chriſt. Under trouble, they ſooth their minds; amidſt temptation, they ſupport their virtue; and, in their dying moments, enable them to ſay, *O death! where is thy ſting? O grave! where is thy victory?*

* *John*, xvi. 33. † *Gen.* iii. 24.

VI. This was the hour when our Lord erected that spiritual kingdom which is never to end. How vain are the counsels and designs of men! How shallow is the policy of the wicked! How short their triumphing! The enemies of Christ imagined, that in this hour they had successfully accomplished their plan for his destruction. They believed, that they had entirely scattered the small party of his followers, and had extinguished his name and his honour for ever. In derision, they addressed him as a King. They clothed him with purple robes; they crowned him with a crown of thorns; they put a reed into his hand; and, with insulting mockery, bowed the knee before him. Blind and impious men! How little did they know, that the Almighty was at that moment *setting him as a King on the hill of Sion; giving him the Heathen for his inheritance, and the uttermost parts of the earth for his possession!* How little did they know, that their badges of mock royalty were at that moment converted into signals of absolute dominion, and the instruments of irresistible power! The reed which they put into his hands became a *rod of iron*, with which he was to *break in pieces his enemies*; a sceptre, with which he was to rule the universe in righteousness. The cross, which they thought was to stigmatize him with infamy, became the ensign of his renown. Instead of being the reproach of his followers, it was to be their boast and their glory. The cross was to shine on palaces and churches, throughout the earth. It was to be assumed as the distinction of the most powerful monarchs, and to wave in the banner of victorious armies, when the memory of Herod and Pilate should be accursed; when Jerusalem should be reduced to ashes; and the Jews be vagabonds over all the world.

These were the triumphs which commenced at this hour. Our Lord saw them already in their birth; he *saw of the travail of his soul, and was satisfied.* He beheld the word of God going forth, conquering, and to conquer; subduing to the obedience of his laws, the subduers of the world; carrying light into the regions of darkness, and mildness into the habitations of cruelty. He beheld the Gentiles waiting below the cross, to receive the Gospel. He beheld *Ethiopia and the Isles stretching out their hands to God; the desert beginning to rejoice, and to blossom as the rose; and the knowledge of the Lord filling the earth, as the waters cover the sea.* Well pleased, he said, *It is finished.* As a conqueror, he retired from the field, reviewing his triumphs: *He bowed his head, and gave up the ghost.*——From that hour, Christ was no longer a mortal man, but *Head over all things to the Church;* the glorious King of men and angels, of whose dominion there shall be no end. His triumphs shall perpetually increase. *His name shall endure for ever; it shall last as long as the sun; men shall be blessed in him, and all nations shall call him blessed.*

Such were the transactions, such the effects of this ever memorable hour. With all those great events was the mind of our Lord filled, when he lifted up his eyes to heaven, and said, *Father, the hour is come.*

From this view which we have taken of this subject, permit me to suggest, what ground it affords to confide in the mercy of God, for the pardon of sin; to trust to his faithfulness, for the accomplishment of all his promises; and to approach to him, with gratitude and devotion, in acts of worship.

In the first place, The death of Christ affords us ground to confide in the Divine mercy, for the pardon of sin. All the steps of that high dispensation of Providence, which we have considered, lead directly to this conclusion, *He that spared not his own Son, but delivered him up for us all, how shall he not with him also freely give us all things* *? This is the final result of the discoveries of the Gospel. On this rests that great system of consolation, which it hath reared up for men. We are not left to dubious and intricate reasonings, concerning the conduct which God may be expected to hold towards his offending creatures. But we are led to the view of important and illustrious facts, which strike the mind with evidence irresistible. For, is it possible to believe, that such great operations, as I have endeavoured to describe, were carried on by the Almighty in vain? Did he excite in the hearts of his creatures, such encouraging hopes, without any intention to fulfil them? After so long a preparation of goodness, could, he mean to deny forgiveness to the penitent and the humble? When, overcome by the sense of guilt, man looks up with an astonished eye to the justice of his Creator, let him recollect that hour of which the Text speaks, and be comforted. The signals of Divine mercy, erected in his view, are too conspicuous to be either distrusted or mistaken.

In the next place, The discoveries of this hour afford the highest reason to trust in the Divine faithfulness, for the accomplishment of every

* *Romans*, viii. 32.

every promife which remains yet unfulfilled. For this was the hour of the completion of God's ancient covenant. It was the *performance of the mercy promifed to the fathers.* We behold the confummation of a great plan, which, throughout a courfe of ages, had been uniformly purfued; and which, againft every human appearance, was, at the appointed moment, exactly fulfilled. *No word that is gone out of the mouth of the Lord, fhall fail.* No length of time alters his purpofe. No obftacles can retard it. Towards the ends accomplifhed in this hour, the moft repugnant inftruments were made to operate. We difcern God, bending to his purpofe the jarring paffions, the oppofite interefts, and even the vices of men; uniting feeming contrarieties in his fcheme; making *the wrath of man to praife him;* obliging the ambition of Princes, the prejudices of the Jews, the malice of Satan, all to concur, either in bringing forward this hour, or in completing its deftined effects. With what entire confidence ought we to wait for the fulfilment of all his other promifes in their due time; even when events are moft embroiled, and the profpect is moft difcouraging? *Although thou fayeft, Thou canft not fee him; yet judgment is before him; therefore truft thou in him.* Be attentive only to perform thy duty; leave the event to God; and be affured, that under the direction of his Providence *all things fhall work together* for a happy iffue.

LASTLY, The confideration of this whole fubject tends to excite gratitude and devotion, when we approach to God in acts of worfhip. The hour of which I have difcourfed, prefents him to us in the amiable light of the Deliverer of mankind, the Reftorer of our forfeited hopes. We behold the greatnefs of the Almighty, foftened by the mild radiance of condefcenfion and mercy. We behold him diminifhing the awful diftance at which we ftand from his prefence, by appointing for us a Mediator and Interceffor, through whom the humble may, without difmay, approach to Him who made them. By fuch views of the Divine nature, Chriftian faith lays the foundation for a worfhip which fhall be at once rational and affectionate; a worfhip, in which the light of the underftanding fhall concur with the devotion of the heart, and the moft profound reverence be united with the moft cordial love. Chriftian faith is not a fyftem of fpeculative truths. It is not a leffon of moral inftruction only. By a train of high difcoveries which it reveals, by a fucceffion of interefting objects which it places in our view, it is calculated to elevate,

elevate the mind, to purify the affections, and, by the assistance of devotion, to confirm and encourage virtue. Such, in particular, is the scope of that divine institution, the Sacrament of our Lord's Supper. To this happy purpose let it conduce, by concentering, in one striking point of light, all that the Gospel has displayed of what is most important to man. Touched with just contrition for past offences, and filled with a grateful sense of Divine goodness, let us come to the altar of God, and, with a humble faith in his infinite mercies, devote ourselves to his service for ever.

SERMON

SERMON VI.

On GENTLENESS.

JAMES, iii. 17.

The wisdom that is from above, is—gentle—

TO be wise in our own eyes, to be wise in the opinion of the world, and to be wise in the sight of God, are three things so very different, as rarely to coincide. One may often be wise in his own eyes, who is far from being so in the judgment of the world; and to be reputed a prudent man by the world, is no security for being accounted wise by God. As there is a worldly happiness, which God perceives to be no other than disguised misery; as there are worldly honours, which in his estimation are reproach; so there is a worldly wisdom, which, *in his sight, is foolishness.* Of this worldly wisdom the characters are given in the context, and placed in contrast with those of the *wisdom which is from above.* The one is the wisdom of the crafty; the other that of the upright. The one terminates in selfishness; the other, in charity. The one is *full of strife and bitter envyings;* the other *of mercy and of good fruits.* One of the chief characters by which the wisdom from above is distinguished, is *gentleness,* of which I am now to discourse. Of this there is the greater occasion to discourse, because it is too seldom viewed in a religious light; and is more readily considered, by the bulk of men, as a mere felicity of nature, or an exterior accomplishment of manners, than as a Christian virtue, which they are bound to cultivate. I shall first explain the nature of this virtue; and shall then offer some arguments to recommend, and some directions to facilitate, the practice of it.

I BEGIN with distinguishing true gentleness from passive tameness of spirit, and from unlimited compliance with the manners of others. That passive tameness, which submits, without struggle, to every encroachment of the violent and assuming, forms no part of Christian duty; but, on the contrary, is destructive of general happiness and
order.

order. That unlimited complaisance, which, on every occasion, falls in with the opinions and manners of others, is so far from being a virtue, that it is itself a vice, and the parent of many vices. It overthrows all steadiness of principle; and produces that sinful conformity with the world which taints the whole character. In the present corrupted state of human manners, always to assent and to comply, is the very worst maxim we can adopt. It is impossible to support the purity and dignity of Christian morals, without opposing the world on various occasions, even though we should stand alone. That gentleness, therefore, which belongs to virtue, is to be carefully distinguished from the mean compliance and fawning assent of sycophants. It renounces no just right from fears. It gives up no important truth from flattery. It is indeed not only consistent with a firm mind, but it necessarily requires a manly spirit, and a fixed principle, in order to give it any real value. Upon this solid ground only, the polish of gentleness can with advantage be superinduced.

It stands opposed, not to the most determined regard for virtue and truth, but to harshness and severity, to pride and arrogance, to violence and oppression. It is, properly, that part of the great virtue of charity, which makes us unwilling to give pain to any of our brethren. Compassion prompts us to relieve their wants. Forbearance prevents us from retaliating their injuries. Meekness restrains our angry passions; candour, our severe judgments. Gentleness corrects whatever is offensive in our manners; and, by a constant train of humane attentions, studies to alleviate the burden of common misery. Its office, therefore, is extensive. It is not, like some other virtues, called forth only on peculiar emergencies; but it is continually in action, when we are engaged in intercourse with men. It ought to form our address, to regulate our speech, and to diffuse itself over our whole behaviour.

I must warn you, however, not to confound this gentle *wisdom which is from above*, with that artificial courtesy, that studied smoothness of manners, which is learned in the school of the world. Such accomplishments, the most frivolous and empty may possess. Too often they are employed by the artful, as a snare; too often affected by the hard and unfeeling, as a cover to the baseness of their minds. We cannot, at the same time, avoid observing the homage which, even in such instances, the world is constrained to pay to virtue. In order to render society agreeable, it is found necessary to assume somewhat, that may at least carry its appearance. Virtue is the universal charm.

charm. Even its shadow is courted, when the substance is wanting. The imitation of its form has been reduced into an art; and, in the commerce of life, the first study of all who would either gain the esteem, or win the hearts of others, is to learn the speech, and to adopt the manners, of candour, gentleness, and humanity. But that gentleness which is the characteristic of a good man, has, like every other virtue, its seat in the heart: And, let me add, nothing, except what flows from the heart, can render even external manners truly pleasing. For no assumed behaviour can at all times hide the real character. In that unaffected civility which springs from a gentle mind, there is a charm infinitely more powerful than in all the studied manners of the most finished courtier.

True gentleness is founded on a sense of what we owe to him who made us, and to the common nature of which we all share. It arises from reflecting on our own failings and wants; and from just views of the condition, and the duty of man. It is native feeling, heightened and improved by principle. It is the heart which easily relents; which feels for every thing that is human; and is backward and slow to inflict the least wound. It is affable in its address, and mild in its demeanour; ever ready to oblige, and willing to be obliged by others; breathing habitual kindness towards friends, courtesy to strangers; long-suffering to enemies. It exercises authority with moderation; administers reproof with tenderness; confers favours with ease and modesty. It is unassuming in opinion, and temperate in zeal. It contends not eagerly about trifles; slow to contradict, and still slower to blame; but prompt to allay dissension, and to restore peace. It neither intermeddles unnecessarily with the affairs, nor pries inquisitively into the secrets of others. It delights above all things to alleviate distress, and if it cannot dry up the falling tear, to sooth at least the grieving heart. Where it has not the power of being useful, it is never burdensome. It seeks to please rather than to shine and dazzle; and conceals with care that superiority, either of talents or of rank, which is oppressive to those who are beneath it. In a word, it is that spirit, and that tenour of manners, which the gospel of Christ enjoins, when it commands us *to bear one another's burdens; to rejoice with those who rejoice, and to weep with those who weep; to please every one his neighbour for his good; to be kind and tender-hearted; to be pitiful and courteous; to support the weak, and to be patient towards all men.*

Having now sufficiently explained the nature of this amiable virtue, I proceed.

I proceed to recommend it to your practice. Let me, for this end, desire you to consider the duty which you owe to God; to consider the relation which you bear one to another; to consider your own interest.

I. CONSIDER the duty which you owe to God. When you survey his works, nothing is so conspicuous as his greatness, and majesty. When you consult his word, nothing is more remarkable, than his attention to soften that greatness, and to place it in the mildest and least oppressive light. He not only characterises himself, as the *God of consolation*, but, with condescending gentleness, he particularly accommodates himself to the situation of the unfortunate. *He dwelleth with the humble and contrite. He hideth not his face when the afflicted cry. He healeth the broken in heart, and bindeth up their wounds.*—When his Son came to be the Saviour of the world, he was eminent for the same attribute of mild and gentle goodness. Long before his birth, it was prophesied of him that he should *not strive, nor cry, nor cause his voice to be heard in the streets; that the bruised reed he should not break, nor quench the smoking flax* *: And after his death, this distinguishing feature in his character was so universally remembered, that the Apostle Paul, on occasion of a request which he makes to the Corinthians, uses those remarkable expressions †, *I beseech you by the meekness and gentleness of Christ.* During all his intercourse with men, no harshness, or pride, or stately distance, appeared in his demeanour. In his access, he was easy; in his manners, simple; in his answers, mild; in his whole behaviour, humble and obliging. *Learn of me,* said he, *for I am meek and lowly in heart.*—As the Son of God is the pattern, so the Holy Ghost is the inspirer of gentleness. His name is *the Comforter,* the *Spirit of grace and peace.* His *fruits,* or operations on the human mind, are *love, meekness, gentleness, and long-suffering* ‡.—Thus, by every discovery of the Godhead, honour is conferred upon gentleness. It is held up to our view, as peculiarly connected with Celestial Nature. And suitable to such discoveries, is the whole strain of the gospel. It were unnecessary to appeal to any single precept. You need only open the New Testament, to find this virtue perpetually inculcated. Charity, or love, is the capital figure ever presented to our view; and gentleness, forbearance, and forgiveness, are the founds ever recurring on our ear.

So predominant, indeed, is this spirit throughout the Christian dispensation, that even the vices and corruptions of men have not been able

* *Matth.* xii. 19, 20. † 2 *Cor.* x. 1. ‡ *Gal.* v. 22.

able altogether to defeat its tendency. Though that difpenfation is far from having hitherto produced its full effect upon the world, yet we can clearly trace its influence, in humanizing the manners of men. Remarkable, in this refpect, is the victory which it has gained over thofe powers of violence and cruelty which belong to the infernal kingdom. Wherever Chriftianity prevails, it has difcouraged, and, in fome degree, abolifhed flavery. It has refcued human nature from that ignominious yoke, under which, in former ages, the one half of mankind groaned. It has introduced more equality between the two fexes, and rendered the conjugal union more rational and happy. It has abated the ferocioufnefs of war. It has mitigated the rigour of defpotifm, mitigated the cruelty of punifhment; in a word, has reduced mankind from their ancient barbarity, into a more humane and gentle ftate.———Do we pretend refpect and zeal for this religion, and at the fame time allow ourfelves in that harfhnefs and feverity, which are fo contradictory to its genius? Too plainly we fhow, that it has no power over our hearts. We may retain the Chriftian name; but we have abandoned the Chriftian fpirit.

II. CONSIDER the relation which you bear to one another. Man, as a folitary individual, is a very wretched being. As long as he ftands detached from his kind, he is poffeffed, neither of happinefs, nor of ftrength. We are formed by nature to unite; we are impelled towards each other, by the compaffionate inftincts in our frame; we are linked by a thoufand connections, founded on common wants. Gentlenefs, therefore, or, as it is very properly termed, humanity, is what man, as fuch, in every ftation, owes to man. To be inacceffible, contemptuous, and hard of heart, is to revolt againft our own nature; is, in the language of fcripture, *to hide ourfelves from our own flefh*. Accordingly, as all feel the claim which they have to mildnefs and humanity, fo all are fenfibly hurt by the want of it in others. On no fide are we more vulnerable. No complaint is more feelingly made, than that of the harfh and rugged manners of perfons with whom we have intercourfe. But how feldom do we transfer the caufe to ourfelves, or examine how far we are guilty of inflicting on others, whofe fenfibility is the fame with ours, thofe very wounds of which we fo loudly complain?

But, perhaps, it will be pleaded by fome, That this gentlenefs on which we now infift, regards only thofe fmaller offices of life, which

in

in their eye are not eſſential to religion and goodneſs. Negligent, they confeſs, on ſlight occaſions, of the government of their temper, or the regulation of their behaviour, they are attentive, as they pretend, to the great duties of beneficence; and ready, whenever the opportunity preſents, to perform important ſervices to their fellow-creatures. But let ſuch perſons reflect, that the occaſions of performing thoſe important good deeds, very rarely occur. Perhaps their ſituation in life, or the nature of their connections, may in a great meaſure exclude them from ſuch opportunities. Great events give ſcope for great virtues; but the main tenour of human life is compoſed of ſmall occurrences. Within the round of theſe, lie the materials of the happineſs of moſt men; the ſubjects of their duty, and the trials of their virtue. Virtue muſt be formed and ſupported, not by unfrequent acts, but by daily and repeated exertions. In order to its becoming either vigorous or uſeful, it muſt be habitually active; not breaking forth occaſionally with a tranſient luſtre, like the blaze of the comet; but regular in its returns, like the light of day: Not like the aromatic gale, which ſometimes feaſts the ſenſe; but like the ordinary breeze, which purifies the air, and renders it healthful.

Years may paſs over our heads, without affording any opportunity for acts of high beneficence or extenſive utility. Whereas not a day paſſes, but in the common tranſactions of life, and eſpecially in the intercourſe of domeſtic ſociety, gentleneſs finds place for promoting the happineſs of others, and for ſtrengthening in ourſelves the habit of virtue. Nay, by ſeaſonable diſcoveries of a humane ſpirit, we ſometimes contribute more materially to the advancement of happineſs, than by actions which are ſeemingly more important. There are ſituations, not a few, in human life, where the encouraging reception, the condeſcending behaviour, and the look of ſympathy, bring greater relief to the heart than the moſt bountiful gift. While, on the other ſide, when the hand of liberality is extended to beſtow, the want of gentleneſs is ſufficient to fruſtrate the intention of the benefit. We four thoſe whom we mean to oblige; and, by conferring favours with oſtentation and harſhneſs, we convert them into injuries. Can any diſpoſition then be held to poſſeſs a low place in the ſcale of virtue, whoſe influence is ſo conſiderable on the happineſs of the world?

Gentleneſs is, in truth, the great avenue to mutual enjoyment. Amidſt the ſtrife of interfering intereſts, it tempers the violence of contention, and keeps alive the ſeeds of harmony. It ſoftens animoſities; renews endearments; and renders the countenance of man a

refreſhment

refreshment to man. Banish gentleness from the earth; suppose the world to be filled with none but harsh and contentious spirits; and what sort of society would remain? the solitude of the desert were preferable to it. The conflict of jarring elements in chaos; the cave, where subterraneous winds contend and roar; the den where serpents hiss, and beasts of the forest howl; would be the only proper representations of such assemblies of men.—*O that I had wings like a dove! for then I would fly away, and be at rest. Lo! then I would wander far off, and remain in the wilderness; I would hasten my escape from the windy storm and tempest: For I have seen violence and strife in the city. Mischief and sorrow are in the midst of it: Deceit and guile depart not from the street**.—Strange! that where men have all one common interest, that they should so often absurdly concur in defeating it! Has not Nature already provided a sufficient quantity of unavoidable evils for the state of man? As if we did not suffer enough from the storm which beats upon us without, must we conspire also, in those societies where we assemble, in order to find a retreat from that storm, to harass one another?—But if the sense of duty, and of common happiness, be insufficient to recommend the virtue of which we treat, then let me desire you,

III. To consider your own interest. Whatever ends a good man can be supposed to pursue, gentleness will be found to favour them. It prepossesses and wins every heart. It persuades, when every other argument fails; often disarms the fierce, and melts the stubborn. Whereas harshness confirms the opposition it would subdue; and, of an indifferent person, creates an enemy. He who could overlook an injury committed in the collision of interests, will long and severely resent the slights of a contemptuous behaviour.—To the man of gentleness, the world is generally disposed to ascribe every other good quality. The higher endowments of the mind we admire at a distance; and when any impropriety of behaviour accompanies them, we admire without love. They are like some of the distant stars, whose beneficial influence reaches not to us. Whereas, of the influence of gentleness, all in some degree partake, and therefore all love it. The man of this character rises in the world without struggle, and flourishes without envy. His misfortunes are universally lamented; and his failings are easily forgiven.

But whatever may be the effect of this virtue on our external condition, its influence on our internal enjoyment is certain and powerful.

* *Psal.* lv. 6, 7, 8.

ful. That inward tranquility which it promotes, is the first requisite to every pleasurable feeling. It is the calm and clear atmosphere, the serenity and sunshine of the mind. When benignity and gentleness reign within, we are always least in hazard of being ruffled from without; every person, and every occurrence, are beheld in the most favourable light. But let some clouds of disgust and ill-humour gather on the mind, and immediately the scene changes: Nature seems transformed; and the appearance of all things is blackened to our view. The gentle mind is like the smooth stream, which reflects every object in its just proportion, and in its fairest colours. The violent spirit, like troubled waters, renders back the images of things distorted and broken; and communicates to them all that disordered motion which arises solely from its own agitation.

Offences must come. As soon may the waves of the sea cease to roll, as provocations to arise from human corruption and frailty. Attacked by great injuries, the man of mild and gentle spirit will feel what human nature feels; and will defend and resent, as his duty allows him. But to those slight provocations, and frivolous offences, which are the most frequent causes of disquiet, he is happily superior. Hence his days flow in a far more placid tenour than those of others, exempted from the numberless discomposures which agitate vulgar minds. Inspired with higher sentiments; taught to regard, with indulgent eye, the frailties of men, the omissions of the careless, the follies of the imprudent, and the levity of the fickle, he retreats into the calmness of his spirit, as into an undisturbed sanctuary; and quietly allows the usual current of life to hold its course.

This virtue has another, and still more important connection with our interest, by means of that relation which our present behaviour bears to our eternal state. Heaven is the region of gentleness and friendship; Hell, of fierceness and animosity. If then, as the scripture instructs us, *according to what we now sow we must hereafter reap,* it follows, that the cultivation of a gentle temper is necessary to prepare us for heavenly felicity; and that the indulgence of harsh dispositions, is the introduction to future misery. Men, I am afraid, too often separate those articles of their belief which relate to eternity, from the ordinary affairs of the world. They connect them with the seasons of seriousness and gravity. They leave them with much respect, as in a high region, to which, only on great occasions, they resort; and, when they descend into common life, consider themselves as at liberty to give free scope to their humours and passions. Whereas, in fact, it is their behaviour in the daily train of social intercourse

which

which, more than any other cause, fixes and determines their spiritual character; gradually instilling those dispositions, and forming those habits, which affect their everlasting condition. With regard to trifles, perhaps their malignant dispositions may chiefly be indulged. But let them remember well, that those trifles, by increasing the growth of peevishness and passion, become pregnant with the most serious mischiefs; and may fit them, before they are aware, for being the future companions of none but infernal spirits.

I mean not to say, that, in order to our preparation for heaven, it is enough to be mild and gentle; or that this virtue alone will cover all our sins. Through the felicity of natural constitution, a certain degree of this benignity may be possessed by some, whose hearts are in other respects corrupt, and their lives irregular. But what I mean to assert, is, That where no attention is given to the government of temper, meekness for Heaven is not yet acquired, and the regenerating power of religion is as yet unknown. One of the first works of the spirit of God is, to infuse into every heart which it inhabits, *that gentle wisdom which is from above. They who are Christ's have crucified the flesh, with its affections and lusts:* But let it not be forgotten, that among the *works of the flesh, hatred, variance, emulations, wrath, strife, and envyings,* are as expressly enumerated, as *uncleanness, murders, drunkenness,* and *revelling**. They who continue either in the one or the other, *shall not inherit,* indeed cannot inherit, *the kingdom of God.*

Having thus shown the importance of gentleness, both as a moral virtue, and as a Christian grace, I shall conclude the subject, with briefly suggesting some considerations which may be of use to facilitate the practice of it.

For this end, let me advise you to view your character with an impartial eye; and to learn, from your own failings, to give that indulgence which in your turn you claim. It is pride which fills the world with so much harshness and severity. In the fulness of self-estimation, we forget what we are. We claim attentions, to which we are not entitled. We are rigorous to offences, as if we had never offended; unfeeling to distress, as if we knew not what it was to suffer. From those airy regions of pride and folly, let us descend to our proper level. Let us survey the natural equality on which Providence has placed man with man, and reflect on the infirmities common to all. If the reflection on natural equality and mutual offences be insufficient to prompt humanity, let us at least remember what we

* *Gal.* v. 19, 20, 21.

we are in the fight of God. Have we none of that forbearance to give to one another, which we all so earnestly intreat from Heaven? Can we look for clemency or gentleness from our Judge, when we are so backward to show it to our own brethren?

Accustom yourselves, also, to reflect on the small moment of those things which are the usual incentives to violence and contention. In the ruffled and angry hour, we view every appearance through a false medium. The most inconsiderable point of interest, or honour, swells into a momentous object; and the slightest attack seems to threaten immediate ruin. But after passion or pride has subsided, we look round in vain for the mighty mischiefs we dreaded. The fabric, which our disturbed imagination had reared, totally disappears. But though the cause of contention has dwindled away, its consequences remain. We have alienated a friend; we have embittered an enemy; we have sown the seeds of future suspicion, malevolence, or disgust.— Suspend your violence, I beseech you, for a moment, when causes of discord occur. Anticipate that period of coolness, which, of itself, will soon arrive. Allow yourselves to think, how little you have any prospect of gaining by fierce contention; but how much of the true happiness of life you are certain of throwing away. Easily, and from the smallest chink, the bitter waters of strife are let forth; but their course cannot be foreseen; and he seldom fails of suffering most from their poisonous effect, who first allowed them to flow.

But gentleness will, most of all, be promoted by frequent views of those great objects which our holy religion presents. Let the prospects of immortality fill your minds. Look upon this world as a state of passage. Consider yourselves as engaged in the pursuit of higher interests; as acting now, under the eye of God, an introductory part to a more important scene. Elevated by such sentiments, your mind will become calm and sedate. You will look down, as from a superiour station, on the petty disturbances of the world. They are the selfish, the sensual, and the vain, who are most subject to the impotence of passion. They are linked so closely to the world; by so many sides they touch every object, and every person around them, that they are perpetually hurt, and perpetually hurting others. But the spirit of true religion removes us to a proper distance from the grating objects of worldly contention. It leaves us sufficiently connected with the world, for acting our part in it with propriety; but disengages us from it so far, as to weaken its power of disturbing our tranquility. It inspires magnanimity; and magnanimity always breathes gentleness. It leads us to view the follies of men with pity,

not

not with rancour; and to treat, with the mildness of a superiour nature, what in little minds would call forth all the bitterness of passion.

Aided by such considerations, let us cultivate that gentle wisdom which is, in so many respects, important both to our duty and our happiness. Let us assume it as the ornament of every age, and of every station. Let it temper the petulence of youth, and soften the moroseness of old age. Let it mitigate authority in those who rule, and promote deference among those who obey. I conclude with repeating the caution, not to mistake for true gentleness, that flimsey imitation of it, called polished manners, which often, among men of the world, under a smooth appearance, conceals much asperity. Let yours be native gentleness of heart, flowing from the love of God, and the love of man. Unite this amiable spirit with a proper zeal for all that is right, and just, and true. Let piety be combined in your character with humanity. Let determined integrity dwell in a mild and gentle breast. A character thus supported, will command more real respect, than can be procured by the most shining accomplishments, when separated from virtue.

SERMON

SERMON VII.

On the DISORDERS of the PASSIONS.

ESTHER, v. 13.

Yet all this availeth me nothing, so long as I see Mordecai the Jew sitting at the King's gate.

THESE are the words of one, who, though high in station and power, confessed himself to be miserable. They relate to a memorable occurrence in the Persian history, under the reign of Ahasuerus, who is supposed to be the Prince known among the Greek historians by the name of Artaxerxes. Ahasuerus had advanced, to the chief dignity in his kingdom, Haman, an Amalekite, who inherited all the ancient enmity of his race to the Jewish nation. He appears, from what is recorded of him, to have been a very wicked minister. Raised to greatness, without merit, he employed his power solely for the gratification of his passions. As the honours which he possessed were next to royal, his pride was every day fed with that servile homage which is peculiar to Asiatic courts; and all the servants of the King prostrated themselves before him. In the midst of this general adulation, one person only stooped not to Haman. This was Mordecai the Jew; who, knowing this Amalekite to be an enemy to the people of God, and, with virtuous indignation, despising that insolence of prosperity with which he saw him lifted up, *bowed not, nor did him reverence.* On this appearance of disrespect from Mordecai, Haman *was full of wrath: But he thought scorn to lay hands on Mordecai alone.* Personal revenge was not sufficient to satisfy him. So violent and black were his passions, that he resolved to exterminate the whole nation to which Mordecai belonged. Abusing, for this cruel purpose, the favour of his credulous Sovereign, he obtained a decree to be sent forth, that, against a certain day, all the Jews throughout the Persian dominions should be put to the sword. Mean while, confident of success, and blind to approaching ruin, he continued exulting in his prosperity. Invited by Ahasuerus to a royal banquet, which Esther the Queen had prepared, *he went forth that day joyful,*

and

and with a glad heart. But behold how flight an incident was sufficient to poifon his joy! As he went forth, he faw Mordecai in the King's gate, and obferved, that ftill he refufed to do him homage: *He ſtood not up, nor was moved for him;* although he well knew the formidable defigns which Haman was preparing to execute. One private man, who defpifed his greatnefs, and difdained fubmiffion, while a whole kingdom trembled before him; one fpirit, which the utmoft ftretch of his power could neither fubdue nor humble, blafted his triumphs. His whole foul was fhaken with a ftorm of paffion. Wrath, pride, and defire of revenge, rofe into fury. With difficulty he reftrained himfelf in public; but as foon as he came to his own houfe, he was forced to difclofe the agony of his mind. He gathered together his friends and family, with Zerifh his wife. *He told them of the glory of his riches, and the multitude of his children; and all the things wherein the King had promoted him, and how he had advanced him above the princes and fervants of the King. He faid, moreover, Yea, Efther the Queen did let no man come in with the King, unto the banquet that fhe had prepared, but myfelf; and to-morrow alfo am I invited unto her with the King.* After all this preamble, what is the conclufion?— *Yet all this availeth me nothing, fo long as I fee Mordecai the Jew fitting at the King's gate.*

The fequel of Haman's hiftory I fhall not now purfue. It might afford matter for much inftruction, by the confpicuous juftice of God in his fall and punifhment. But, contemplating only the fingular fituation in which the Text prefents him, and the violent agitation of his mind which it difplays, the following reflections naturally arife, which, together with fome practical improvements, fhall make the fubject of this difcourfe. I. How miferable is vice, when one guilty paffion creates fo much torment! II. How unavailing is profperity, when, in the height of it, a fingle difappointment can deftroy the relifh of all its pleafures! III. How weak is human nature, which, in the abfence of real, is thus prone to form to itfelf imaginary woes!

I. How miferable is vice, when one guilty paffion is capable of creating fo much torment! When we difcourfe to you of the internal mifery of finners; when we reprefent the pangs which they fuffer, from violent paffions, and a corrupted heart; we are fometimes fufpected of chufing a theme for declamation, and of heightening the picture which we draw, by colours borrowed from fancy. They whofe minds are, by nature, happily tranquil, or whofe fituation in life removes them

P

them from the disturbance and tumult of passion, can hardly conceive, that as long as the body is at ease, and the external condition prosperous, any thing which passes within the mind should cause such exquisite woe. But, for the truth of our assertions, we appeal to the history of mankind. We might reason from the constitution of the rational frame; where the understanding is appointed to be supreme, and the passions be subordinate; and where, if this due arrangement of its parts be overthrown, misery as necessarily ensues, as pain is consequent in the animal frame, upon the distortion of its members. But laying speculations of this kind aside, it is sufficient to lead you to the view of facts, the import of which can neither be controverted, nor mistaken. This is, indeed, the great advantage of history, that it is a mirror which holds up mankind to their own view. For, in all ages, human nature has been the same. In the circle of worldly affairs, the same characters and situations are perpetually returning; and in the follies and passions, the vices and crimes, of the generations that are past, we read those of the present.

Attend, then, to the instance now before us; and conceive, if you can, a person more thoroughly wretched, than one reduced to make this humiliating confession, that though surrounded with power, opulence, and pleasure, he was lost to all happiness, through the fierceness of his resentment; and was at that moment stung by disappointment, and torn by rage, beyond what he could bear. *All this availeth me nothing, so long as I see Mordecai the Jew sitting at the King's gate.* Had this been a soliloquy of Haman's within himself, it would have been a sufficient discovery of his misery. But when we consider it as a confession which he makes to others, it is a proof that his misery was become insupportable. For such agitations of the mind every man strives to conceal, because he knows they dishonour him. Other griefs and sorrows, he can, with freedom, pour out to a confident. What he suffers from the injustice or malice of the world, he is not ashamed to acknowledge. But when his suffering arises from the bad dispositions of his own heart; when, in the height of prosperity, he is rendered miserable, solely by disappointed pride, every ordinary motive for communication ceases. Nothing but the violence of anguish can drive him to confess a passion which renders him odious, and a weakness which renders him despicable. To what extremity, in particular, must he be reduced, before he can disclose to his own family the infamous secret of his misery? In the eye of his family every man wishes to appear respectable, and to cover from their knowledge whatever may vilify or degrade him. Attacked or reproached abroad, he consoles

himself

himself with his importance at home; and in domeftic attachment and refpect, feeks for fome compenfation for the injuftice of the world. Judge then of the degree of torment which Haman endured, by its breaking through all thefe reftraints, and forcing him to publifh his fhame before thofe from whom all men feek moft to hide it. How fevere muft have been the conflict which he underwent within himfelf, before he called together his wife and all his friends for this purpofe! How dreadful the agony he fuffered at the moment of his confeffion, when, to the aftonifhed company, he laid open the caufe of his diftrefs!

Affemble all the evils which poverty, difeafe, or violence can inflict, and their ftings will be found by far lefs pungent, than thofe which fuch guilty paffions dart into the heart. Amidft the ordinary calamities of the world, the mind can exert its powers, and fuggeft relief: And the mind is properly the man; the fufferer, and his fufferings, can be diftinguifhed. But thofe diforders of paffion, by feizing directly on the mind, attack human nature in its ftrong hold, and cut off its laft refource. They penetrate to the very feat of fenfation; and convert all the powers of thought into inftruments of torture.

Let us remark, in the event that is now before us, the awful hand of God; and admire his juftice, in thus making the finner's *own wickednefs to reprove him, and his backflidings to correct him.* Sceptics reafon in vain againft the reality of divine government. It is not a fubject of difpute. It is a fact which carries the evidence of fenfe, and difplays itfelf before our eyes. We fee the Almighty manifeftly *purfuing the finner with evil.* We fee him connecting with every fingle deviation from duty, thofe wounds of the fpirit which occafion the moft exquifite torments. He hath not merely promulgated his laws now, and delayed the diftribution of rewards and punifhments until a future period of being. But the fanctions of his laws already take place; their effects appear; and with fuch infinite wifdom are they contrived, as to require no other executioners of juftice againft the finner, than his own guilty paffions. God needs not come forth from his fecret place, in order to bring him to punifhment. He need not call thunder down from the heavens, nor raife any minifter of wrath from the abyfs below. He needs only fay, *Ephraim is joined to his idols; let him alone:* And, at that inftant, the finner becomes his own tormentor. The infernal fire begins, of itfelf, to kindle within him. The worm that never dies, feizes on his heart.

Let us remark alfo, for this example, how imperfectly we can judge from external appearances, concerning real happinefs or mifery. All Perfia, it is probable, envied Haman as the happieft perfon in the empire;

pire; while yet, at the moment of which we now treat, there was not within its bounds one more thoroughly wretched. We are seduced and deceived by that false glare which prosperity sometimes throws around bad men. We are tempted to imitate their crimes, in order to partake of their imagined felicity. But remember Haman, and beware of the snare. Think not, when you behold a pageant of grandeur displayed to public view that you discern the ensign of certain happiness. In order to form any just conclusion, you must follow the great man into the retired apartment, where he lays aside his disguise; you must not only be able to penetrate into the interiour of families, but you must have a faculty by which you can look into the inside of hearts. Were you endowed with such a power, you would most commonly behold good men, in proportion to their goodness, satisfied and easy; you would behold atrocious sinners always wretchless and unhappy.

Unjust are our complaints, of the promiscuous distribution made by Providence, of its favours among men. From superficial views such complaints arise. The distribution of the goods of fortune, indeed, may often be promiscuous; that is, disproportioned to the moral characters of men; but the allotment of real happiness is never so. For *to the wicked there is no peace. They are like the troubled sea when it cannot rest. They travel with pain all their days. Trouble and anguish prevail against them. Terrours make them afraid on every side. A dreadful sound is in their ears; and they are in great fear where no fear is.*———— Hitherto we have considered Haman under the character of a very wicked man, tormented by criminal passions. Let us now consider him, merely as a child of fortune, a prosperous man of the world; and proceed to observe,

II. How unavailing worldly prosperity is, since, in the midst of it, a single disappointment is sufficient to embitter all its pleasures. We might at first imagine, that the natural effect of prosperity would be, to diffuse over the mind a prevailing satisfaction, which the lesser evils of life could not ruffle or disturb. We might expect, that as one in the full glow of health, despises the inclemency of weather; so one in possession of all the advantages of high power and station, should disregard slight injuries; and, at perfect ease with himself, should view, in the most favourable light, the behaviour of others around him. Such effects would indeed follow, if worldly prosperity contained in itself the true principles of human felicity. But as it possesses them not, the very reverse of those consequences generally obtains. Prosperity debilitates, instead of strengthening the mind. Its most common

mon effect is, to create an extreme fenfibility to the flighteft wound. It foments impatient defires; and raifes expectations which no fuccefs can fatisfy. It fofters a falfe delicafy, which fickens in the midft of indulgence. By repeated gratification, it blunts the feelings of men to what is pleafing; and leaves them unhappily acute to whatever is uneafy. Hence, the gale which another would fcarcely feel, is, to the profperous, a rude tempeft. Hence, the rofe-leaf doubled below them on the couch, as it is told of the effeminate Sybarite, breaks their reft. Hence, the difrefpect fhown by Mordecai, preyed with fuch violence on the heart of Haman. Upon no principle of reafon can we affign a fufficient caufe for all the diftrefs which this incident occafioned to him. The caufe lay not in the external incident. It lay within himfelf; it arofe from a mind diftempered by profperity.

Let this example correct that blind eagernefs, with which we rufh to the chafe of worldly greatnefs and honours. I fay not, that it fhould altogether divert us from purfuing them; fince, when enjoyed with temperance and wifdom, they may doubtlefs both enlarge our utility, and contribute to our comfort. But let it teach us not to over-rate them. Let it convince us, that unlefs we add to them the neceffary correctives of piety and virtue, they are, by themfelves, more likely to render us wretched, than to make us happy.

Let the memorable fate of Haman fuggeft to us alfo, how often, befides corrupting the mind, and engendering internal mifery, they lead us among precipices, and betray us into ruin. At the moment when fortune feemed to fmile upon him with the moft ferene and fettled afpect, fhe was digging in fecret the pit for his fall. Profperity was weaving around his head the web of deftruction. Succefs inflamed his pride; pride increafed his thirft of revenge; the revenge which, for the fake of one man, he fought to execute on a whole nation, incenfed the Queen; and he is doomed to fuffer the fame death which he had prepared for Mordecai.—Had Haman remained in a private ftation, he might have arrived at a peaceable old age. He might have been, I fhall not fay, a good or a happy man, yet probably far lefs guilty, and lefs wretched, than when placed at the head of the greateft empire in the Eaft. *Who knoweth what is good for man in this life; all the days of his vain life, which he fpendeth as a fhadow?*

An extenfive contemplation of human affairs will lead us to this conclufion, That, among the different conditions and ranks of men, the balance of happinefs is preferved in a great meafure equal; and that the high and the low, the rich and the poor, approach, in point of real enjoyment, much nearer to each other than is commonly imagined. In the

the lot of man, mutual compenfations, both of pleafure and of pain, univerfally take place. Providence never intended, that any ftate here fhould be either completely happy, or entirely miferable. If the feelings of pleafure are more numerous, and more lively, in the higher departments of life, fuch alfo are thofe of pain. If greatnefs flatters our vanity, it multiplies our dangers. If opulence increafes our gratifications, it increafes, in the fame proportion, our defires and demands. If the poor are confined to a more narrow circle, yet within that circle lie moſt of thofe natural fatisfactions, which, after all the refinements of art, are found to be the moſt genuine and true.—In a ftate, therefore, where there is neither fo much to be coveted on the one hand, nor to be dreaded on the other, as at firft appears, how fubmiffive ought we to be to the difpofal of Providence! How temperate in our defires and purfuits! How much more attentive to preferve our virtue, and to improve our minds, than to gain the doubtful and equivocal advantages of worldly profperity!——But now, laying afide the confideration of Haman's great crimes; laying afide his high profperity; viewing him fimply as a man, let us obferve, from his hiftory,

III. How weak human nature is, which, in the abfence of real, is thus prone to create to itfelf imaginary woes. *All this availeth me nothing, fo long as I fee Mordecai the Jew fitting at the King's gate.*—— What was it, O Haman! to thee, though Mordecai had continued to fit there, and neglected to do thee homage? Would the banquet have been on that account the lefs magnificent, thy palace lefs fplendid, or thy retinue lefs numerous? Could the difrefpect of an obfcure ftranger difhonour the favourite of a mighty King? In the midft of a thoufand fubmiffive courtiers, was one fullen countenance an object worthy of drawing thy notice, or of troubling thy repofe?—Alas! in Haman we behold too juft a picture of what often paffes within ourfelves. We never know what it is to be long at eafe. Let the world ceafe from changing around us. Let external things keep that fituation in which we moft wifh them to remain; yet fomewhat from within fhall foon arife, to difturb our happinefs. A *Mordecai* appears, or feems to appear, *fitting at the gate.* Some vexation, which our fancy has either entirely created, or at leaſt has unreafonably aggravated, corrodes us in fecret; and until that be removed, all that we enjoy *availeth us nothing.* Thus, while we are inceffantly complaining of the vanity and the evils of human life, we make that vanity, and we increafe thofe evils. Unfkilled in the art of extracting happinefs from the objects around us, our ingenuity folely appears in converting them into mifery.

Let

Let it not be thought, that troubles of this kind are incident only to the great and the mighty. Though they, perhaps, from the intemperance of their paſſions, are peculiarly expoſed to them; yet the diſeaſe itſelf belongs to human nature, and ſpreads through all ranks. In the humble and ſeemingly quiet ſhade of private life, diſcontent broods over its imaginary ſorrows; preys upon the citizen, no leſs than upon the courtier; and often nouriſhes paſſions equally malignant in the cottage and in the palace. Having once ſeized the mind, it ſpreads its own gloom over every ſurrounding object; it every where ſearches out materials for itſelf; and in no direction more frequently employs its unhappy activity, than in creating diviſions amongſt mankind, and in magnifying ſlight provocations into mortal injuries. Thoſe ſelf-created miſeries, imaginary in the cauſe, but real in the ſuffering, will be found to form a proportion of human evils, not inferiour, either in ſeverity or in number, to all that we endure from the unavoidable calamities of life. In ſituations where much comfort might be enjoyed, this man's ſuperiority, and that man's neglect, our jealouſy of a friend, our hatred of a rival, an imagined affront, or a miſtaken point of honour, allow us no repoſe. Hence, diſcords in families, animoſities among friends, and wars among nations. Hence, Haman miſerable in the midſt of all that greatneſs could beſtow. Hence multitudes in the moſt obſcure ſtations, for whom Providence ſeemed to have prepared a quiet life, no leſs eager in their petty broils, nor leſs tormented by their paſſions, than if princely honours were the prize for which they contended.

From this train of obſervation, which the Text has ſuggeſted, can we avoid reflecting upon the diſorder in which human nature plainly appears at preſent to lie? We have beheld, in Haman, the picture of that miſery which ariſes from evil paſſions; of that unhappineſs, which is incident to the higheſt proſperity; of that diſcontent, which is common to every ſtate. Whether we conſider him as a bad man, a proſperous man, or ſimply as a man, in every light we behold reaſon too weak for paſſion. This is the ſource of the reigning evil; this is the root of the univerſal diſeaſe. The ſtory of Haman only ſhows us, what human nature has too generally appeared to be in every age. Hence, when we read the hiſtory of nations, what do we read but the hiſtory of the follies and crimes of men? We may dignify thoſe recorded tranſactions, by calling them the intrigues of ſtateſmen, and the exploits of conquerours; but they are in truth, no other than the efforts of diſcontent to eſcape from its miſery, and the ſtruggles of contending paffions among unhappy men. The hiftory of mankind has ever been a continued tragedy; the world, a great theatre exhibiting the fame repeated fcene, of the follies of men fhooting forth into guilt, and of their paffions fermenting, by a quick procefs, into mifery.

But can we believe, that the nature of man came forth in this ftate from the hands of its gracious Creator? Did he frame this world, and ftore it with inhabitants, folely that it might be replenifhed with crimes and misfortunes?—In the moral, as well as in the natural world, we may plainly difcern the figns of fome violent convulfion, which has fhattered the original workmanfhip of the Almighty. Amidft this wreck of human nature, traces ftill remain which indicate its Author. Thofe high powers of confcience and reafon, that capacity for happinefs, that ardour of interprife, that glow of affection, which often break through the gloom of human vanity and guilt, are like the fcattered columns, the broken arches, and defaced fculptures of fome fallen temple, whofe ancient fplendour appears amidft its ruins. So confpicuous in human nature are thofe characters, both of a high origin, and of a degraded ftate, that, by many religious fects throughout the earth, they have been feen and confeffed. A tradition feems to have pervaded almoft all nations, that the human race had either, through fome offence, forfeited, or, through fome misfortune, loft that ftation of primæval honour which they once poffeffed. But while, from this doctrine, ill underftood, and involved in many fabulous tales, the nations wandering in Pagan darknefs could draw no confequences that were juft; while totally ignorant of the nature of the difeafe, they fought in vain for the remedy; the fame divine revelation, which has informed us in what manner our apoftacy arofe, from the abufe of our rational powers, has inftructed us alfo how we may be reftored to virtue and to happinefs.

LET us, therefore, ftudy to improve the affiftance which this revelation affords, for the reftoration of our nature, and the recovery of our felicity. With humble and greatful minds, let us apply to thofe medicinal fprings which it hath opened, for curing the diforders of our heart and paffions. In this view, let us, with reverence, look up to that Divine Perfonage, who defcended into this world on purpofe to be *the light and the life of men;* who came in the fulnefs of grace and truth, to *repair the defolation of many generations,* to reftore order among the works of God, and to raife up a *new earth and new heavens, wherein righteoufnefs fhould dwell for ever.* Under his tuition let us put ourfelves; and, amidft the ftorms of paffion to which we are here expofed, and

the

the slippery paths which we are left to tread, never trust presumptuously to our own understanding. Thankful that a Heavenly Conductor vouchsafes his aid, let us earnestly pray, that from him may descend divine light to guide our steps, and divine strength to fortify our minds. Let us pray, that his grace may keep us from all intemperate passions, and mistaken pursuits of pleasure; that whether it shall be his will to give or to deny us earthly prosperity, he may bless us with a calm, a sound, and well regulated mind; may give us moderation in success, and fortitude under disappointment; and may enable us so to take warning from the crimes and miseries of others, as to escape the snares of guilt.

WHILE we thus maintain a due dependence on God, let us also exert ourselves with care in acting our own part. From the whole of what has been said, this important instruction arises, that the happiness of every man depends more upon the state of his own mind, than upon any one external circumstance; nay, more than upon all external things put together. We have seen, that inordinate passions are the great disturbers of life; and that, unless we possess a good conscience, and a well-governed mind, discontent will blast every enjoyment, and the highest prosperity will prove only disguised misery. Fix then this conclusion in your minds, that the destruction of your virtue is the destruction of your peace. *Keep thy heart with all diligence;* govern it with the greatest care; *for out of it are the issues of life.* In no station, in no period, think yourselves secure from the dangers which spring from your passions. Every age, and every station they beset; from youth to grey hairs, and from the peasant to the prince.

At your first setting out in life, especially when yet unacquainted with the world and its snares, when every pleasure enchants with its smile, and every object shines with the gloss of novelty; beware of the seducing appearances which surround you, and recollect what others have suffered from the power of headstrong desire. If you allow any passion, even though it be esteemed innocent, to acquire an absolute ascendant, your inward peace will be impaired. But if any, which has the taint of guilt, take early possession of your mind, you may date from that moment the ruin of your tranquillity. Nor with the season of youth does the peril end. To the impetuosity of youthful desire, succeed the more sober, but no less dangerous, attachments of advancing years; when the passions which are connected with interest

rest and ambition begin their reign, and too frequently extend their malignant influence, even over those periods of life which ought to be most tranquil. From the first to the last of man's abode on earth, the discipline must never be relaxed, of guarding the heart from the dominion of passion. Eager passions, and violent desires, were not made for man. They exceed his sphere. They find no adequate objects on earth; and of course can be productive of nothing but misery. The certain consequence of indulging them is, that there shall come an evil day, when the anguish of disappointment shall drive us to acknowledge, that all which we enjoy *availeth us nothing*.

You are not to imagine, that the warnings which I have given in this discourse, are applicable only to the case of such signal offenders as he was, of whom the Text treats. Think not, as I am afraid too many do, that because your passions have not hurried you into atrocious deeds, they have therefore wrought no mischief, and have left no sting behind them. By a continued series of loose, though apparently trivial, gratifications, the heart is often as thoroughly corrupted, as by the commission of any one of those enormous crimes which spring from great ambition, or great revenge. Habit gives the passions strength, while the absence of glaring guilt seemingly justifies them; and, unawakened by remorse, the sinner proceeds in his course, till he wax bold in guilt, and become ripe for ruin. For by gradual and latent steps, the destruction of our virtue advances. Did the evil unveil itself at the beginning; did the storm which is to overthrow our peace, discover as it rose, all its horrors, precautions would more frequently be taken against it. But we are imperceptibly betrayed; and from one licentious attachment, one criminal passion, are, by a train of consequences, drawn on to another, till the government of our minds is irrecoverably lost. The enticing and the odious passions are, in this respect, similar in their process; and, though by different roads, conduct at last to the same issue. David, when he first beheld Bathsheba, did not plan the death of Uriah. Haman was not delivered up all at once to the madness of revenge. His passions rose with the rising tide of prosperity; and pride completed what prosperity began. What was originally no more than displeasure at Mordecai's disrespect, increased with every invitation he received to the banquet of the Queen; till it impelled him to devise the slaughter of a whole nation, and ended in a degree of rage which confounded his reason, and hurried him to ruin. In this manner, every criminal passion, in its progress, swells and blackens; and what was at first a small cloud, such as the Prophet's servant saw, *no bigger than a man's hand, rising from the sea**, is soon found to carry the tempest in its womb.

* 1 *Kings*, xviii. 44.

SERMON VIII.

On our IGNORANCE of GOOD and EVIL in this Life.

ECCLES. vi. 12.

Who knoweth what is good for man in this life, all the days of his vain life, which he spendeth as a shadow?

THE measure according to which knowledge is dispensed to man, affords conspicuous proofs of divine wisdom. In many instances we clearly perceive, that either more or less would have proved detrimental to his state; that entire ignorance would have deprived him of proper motives to action; and that complete discovery would have raised him to a sphere too high for his present powers. He is, therefore, permitted to *know only in part; and to see through a glass, darkly.* He is left in that state of conjecture, and partial information, which, though it may occasionally subject him to distress, yet, on the whole, conduces most to his improvement; which affords him knowledge sufficient for the purposes of virtue, and of active life, without disturbing the operations of his mind, by a light too bright and dazzling. This evidently holds with respect to that degree of obscurity which now covers the great laws of Nature, the decrees of the Supreme Being, the state of the invisible world, the future events of our own life, and the thoughts and designs which pass within the breasts of others *.

But there is an ignorance of another kind, with respect to which application of this remark may appear more dubious; the ignorance under which men labour concerning their happiness in the present life, and the means of attaining it. If there be foundation for Solomon's complaint in the Text, *who knoweth what is good for man in this life?* this consequence may be thought inevitably to follow, That the *days of his life* must be *vain* in every sense; not only because they are fleeting, but because they are empty too, like the *shadow*. For, to what purpose are all his labours in the pursuit of an object, which it is not in his power to discover or ascertain?—Let us then seriously enquire, what

* *Vid. Serm.* iv.

what account can be given of our present ignorance, respecting what is good for us in this life; whether nothing be left, but only to wander in uncertainty amidst this darkness, and to lament it as the sad consequence of our fallen state; or whether such instructions may not be derived from it, as give ground for acknowledging, that by this, as by all its other appointments, the wisdom of Providence brings real good out of seeming evil. I shall, in order to determine this point, first, endeavour to illustrate the doctrine of the Text, That we know not, or at most know imperfectly, *what is good for us in this life*: I shall next explain the causes to which this defect in our knowledge is owing: And then shall show the purposes which it was intended to serve, and the effects which it ought to produce on our conduct.

The whole history of mankind seems a comment on the doctrine of the Text. When we review the course of human affairs, one of the first objects which every where attracts our notice, is, the mistaken judgment of men concerning their own interest. The *sore evil*, which Solomon long ago remarked with respect to riches, of their being *kept by the owners thereof to their hurt*, takes place equally with respect to dominion and power, and all the splendid objects and high stations of life. We every day behold men climbing, by painful steps, to that dangerous height, which, in the end, renders their fall more severe, and their ruin more conspicuous. But it is not to high stations that the doctrine of the Text is limited. In the crimes by which too often these are gained, and in the misfortunes which they afterwards bring forth, the greater part of every audience may think themselves little concerned. Leaving such themes, therefore, to the poet and the historian, let us come nearer to ourselves, and survey the ordinary walk of life.

Around us, we every where behold a busy multitude. Restless and uneasy in their present situation, they are incessantly employed in accomplishing a change of it; and, as soon as their wish is fulfilled, we discern, by their behaviour, that they are as dissatisfied as they were before. Where they expected to have found a paradise, they find a desert. The man of business pines for leisure. The leisure for which he had longed, proves an irksome gloom; and, through want of employment, he languishes, sickens, and dies. The man of retirement fancies no state to be so happy, as that of active life. But he has not engaged long in the tumults and contests of the world, until he finds cause to look back with regret on the calm hours of his former privacy and retreat. Beauty, wit, eloquence, and fame, are eagerly desired by persons in every rank of life. They are the parent's fondest wish for his child; the ambition

ambition of the young, and the admiration of the old. And yet, in what numberlefs inftances have they proved, to thofe who poffeffed them, no other than fhining fnares; feductions to vice, inftigations to folly, and, in the end, fources of mifery? Comfortably might their days have paffed, had they been lefs confpicuous. But the diftinctions which brought them forth to notice, conferred fplendour, and withdrew happinefs. Long life is, of all others, the moft general, and feemingly the moft innocent object of defire. With refpect to this too, we fo frequently err, that it would have been a bleffing to many to have had their wifh denied. There was a period, when they might have quitted the ftage with honour, and in peace. But by living too long, they outlived their reputation; outlived their family, their friends, and comforts; and reaped nothing from the continuance of days, except to feel the preffure of age, to tafte the dregs of life, and to behold a wider compafs of human mifery.

Man walketh in a vain fhow. His fears are often as vain as his wifhes. As what flattered him in expectation, frequently wounds him in poffeffion; fo the event to which he looked forward with an anxious and fearful eye, has often, when it arrived, laid its terrours afide; nay, has brought in its train unexpected bleffings. Both good and evil are beheld at a diftance, through a perfpective which deceives. The colours of objects when nigh, are entirely different from what they appeared, when they were viewed in futurity.

THE fact then being undoubtedly certain, that it is common for men to be decived in their profpects of happinefs, let us next enquire into the caufes of that deception. Let us attend to thofe peculiar circumftances in our ftate, which render us fuch incompetent judges of future good or evil in this life.

Firft, We are not fufficiently acquainted with ourfelves, to forefee our future feelings. We judge by the fenfations of the prefent moment; and, in the fervour of defire, pronounce confidently concerning the defired object. But we reflect not, that our minds, like our bodies, undergo great alteration from the fituations into which they are thrown, and the progreffive ftages of life through which they pafs. Hence, concerning any condition which is yet untried, we conjecture with much uncertainty. In imagination, we carry our prefent wants, inclinations, and fentiments, into the ftate of life to which we afpire. But no fooner have we entered on it, than our fentiments and inclinations change. New wants and defires arife; new objects are required to gratify them; and by confequence our old diffatisfaction

returns,

returns, and the void, which was to have been filled, remains as great as it was before.

But, next, suppofing our knowledge of ourfelves fufficient to direct us in the choice of happinefs, yet ftill we are liable to err, from our ignorance of the connections which fubfift between our own condition and that of others. No individual can be happy, unlefs the circumftances of thofe around him be fo adjufted as to confpire with his intereft. For, in human fociety, no happinefs or mifery ftands unconnected and independent. Our fortunes are interwoven by threads innumerable. We touch one another on all fides. One man's misfortune or fuccefs, his wifdom or his folly, often, by its confequences, reaches through multitudes. Such a fyftem is far too complicated for our arrangement. It requires adjuftments beyond our fkill and power. It is a chaos of events, into which our eye cannot pierce; and is capable of regulation, only by him who perceives at one glance the relation of each to all.

Farther, As we are ignorant of the events which will arife from the combination of our circumftances with thofe of others, fo we are equally ignorant of the influence which the prefent tranfactions of our life may have upon thofe which are future. The important queftion is not, What is good for a man one day; but What is *good for him all the days of his life*? Not, what will yield him a few fcattered pleafures; but what will render his life happy on the whole amount? And is he able to anfwer that queftion, who knoweth not what *one day may bring forth;* who cannot tell, whether the events of it may not branch out into confequences, which will affume a direction quite oppofite to that in which they fet forth, and fpread themfelves over all his life to come? There is not any prefent moment that is unconnected with fome future one. The life of every man is a continued chain of incidents, each link of which hangs upon the former. The tranfition from caufe to effect, from event to event, is often carried on by fecret fteps, which our forefight cannot divine, and our fagacity is unable to trace. Evil may, at fome future period, bring forth good; and good may bring forth evil, both equally unexpected. Had the Patriarch, Jofeph, continued to loiter under his father's fond indulgence, he might have lived an obfcure and infignificant life. From the pit and the prifon, arofe the incidents which made him the ruler of Egypt, and the faviour of his father's houfe.

Laftly, Suppofing every other incapacity to be removed, our ignorance of the dangers to which our fpiritual ftate is expofed, would difqualify us for judging foundly concerning our true happinefs. Higher interefts terests than those of the present world are now depending. All that is done or suffered by us here, ultimately refers to that immortal world, for which good men are trained up, under the care of an Almighty Parent. We are as incompetent judges of the measures necessary to be pursued for this end, as children are, of the proper conduct to be held in their education. We foresee the dangers of our spiritual, still less than we do those of our natural state; because we are less attentive to trace them. We are still more exposed to vice than to misery; because the confidence which we place in our virtue, is yet worse founded than that which we place in our wisdom. Can you esteem him prosperous, who is raised to a situation which flatters his passions, but which corrupts his principles, disorders his temper, and, finally, oversets his virtue? In the ardour of pursuit, how little are these effects foreseen? And yet, how often are they accomplished by a change of condition? Latent corruptions are called forth; seeds of guilt are quickened into life; a growth of crimes arises, which, had it not been for the fatal culture of prosperity, would never have seen the light. How often is man, boastful as he is of reason, merely the creature of his fortune; formed, and moulded, by the incidents of his life?—Hazael, when yet a private man, detested the thoughts of cruelty. *Thou shalt slay the young men with the sword*, said the Prophet: *Thou shalt dash the children, and rip up the women with child. Is thy servant a dog*, replied Hazael, *that he should do these things?* But no sooner was he clothed with the coveted purple, than it seemed to taint his nature. He committed the crimes of which, at a distance, he believed himself incapable; and became the bloody tyrant, whose character his soul once abhorred [*].

Such then at present is man; thus incapable of pronouncing with certainty concerning his own good or evil. Of futurity he discerns little; and even that little he sees through a cloud. Ignorant of the alteration which his sentiments and desires will undergo from new situations in life; ignorant of the consequences which will follow from the combination of his circumstances with those of others around him; ignorant of the influence which the present may have on the future events of his life; ignorant of the effect which a change of condition may produce on his moral character, and his eternal interests: How can he know *what is good for him all the days of his vain life, which he spendeth as a shadow?*

Instead of only lamenting this ignorance, let us, in the last place, consider how it ought to be improved; what duties it suggests, and what wise ends it was intended by Providence to promote.

[*] 2 *Kings*, viii. 12, 13.

I. LET this doctrine teach us to proceed with caution and circumspection, through a world where evil so frequently lurks under the form of good. To be humble and modest in opinion, to be vigilant and attentive in conduct, to distrust fair appearances, and to restrain rash desires, are instructions which the darkness of our present state should strongly inculcate. God hath appointed our situation to be so ambiguous, in order both to call forth the exertion of those intelligent powers which he hath given us, and to enforce our dependence on his gracious aid. *It is not in man that walketh, to direct his steps.* Surrounded with so many bewildering paths, among which the wisest are ready to stray, how earnestly should we implore, and how thankfully should we receive, that divine illumination which is promised in scripture to the pious and the humble! *The secret of the Lord is with them that fear him. He will guide them with his counsel. He will teach them the way that they should chuse.* But what must be the fate of him, who, amidst all the dangers attending human conduct, neither looks up to Heaven for direction, nor properly exerts that reason which God hath given him? If to the most diligent enquirer, it proves so difficult a task to distinguish true good, from those fallacious appearances with which it is ever blended, how should he discover it, who brings neither patience nor attention to the search; who applies to no other counsellor than present pleasure, and, with a rash and credulous mind, delivers himself up to every suggestion of desire?

This admonition I particularly direct to those, who are in a period of life too often characterised by forward presumption and headlong pursuit. The selfconceit of the young, is the great source of those dangers to which they are exposed; and it is peculiarly unfortunate, that the age which stands most in need of the counsel of the wise, should be the most prone to contemn it. Confident in the oppinions which they adopt, and in the measures which they pursue, they seem as if they understood Solomon to say, not, *Who knoweth,* but, Who is ignorant of *what is good for man all the days of his life?* The bliss to be aimed at, is, in their oppinion, fully apparent. It is not the danger of mistake, but the failure of success, which they dread. Activity to seize, not sagacity to discern, is the only requisite which they value.

——How long shall it be, ere the fate of your predecessors in the same course teach you wisdom? How long shall the experience of all ages continue to lift its voice to you in vain? Beholding the ocean on which you are embarked covered with wrecks, are not those fatal signals sufficient to admonish you of the hidden rock? If, in Paradise itself, there was a tree which bare fruit fair to the eye, but mortal in its
effects,

Good and Evil in this Life.

effects, how much more, in this fallen state, may such deceiving appearances be expected to abound! The whole state of Nature is now become a scene of delusion to the sensual mind. Hardly any thing is what it appears to be. And what flatters most, is always farthest from reality. There are voices which sing around you; but whose strains allure to ruin. There is a banquet spread, where poison is in every dish. There is a couch which invites you to repose; but to slumber upon it, is death. In such a situation, *be not high-minded, but fear.* Let sobriety temper your unweary ardour. Let modesty check your rash presumption. Let wisdom be the offspring of reflection now, rather than the fruit of bitter experience hereafter.

II. LET our ignorance of what is good or evil, correct anxiety about worldly success. As rashness is the vice of youth, the opposite extreme of immoderate care is the vice of advancing years. The doctrine which I have illustrated, is equally adapted for checking both. Since we are so often betrayed into evil by the mistaken pursuit of good, care and attention are requisite, both informing our choice, and in conducting our pursuit; but since our attention and care are liable to be so often frustrated, they should never be allowed to deprive us of tranquility. The ignorance in which we are left concerning good and evil, is not such as to supersede prudence in conduct: For wisdom is still found to *excel folly as far as light excelleth darkness.* But it is that degree of uncertainty, which ought to render us temperate in pursuit; which ought to calm the perturbation of hope and fear, and to cure the pain of anxiety. Anxiety is the poison of human life. It is the parent of many sins, and of more miseries. In a world where every thing is so doubtful; where you may succeed in your with, and be miserable; where you may be disappointed, and be blest in the disappointment; what means this restless stir and commotion of mind? Can your solicitude alter the course, or unravel the intricacy of human events? Can your curiosity pierce through the cloud which the Supreme Being hath made impenetrable to mortal eye?—To provide against every apparent danger, by the employment of the most promising means, is the office of wisdom. But at this point wisdom stops. It commands you to retire, after you have done all that was incumbent on you, and to possess your mind in peace. By going beyond this point; by giving yourselves up to immoderate concern about unknown events, you can do nothing to advance your success, and you do much to ruin your peace. You plant within your breast the thorn which is long to gall you. To the vanity of life, you add a vexation of spirit, which is wholly of your own creation, not of Divine appointment

ment. For the dubious goods of this world were never designed by God to raise such eager attachment. They were given to man for his occasional refreshment, not for his chief felicity. By setting an excessive value upon objects which were intended only for your secondary regard, you change their nature. Seeking more satisfaction from them than they are able to afford, you receive less than they might give. From a mistaken care to secure your happiness, you bring upon yourselves certain misery.

III. LET our ignorance of good and evil determine us to follow Providence, and to resign ourselves to God. One of the most important lessons which can be given to man, is resignation to his Maker; and nothing inculcates it more, than the experience of his own inability to guide himself.—You know not what is good for you, in the future periods of life. But God perfectly knows it; and if you faithfully serve him, you have reason to believe that he will always consult it. Before him lies the whole succession of events, which are to fill up your existence. It is in his power to arrange and model them at his pleasure; and so to adapt one thing to another, as to fulfil his promise of making them *all work together for good to those who love him.* Here then, amidst the agitation of desire, and the perplexities of doubt, is one fixed point of rest. By this let us abide; and dismiss our anxiety about things uncertain and unknown. *Acquaint yourselves with God, and be at peace.* Secure the *one thing needful.* Study to acquire an interest in the Divine favour; and you may safely surrender yourselves to the Divine administration.

When tempted to repine at your condition, reflect how uncertain it is, whether you should have been happier in any other. Remembering the vanity of many of your former wishes, and the fallacy which you have so often experienced in your schemes of happiness, be thankful that you are placed under a wiser direction than your own. Be not too particular in your petitions to Heaven, concerning your temporal interest. Suffer God to govern the world according to his own plan; and only pray, that he would bestow what his unerring wisdom sees to be best for you on the whole. In a word, *Commit your way unto the Lord. Trust in him, and do good.* Follow wherever his Providence leads; comply with whatever his will requires; and leave all the rest to him.

IV. LET our ignorance of what is good for us in this life, prevent our taking any unlawful step, in order to compass our most favourite designs.

designs. Were the sinner bribed with any certain and unquestionable advantage; could the means which he employs ensure his success, and could that success ensure his comfort; he might have some apology to offer for deviating from the path of virtue. But the doctrine which I have illustrated, deprives him of all excuse, and places his folly in the most striking light. He climbs the steep rock, and treads on the edge of a precipice, in order to catch a shadow. He has cause to dread, not only the uncertainty of the event which he wishes to accomplish, but the nature also of that event when accomplished. He is not only liable to that disappointment of success, which so often frustrates all the designs of men; but liable to a disappointment still more cruel, that of being successful and miserable at once. Riches and pleasures are the chief temptations to criminal deeds. Yet those riches, when obtained, may very possibly overwhelm him with unforeseen miseries. Those pleasures may cut short his health and life. And is it for such doubtful and fallacious rewards, that the deceiver fills his mouth with lies, the friend betrays his benefactor, the apostate renounces his faith, and the assassin covers himself with blood?

Whoever commits a crime, incurs a certain evil for a most uncertain good. What will turn to his advantage in the course of his life, he cannot with any assurance know. But this he may know, with full certainty, that by breaking the Divine commandments, he will draw upon his head that displeasure of the Almighty, which shall crush him for ever. The advantages of this world, even when innocently gained, are uncertain blessings; when obtained by criminal means, they carry a curse in their bosom. To the virtuous, they are often no more than chaff. To the guilty, they are always poison.

V. LET our imperfect knowledge of what is good or evil, attach us the more to those few things, concerning which there can be no doubt of their being truly good. Of temporal things which belong to this class, the catalogue, it must be confessed, is small. Perhaps the chief worldly good we should wish to enjoy, is a sound mind in a sound body. Health and peace, a moderate fortune, and a few friends, sum up all the undoubted articles of temporal felicity. Wise was the man who addressed this prayer to God; *Remove far from me vanity and lies. Give me neither poverty nor riches. Feed me with food convenient for me. Lest I be full and deny thee, and say, who is the Lord? or lest I be poor and steel, and take the name of my God in vain* *. He whose wishes, respecting the possessions of this world, are the most reasonable and bounded, is likely to lead the safest, and, for that reason, the most

* *Prov.* xxx. 8, 9.

most desirable life. By aspiring too high, we frequently miss the happiness which, by a less ambitious aim, we might have gained. High happiness on earth, is rather a picture which the imagination forms, than a reality which man is allowed to possess.

But with regard to spiritual felicity, we are not confined to such humble views. Clear and determinate objects are proposed to our pursuit; and full scope is given to the most ardent desire. The forgiveness of our sins, and the assistance of God's holy grace to guide our life; the improvement of our minds in knowledge and wisdom, in piety and virtue; the protection and favour of the great Father of all, of the blessed Redeemer of mankind, and of the Spirit of sanctification and comfort; these are objects, in the pursuit of which there is no room for hesitation and distrust, nor any ground for the question in my Text, *Who knoweth what is good for man?* Had Providence spread an equal obscurity over happiness of every kind, we might have had some reason to complain of the vanity of our condition. But we are not left to so hard a fate. The Son of God hath descended from heaven, to be the *Light of the world.* He hath removed that veil which covered true bliss from the search of wandering mortals, and hath taught them the way which leads to life. Worldly enjoyments are shown to be hollow and deceitful, with an express intention to direct their affections towards those which are spiritual. The same discoveries which diminish the value of the one, serve to increase that of the other. Finally,

VI. LET our ignorance of what is good or evil here below, lead our thoughts and desires to a better world. I have endeavoured to vindicate the wisdom of Providence, by showing the many useful purposes which this ignorance at present promotes. It serves to check presumption and rashness, and to enforce a diligent exertion of our rational powers, joined with a humble dependence on Divine aid. It moderates eager passions respecting worldly success. It inculcates resignation to the disposal of a Providence which is much wiser than man. It restrains us from employing unlawful means in order to compass our most favourite designs. It tends to attach us more closely to those things which are unquestionably good. It is therefore such a degree of ignorance as suits the present circumstances of man better than more complete information concerning good and evil.

At the same time the causes which render this obscurity necessary, too plainly indicate a broken and corrupted state of human nature. They show this life to be a state of trial. They suggest the ideas of a land of pilgrimage, not of the houſe of reſt. Low-minded and baſe is he; who aſpires to no higher portion; who could be ſatisfied to ſpend his whole exiſtence, in chaſing thoſe treacherous appearances of good, which ſo often mock his purſuit. What ſhadow can be more vain than the life of the greateſt part of mankind? Of all that eager and buſtling crowd which we behold on the earth, how few diſcover the path of true happineſs! How few can we find, whoſe activity has not been miſemployed, and whoſe courſe terminates not in confeſſions of diſappointments? Is this the ſtate, are theſe the habitations, to which a rational ſpirit, with all its high hopes and great capacities, is to be limited for ever ?—Let us bleſs that God who hath ſet nobler proſpects before us; who, by the death and reſurrection of his Son Jeſus Chriſt, hath *begotten us to the lively hope of an inheritance incorruptible, undefiled, and that fadeth not away, reſerved in the heavens.* Let us ſhow ourſelves worthy of ſuch a hope, by *ſetting our affections upon the things above, not upon things on the earth.* Let us *walk by faith, and not by ſight ;* and, amidſt the obſcurity of this faint and dubious twilight, conſole ourſelves with the expectation of a brighter day which is ſoon to open. This earth is the land of ſhadows. But we hope to paſs into the world of realities; where the proper objects of human deſire ſhall be diſplayed ; where the ſubſtance of that bliſs ſhall be found, whoſe image only we now purſue ; where no fallacious hopes ſhall any longer allure, no ſmiling appearances ſhall betray, no inſidious joys ſhall ſting ; but where truth ſhall be inſeparably united with pleaſure, and the miſts which hang over this preliminary ſtate being diſſipated, the perfect knowledge of good ſhall lead to the full enjoyment of it for ever.

SERMON

SERMON IX.

On Religious Retirement.

PSALM iv. 4.

Commune with your own heart, upon your bed, and be still.

MUCH communing with themselves there has always been among mankind; though frequently, God knows, to no purpose, or to a purpose worse than none. Could we discover the employments of men in retirement, how often should we find their thoughts occupied with subjects which they would be ashamed to own? What a large share have ambition and avarice, at some times the grossest passions, and at other times the meanest trifles, in their solitary musings? They carry the world, with all its vices, into their retreat; and may be said to dwell in the midst of the world, even when they seem to be alone.

This, surely, is not that sort of communing which the Psalmist recommends. For this it not properly *communing with our heart*, but rather holding secret intercourse with the world. What the Psalmist means to recommend, is religious recollection; that exercise of thought which is connected with the precept given in the proceeding words, *to stand in awe, and sin not.* It is to commune with ourselves, under the character of spiritual and immortal beings; and to *ponder those paths of our feet,* which are leading us to eternity. I shall, in the first place, show the advantages of such serious retirement and meditation; and shall in the second place point out some of the principal subjects which ought to employ us in our retreat.

The advantages of retiring from the world, *to commune with our heart,* will be found to be great, whether we regard our happiness in this world, or our preparation for the world to come.

Let us consider them, first, with respect to our happiness in this world. It will readily occur to you, that an entire retreat from worldly affairs, is not what religion requires; nor does it even enjoin a great retreat from them. Some stations of life would not permit this; and there are few stations which render it necessary. The chief field, both of the duty and of the improvement of man, lies in active life. By the graces and virtues which he exercises amidst his fellow-creatures, he is trained up for heaven. A total retreat from the world is so far from being, as the Roman Catholic Church holds, the perfection of religion, that, some particular cases excepted, it is no other than the abuse of it.

But, though entire retreat would lay us aside from the part for which Providence chiefly intended us, it is certain, that, without occasional retreat, we must act that part very ill. There will be neither consistency in the conduct, nor dignity in the character, of one who sets apart no share of his time for meditation and reflection. In the heat and bustle of life, while passion is every moment throwing false colours on the objects around us, nothing can be viewed in a just light. If you with that reason should exert her native power, you must step aside from the crowd, into the cool and silent shade. It is there that, with sober and steady eye, she examines what is good or ill, what is wise or foolish in human conduct; she looks back on the past, she looks forward to the future; and forms plans, not for the present moment only, but for the whole of life. How should that man discharge any part of his duty aright, who never suffers his passions to cool? And how should his passions cool, who is engaged, without interruption, in the tumult of the world? This incessant stir may be called the perpetual drunkenness of life. It raises that eager fermentation of spirit, which will be ever sending forth the dangerous fumes of rashness and folly. Whereas he who mingles religious retreat with worldly affairs, remains calm, and master of himself. He is not whirled round, and rendered giddy, by the agitation of the world; but, from that sacred retirement, in which he has been conversant among higher objects, comes forth into the world with manly tranquillity, fortified by the principles which he has formed, and prepared for whatever may befal.

As he who is unacquainted with retreat, cannot sustain any character with propriety, so neither can he enjoy the world with any advantage. Of the two classes of men who are most apt to be negligent of this duty, the men of pleasure, and the men of business, it is hard to say which suffer most in point of enjoyment from that neglect. To the former, every moment appears to be lost, which partakes not of the vivacity of amusement. To connect one plan of gaiety with another, is their whole study; till, in a very short time, nothing remains but to tread the same beaten round; to enjoy what they have already enjoyed, and to see what they have often seen. Pleasures thus drawn to the dregs, become vapid and tasteless. What might have pleased long, if enjoyed with temperance and mingled with retirement,

being

being devoured with such eager haste, speedily surfeits and disgusts. Hence, these are the persons, who, after having run through a rapid course of pleasure, after having glittered for a few years in the foremost line of public amusements, are the most apt to fly at least to a melancholy retreat; not led by religion or reason, but driven by disappointed hopes, and exhausted spirits, to the pensive conclusion, that *all is vanity.*

If uninterrupted intercourse with the world wears out the man of pleasure, it no less oppresses the man of business and ambition. The strongest spirits must at length sink under it. The happiest temper must be soured by incessant returns of the opposition, the inconstancy, and treachery of men. For he who lives always in the bustle of the world, lives in a perpetual warfare. Here an enemy encounters; there a rival supplants him. The ingratitude of a friend stings him this hour; and the pride of a superior wounds him the next. In vain he flies for relief to trifling amusements. These may afford, a temporary opiate to care; but they communicate no strength to the mind. On the contrary, they leave it more soft and defenceless, when molestations and injuries renew their attack.

Let him who wishes for an effectual cure to all the wounds which the world can inflict, retire from intercourse with men to intercourse with God. When he enters into his closet, and shuts the door, let him shut out, at the same time, all intrusion of worldly care; and dwell among objects divine and immortal.——Those fair prospects of order and peace shall there open to his view, which form the most perfect contrast to the confusion and misery of this earth. The celestial inhabitants quarrel not; among them there is neither ingratitude, nor envy, nor tumult. Men may harrass one another; but in the kingdom of God concord and tranquility reign for ever.—From such objects there beams upon the mind of the pious man, a pure and enlivening light; there is diffused over his heart a holy calm. His agitated spirit reassumes its firmness, and regains its peace. The world sinks in its importance; and the load of mortality and misery loses almost all its weight. The *green pastures* open, and the *still waters* flow around him, beside which the *Shepherd of Israel* guides his flock. The disturbances and alarms, so formidable to those who are engaged in the tumults of the world, seem to him only like thunder rolling afar off; like the noise of distant waters, whose sound he hears, whose course he traces, but whose waves touch him not.—As religious retirement is thus evidently conducive to our happiness in this life, so,

IN

On Religious Retirement.

In the second place, it is absolutely necessary in order to prepare us for the life to come. He who lives always in public, cannot live to his own soul. The world *lieth in wickedness;* and with good reason the Christian is exhorted, *not to be conformed to it, but transformed by the renewing of his mind.* Our conversation and intercourse with the world, is, in several respects, an education for vice. From our earliest youth, we are accustomed to hear riches and honours extolled as the chief possessions of man; and proposed to us, as the principal aim of our future pursuits. We are trained up, to look with admiration on the flattering marks of distinction which they bestow. In quest of those fancied blessings, we see the multitude around us eager and fervent. Principles of duty, we may, perhaps, hear sometimes inculcated; but we seldom behold them brought into competition with worldly profit. The soft names, and plausible colours, under which deceit, sensuality, and revenge, are presented to us in common discourse, weaken, by degrees, our natural sense of the distinction between good and evil. We often meet with crimes authorised by high examples, and rewarded with the caresses and smiles of the world. We discover, perhaps, at last, that those whom we are taught to reverence, and to regard as our patterns of conduct, act upon principles no purer than those of others. Thus breathing habitually a contagious air, how certain is our ruin unless we sometimes retreat from this pestilential region, and seek for proper correctives of the disorders which are contracted there? Religious retirement both abates the disease, and furnishes the remedy. It lessens the corrupting influence of the world; and it gives opportunity for better principles to exert their power. He who is accustomed to turn aside, and commune with himself, will, sometimes at least, hear the truths which the multitude do not tell him. A more sound instructor will lift his voice, and awaken within the heart those latent suggestions, which the world had overpowered and suppressed.

The acts of prayer and devotion, the exercises of faith and repentance, all the great and peculiar duties of the religion of Christ, necessarily suppose retirement from the world. This was one chief end of their institution, that they might be the means of occasionally sequestering us from that great scene of vice and folly, the continued presence of which is so hurtful. Solitude is the hallowed ground which Religion hath, in every age, chosen for her own. There, her inspiration is felt, and her secret mysteries elevate the soul. There, falls the tear of contrition; there, rises towards heaven the sigh of the heart; there, melts the soul with all the tenderness of devotion, and pours itself forth before him who made, and him who redeemed it. How can any one who

who is unacquainted with such employments of mind, be fit for heaven? If heaven be the habitation of pure affections, and of intellectual joy, can such a state be relished by him who is always immersed among sensible objects, and has never acquired any taste for the pleasures of the understanding, and the heart?

The great and the worthy, the pious and the virtuous, have ever been addicted to serious retirement. It is the characteristic of little and frivolous minds, to be wholly occupied with the vulgar objects of life. These fill up their desires, and supply all the entertainment which their coarse apprehensions can relish. But a more refined and enlarged mind leaves the world behind it, feels a call for higher pleasures, and seeks them in retreat. The man of public spirit has recourse to it, in order to form plans for general good; the man of genius, in order to dwell on his favourite themes; the philosopher, to pursue his discoveries; the saint to improve himself in grace. *Isaac went out to meditate in the fields, at the evening tide.* David, amidst all the splendour of royalty, often bears witness both to the pleasure which he received, and to the benefit which he reaped, from devout meditation. *I communed with my own heart, and my spirit made diligent search. I thought on my ways, and turned my feet unto God's testimonies. In the multitude of thoughts within me, his comforts delight my soul.* Our blessed Saviour himself, though of all who ever lived on earth he needed least the assistance of religious retreat, yet by his frequent practice, has done it signal honour. Often were the garden, the mountain, and the silence of the night, sought by him, for intercourse with heaven. *When he had sent the multitude away, he went up into a mountain, apart, to pray.*

The advantages of religious retirement will still more clearly appear, by considering, as was proposed, in the next place, some of those great objects which should there employ our thoughts. I shall mention only three, which are of the most plain and acknowledged importance; God, the world, and our own character.

I. WHEN you retire from the world, *commune with your hearts* concerning God. Impressions of Deity, besides there being the principle of what is strictly termed religion, are the great support of all moral sentiment, and virtuous conduct, among men. But with what difficulty are they preserved in any due degree of force, amidst the affairs and avocations of the world? While the crowd of surrounding objects is ever rushing on the imagination, and occupying the senses and the heart, what is not only absent from view, but, by its nature, invisible, is apt to vanish like a shadow. Hence it is given as the character of wicked men,

men, in scripture, that they are *without God in the world*. They deny not, perhaps, that he does exist; but it is the same to them as though he did not: For having lost him from their view, his existence has no effect on their conduct. If, at any time, the idea of God rise in their mind, it rises like a terrifying phantom which they hasten to expel; and which they gladly fancy to be unreal, because they see it make so little impression on others around them.

Let him who retires to serious meditation, begin with impressing deeply on his mind this important truth, that there is undoubtedly a Supreme Governour, who presides over the universe. But let him not imagine, that to commune with his heart concerning God, is to search into the mysteries of the Divine nature, or to attempt a discovery of the whole plan of Providence. Long enough he may bewilder himself in this maze, without making any proficiency in the practical knowledge of God. Shall he who knows so little of his own nature, or of the nature of the objects with which he is surrounded, expect to comprehend the Being who made him? To commune with ourselves, to any useful purpose, on this subject, is to bring home to our souls the internal, authoritative sense of God, as of a Sovereign and a Father. It is not to speculate about what is mysterious in his essence, but to contemplate what is displayed of his perfections. It is to realize the presence of the Supreme Being, so as to produce the most profound veneration; and to awaken the earnest desire of as near an approach as our nature will permit, to that great Fountain of happiness and life.

After this manner was that holy man affected, who uttered this ardent * wish, *O that I knew where I might find him, that I might come even to his seat!*—If with such a frame of mind you seek after God, be assured that he is not far from you; and that, though you are not permitted as yet to *come to his seat*, you may, at least reach the footstool of his throne, and touch the robe that covers him. In the midst of your solitary musings lift your eyes, and behold all nature full of God. Look up to the firmament, and admire his glory. Look round on the earth, and observe his presence every where displayed. If the gay landscape, or the fruitful field, present themselves to your eye, behold him smiling upon his works. If the mountain raise its lofty head, or the expanse of waters roll its tide before you, contemplate, in those great and solemn objects, his power and majesty. Nature, in all its diversities, is a varied manifestation of the Deity. If you were to *take the wings of the morning, and dwell in the uttermost parts of the sea*, even there you would

* *Job*, xxiii. 3.

would find him. For *in him you live and move.* He fills and animates all space. In the barren wilderness, as in the peopled region, you can trace his footsteps; and in the deepest solitude, you may hear a voice which testifies of him.

Him, indeed, you are never to confound with the workmanship of his hands. Nature in its most awful or most pleasing scenes, exhibits no more than different forms of inanimate matter. But on these dead forms is impressed the glory of a living spirit. The beauty, or the greatness, which appears in them, flows from the Fountain of all greatness and beauty; in him it centers; of his perfection it reflects an image; and towards him should lead your view.—In conversing with a fellow-creature on earth, it is not with his body we converse, though it is his body only which we see. From his words and actions we conceive his mind; with his mind, though invisible, we hold correspondence; and direct towards this Spiritual Essence our affection and regard. In like manner, though here we behold no more of God than what his works display, yet in those displays, we are capable of perceiving the universal Spirit, and of holding correspondence with this unseen Being, in veneration, gratitude, and love.

It is thus that a pious man, in his retired meditations, viewing natural objects with a spiritual eye, communes with his heart concerning God. He walks among the various scenes of nature, as within the precincts of a great temple, in the habitual exercise of devotion. To those discoveries of the Supreme Being in his works, let him apply the comment of his word. From the world of Nature, let him follow God into the world of Grace. When conducted from the outer courts, into this inmost sanctuary of the temple, he shall feel himself brought still more nigh to the sacred Presence. In the great plan of Divine Wisdom, for extirpating the evils produced by sin, he shall receive the interpretation of many of the hidden mysteries of Nature. He shall discover in Christ, the Deity made, in some degree, visible to sense. In the beneficent works which he performed, and the gracious undertaking which he accomplished, he shall behold *the brightness of the Father's glory,* and shall discern it to be *full of grace and truth.*—From the sacred retreat, wherein his thoughts have been thus employed, he returns to the world like a superiour being. He carries into active life those pure and elevating sentiments, to which the giddy crowd are strangers. A certain odour of sanctity remains upon his mind, which, for awhile at least, will repel the contagion of the world.

II. COMMUNE with your heart, in the season of retirement, concerning

On Religious Retirement.

concerning the world. The world is the great deceiver, whose fallacious arts it highly imports us to detect. But in the midst of its pleasures and pursuits, the detection is impossible. We tread, as within an enchanted circle, where nothing appears as it truly is. It is only in retreat, that the charm can be broken. Did men employ that retreat, not in carrying on the delusion which the world has begun, not in forming plans of imaginary bliss, but in subjecting the happiness which the world affords to a strict discussion, the spell would dissolve; and in the room of the unreal prospects, which had long amused them, the nakedness of the world would appear.

Prepare yourselves, then, to encounter the light of truth. Resolve rather to bear the disappointment of some flattering hopes, than to wander for ever in the paradise of fools. While others meditate in secret on the means of attaining worldly success, let it be your employment to scrutinize that success itself. Calculate fairly to what it amounts; and whether you are not losers on the whole, by your apparent gain. Look back for this purpose on your past life. Trace it from your earliest youth; and put the question to yourselves, What have been its happiest periods? Were they those of quiet and innocence, or those of ambition and intrigue? Has your real enjoyment uniformly kept pace with what the world calls prosperity? As you are advanced in wealth or station, did you proportionably advance in happiness? Has success, almost in any one instance, fulfilled your expectation? Where you reckoned upon most enjoyment, have you not often found least? Wherever guilt entered into your pleasures, did not its sting long remain, after the gratification was past?——Such questions as these, candidly answered, would in a great measure unmask the world. They would expose the vanity of its pretensions; and convince you, that there are other springs than those which the world affords, to which you must apply for happiness.

While you commune with your heart concerning what the world now is, consider also what it will one day appear to be. Anticipate the awful moment of your bidding it an eternal farewell. Think, what reflections shall most probably arise, when you are quitting the field, and looking back on the scene of action. In what light will your closing eyes contemplate those vanities which now shine so bright, and those interests which now swell into such high importance? What part will you then wish to have acted? What shall then appear momentous, what trifling, in human conduct?—Let the sober sentiments which such anticipations suggest, temper now your mis-

placed

placed ardour. Let the laſt concluſions which you ſhall form, enter into the preſent eſtimate which you make of the world, and of life.

Moreover, in communing with yourſelves concerning the world, contemplate it as ſubject to the Divine dominion. The greater part of men behold nothing more than the rotation of human affairs. They ſee a great crowd ever in motion; the fortunes of men alternately riſing and falling; virtue often diſtreſſed, and proſperity appearing to be the purchaſe of worldly wiſdom. But this is only the outſide of things. Behind the curtain there is a far greater ſcene, which is beheld by none but the retired, religious ſpectator. Lift up that curtain, when you are alone with God. View the world with the eye of a Chriſtian; and you ſhall ſee, that while *man's heart deviſeth his way, it is the Lord who directeth his ſteps.* You ſhall ſee, that however men appear to move and act after their own pleaſure, they are, nevertheleſs, retained in ſecret bonds by the Almighty, and all their operations rendered ſubſervient to the ends of his moral government. You ſhall behold him obliging *the wrath of man to praiſe him;* puniſhing the ſinner by means of his own iniquities; from the trials of the righteous, bringing forth their reward; and to a ſtate of ſeeming univerſal confuſion, preparing the wiſeſt and moſt equitable iſſue. While the *faſhion of this world* is paſſing faſt away, you ſhall diſcern the glory of another riſing to ſucceed it. You ſhall behold all human events, our griefs and our joys, our love and our hatred, our character and our memory, abſorbed in the ocean of eternity; and no trace of our preſent exiſtence left, except its being for ever *well with the righteous, and ill with the wicked.*—Such a view of the world, frequently preſented to our minds, could not fail to enforce thoſe ſolemn concluſions; *There is no wiſdom, nor counſel, againſt the Lord. Fear God, and keep his commandments; for this is the whole of man. What is a man profited, if he ſhall gain the whole world, and loſe his own ſoul?*

III. COMMUNE with your heart, concerning yourſelves, and your real character. To acquire a thorough knowledge of ourſelves, is an attainment no leſs difficult than important. For men are generally unwilling to ſee their own imperfections; and when they are willing to enquire into them, their ſelf-love impoſes on their judgment. Their intercourſe with one another aſſiſts the deluſion to which, of themſelves, they are prone. For the ordinary commerce of the world is a commerce of flattery and falſehood; where reciprocally they deceive and are deceived, where every one appears under an aſſumed form, profeſſes eſteem which he does not feel, and beſtows praiſe in order to receive it.

it. It is only in retreat where those false semblances disappear, and those flattering voices are silent, that a man can learn to *think soberly of himself, and as he ought to think.*

It has been said, that there are three characters which every man sustains; and these often extremely different from one another: One, which he possesses in his own oppinion; another, which he carries in the estimation of the world; and a third, which he bears in the judgment of God. It is only the last which ascertains what he really is.—Whether the character which the world forms of you be above or below the truth, it imports you not much to know. But it is of eternal consequence, that the character which you possess in your own eyes, be formed upon that which you bear in the sight of God. In order to try it by this great standard, you must lay aside, as much as possible, all partiality to yourselves; and in the season of retirement, explore your heart with such accurate scrutiny, as may bring your hidden defects to light.

Enquire, for this purpose, whether you be not conscious, that the fair opinion which the world entertains of you, is founded on their partial knowledge both of your abilities and your virtues? Would you be willing that all your actions should be publicly canvassed? Could you bear to have your thoughts laid open? Are there no parts of your life which you would be uneasy if an enemy could discover? In what light, then, must these appear to God? When you have kept free of vice, has your innocence proceeded from purity of principle, or from worldly motives? Rise there no envy or malignity within you, when you compare your own condition with that of others? Have you been as solicitous to regulate your heart, as to preserve your manners from reproach? Professing yourselves to be Christians, has the Spirit of Christ appeared in your conduct? Declaring that you hope for immortality, has that hope surmounted undue attachments to the present life!

Such investigation as this, seriously pursued, might produce to every man many discoveries of himself; discoveries, not pleasing perhaps to vanity, but salutary and useful. For he can be only a flatterer, but no true friend to himself, who aims not at knowing his own defects as well as virtues. By imposing on the world, he may carry on some plan of fancied profit; but by imposing on his heart, what can he propose to gain? He *feedeth on ashes: A deceived heart hath turned him aside, that he cannot deliver his soul, nor say, Is there not a lie in my right hand**?

THUS I have set before you, some of those great objects which ought to employ your meditation in religious retirement. I have endeavoured

* *Isa.* xliv. 20.

deavoured to introduce you into a proper intercourse with your heart, concerning God, the world, and your own character. Let this intercourse terminate in fixing the principles of your future conduct. Let it serve to introduce consistency into your life. Nothing can be more wavering and disjointed, than the behaviour of those who are wholly men of the world, and have never been inured to commune with themselves. Dissipation is a more frequent cause of their ruin, than determined impiety. It is not so much because they have adopted bad principles, as because they have never attended to principles of any kind, that their lives are so full of incoherence and disorder.—You hover on the borders of sin and duty. One day, you read the scriptures, you hear religious discourses, and form good resolutions. Next day, you plunge into the world, and forget the serious impression, as if it had never been made. The impression is again renewed, and again effaced; and in this circle your life revolves. Is such conduct worthy of creatures endowed with entelligent powers? Shall the close of life overtake you, before you have determined how to live? Shall the day never come, that is to find you steady in your views, decided in your plans, and engaged in a course of action which your mind approves? —If you wish that day ever to arrive, retirement and meditation must first bring you home to yourselves, from the dissipation in which you are now scattered; must teach you to fix such aims, and to lay down such rules of conduct, as are suitable to rational and immortal beings. Then will your character become uniform and respectable. Then you may hope that your life will proceed in such a train as shall prepare you, when it is finished, for joining the society of more exalted spirits.

SERMON

ACTS, x. 2.

Cornelius——A devout man—

THAT religion is essential to the welfare of man, can be proved by the most convincing arguments. But these, how demonstrative soever, are insufficient to support its authority over human conduct. For arguments may convince the understanding, when they cannot conquer the passions. Irresistible they seem in the calm hours of retreat; but in the season of action, they often vanish into smoke. There are other and more powerful springs, which influence the great movements of the human frame. In order to operate with success on the active powers, the heart must be gained. Sentiment and affection must be brought to the aid of reason. It is not enough that men believe religion to be a wise and rational rule of conduct, unless they relish it as agreeable, and find it to carry its own reward. Happy is the man, who, in the conflict of desire between God and the world, can oppose, not only argument to argument, but pleasure to pleasure; who, to the external allurements of sense, can oppose the internal joys of devotion; and to the uncertain promises of a flattering world, the certain experience of that *peace of God which passeth understanding, keeping his mind and heart.*—Such is the temper and spirit of *a devout man.* Such was the character of Cornelius, that good centurion, whose *prayers and alms* are said to have *come up in memorial before God.* Of this character I intend, through Divine assistance, to discourse; and shall endeavour, I. To explain the nature of devotion; II. To justify, and recommend it; and, III. To rectify some mistakes concerning it.

I. DEVOTION is the lively exercise of those affections, which we owe to the Supreme Being. It comprehends several emotions of the heart, which all terminate on the same great object. The chief of them are, veneration, gratitude, desire, and resignation.

It implies, first, profound veneration of God. By veneration, I understand an affection compounded of awe and love; the affection which, of all others, it best becomes creatures to bear towards their

infinitely

infinitely perfect Creator. Awe is the first sentiment that rises in the soul, at the view of his greatness. But, in the heart of a devout man, it is a solemn and elevating, not a dejecting, emotion; for, he glows, rather than trembles, in the Divine presence. It is not the superstitious dread of unknown power, but the homage yielded by the heart to him who is, at once, the greatest, and the best of beings. Omnipotence, viewed alone, would be a formidable object. But, considered in conjunction with the moral perfections of the Divine nature, it serves to heighten devotion. Goodness affects the heart with double energy, when residing in One so exalted. The goodness which we adore in him, is not like that which is common among men, a weak, mutable, undiscerning fondness, ill qualified to be the ground of assured trust. It is the goodness of a perfect Governour, acting upon a regular extensive plan; a steady principle of benevolence, conducted by wisdom; which, subject to no *variableness or shadow of turning*, free from all partiality and caprice, incapable of being either soothed by flattery or ruffled by resentment, resembles, in its calm and equal lustre, the eternal serenity of the highest heavens. *Thy mercy, O Lord! is in the heavens, and thy faithfulness reacheth unto the clouds. Thy righteousness is like the great mountains, and thy judgments are a great depth.*

Such are the conceptions of the great God, which fill with veneration the heart of a devout man. His veneration is not confined to acts of immediate worship. It is the habitual temper of his soul. Not only when engaged in prayer or praise, but in the silence of retirement, and even amidst the occupations of the world, the Divine Being dwells upon his thoughts. No place, and no object, appear to him void of God. On the works of Nature he views the impression of his hand; and in the actions of men, he traces the opperation of his Providence. Whatever he beholds on earth, that is beautiful or fair, that is great or good, he refers to God, as to the supreme origin of all the excellence which is scattered throughout his works. From those effects he rises to the first cause. From those streams he ascends to the fountain whence they flow. By those rays he is lead to that eternal source of light in which they centre.

DEVOTION implies, secondly, sincere gratitude to God, for all his benefits. This is a warmer emotion than simple veneration. Veneration looks up to the Deity, as he is in himself; Gratitude regards what he is towards us. When a devout man surveys this vast universe, where beauty and goodness are every where predominant; when he reflects on those numberless multitudes of creatures who, in their different stations, enjoy the blessings of existence; and when at the same time he looks up to an Universal Father, who hath thus filled creation with life and happiness, his heart glows within him.

He

He adores that difinterefted goodnefs, which prompted the Almighty to raife up fo many orders of intelligent beings, not that he might receive, but that he might give and impart; that he might pour forth himfelf, and communicate to the fpirits which he formed, fome emanations of his felicity.

The goodnefs of this Supreme Benefactor he gratefully contemplates, as difplayed in his own ftate. He reviews the events of his life; and in every comfort which has fweetened it, he difcerns the Divine hand. Does he remember with affection, the parents under whofe care he grew up, and the companions with whom he paffed his youthful life? Is he now happy, in his family rifing around him; in the fpoufe who loves him, or in the children who give him comfort and joy? Into every tender remembrance of the paft, and every pleafing enjoyment of the prefent, devotion enters; for in all thofe beloved objects, it recognizes God. The communication of love from heart to heart, is an effufion of his goodnefs. From his infpiration defcends all the friendfhip which ever glowed on earth; and therefore, to him it juftly returns in gratitude, and terminates on him.

But this life, with all its interefts, is but a fmall part of human exiftence. A devout man looks forward to immortality, and difcovers ftill higher fubjects of gratitude. He views himfelf as a guilty creature, whom Divine benignity has received into grace; whofe forfeited hopes it has reftored; and to whom it has opened the moft glorious profpects of future felicity. Such generofity fhewn to the fallen and miferable, is yet more affecting to the heart, than favours conferred on the innocent. He contemplates, with aftonifhment, the labours of the Son of God, in accomplifhing redemption for men; and his foul overflows with thankfulnefs to him, *who loved us, and wafhed us from our fins in his own blood.—What fhall I render to the Lord for all his benefits? Blefs the Lord, O my foul! and all that is within me, blefs his holy name; who forgiveth all thine iniquities, and healeth all thy difeafes; who redeemeth thy life from deftruction, and crowneth thee with loving kindnefs, and with tender mercies.*

DEVOTION implies, thirdly, the defire of the foul after the favour of the Supreme Being, as its chief good, and final reft. To interiour enjoyments, the devout man allots inferiour and fecondary attachment. He difclaims not every earthly affection. He pretends not to renounce all pleafure in the comforts of his prefent ftate. Such an unnatural renunciation humanity forbids, and religion cannot require. But from thefe he expects not his fupreme blifs. He difcerns the vanity which belongs to them all; and beyond the circle of mutable objects

jects which surround him, he aspires after some principles of more perfect felicity, which shall not be subject to change or decay. But where is this complete and permanent good to be found? Ambition pursues it in courts and palaces; and returns from the pursuit, loaded with sorrows. Pleasure seeks it among sensual joys; and retires with the confession of disappointment. *The deep saith, it is not in me; and the sea saith, it is not in me. It cannot be gotten for gold; neither shall silver be weighed for the price thereof. Its place is not in the land of the living.* True happiness dwells with God; and from *the light of his countenance,* it beams upon the devout man. His voice is, *Whom have I in heaven but thee? and there is none upon earth that I desire beside thee.* After exploring heaven and earth for happiness, they seem to him a mighty void, a wilderness of shadows, where all would be empty and unsubstantial without God. But in his favour and love, he finds what supplies every defect of temporal objects; and assures tranquility to his heart, amidst all the changes of his existence. *Thou shalt guide me with thy counsel; and thou shalt receive me to thy glory. My flesh and my heart faileth; but God is the strength of my heart, and my portion for ever.*

FROM these sentiments and affections, Devotion advances, fourthly, to an entire resignation of the soul to God. It is the consummation of trust and hope. It banishes anxious cares and murmuring thoughts. It reconciles us to every appointment of Divine Providence; and resolves every wish into the desire of pleasing him, whom our hearts adore. Its genuine breathings are to this effect: " Conduct me, O God! in what path soever seemeth good to thee. In nothing shall I ever arraign thy sacred will. Dost thou require me to part with any wordly advantages, for the sake of virtue and a good conscience? I give them up. Dost thou command me to relinquish my friends, or my country? At thy call I cheerfully leave them. Dost thou summon me away from this world? Lo! I am ready to depart. Thou hast made, thou hast redeemed me, and I am thine. Myself, and all that belongs to me, I surrender to thy disposal. Let the men of the world have *their portion in this life.* Be it mine, to *behold thy face in righteousness; and when I awake, to be satisfied with thy likeness.*"

This, surely, is one of the noblest acts of which the human mind is capable, when thus, if we may be allowed the expression, it unites itself with God. Nor can any devotion be genuine, which inspires not sentiments of this nature. For devotion is not to be considered as a transient glow of affection, occasioned by some casual impressions of divine goodness, which are suffered to remain unconnected with the conduct of life. It is a powerful principle, which penetrates the soul; which purifies the affections from debasing attachments; and,

by

by a fixed and steady regard to God, subdues every sinful passion, and forms the inclinations to piety and virtue.

Such in general are the dispositions that constitute devotion. It is the union of veneration, gratitude, desire, and resignation. It expresses, not so much the performance of any particular duty, as the spirit which must animate all religious duties. It stands opposed, not merely to downright vice; but to a heart which is cold, and insensible to sacred things; which, from compulsion, perhaps, and a sense of interest, preserves some regard to the divine commands, but obeys them without ardour, love, or joy. I proceed,

II. To recommend this devout spirit to your imitation. I begin with observing, That it is of the utmost consequence to guard against extremes of every kind in religion. We must beware, lest, by seeking to avoid one rock, we split upon another. It has been long the subject of remark, that superstition and enthusiasm are two capital sources of delusion; superstition on the one hand, attaching men, with immoderate zeal, to the ritual and external part of religion; and enthusiasm, on the other, directing their whole attention to internal emotions, and mystical communications with the spiritual world; while neither the one, nor the other, has paid sufficient regard to the great moral duties of the Christian life. But, running with intemperate eagerness from these two great abuses of religion, men have neglected to observe, that there are extremes opposite to each of them, into which they are in hazard of precipitating themselves. Thus the horrour of superstition has sometimes reached so far as to produce contempt for all external institutions; as if it were possible for religion to subsist in the world, without forms of worship, or public acknowledgment of God. It has also happened that some, who in the main are well affected to the cause of goodness, observing that persons of a devout turn have at times been carried, by warm affections, into unjustifiable excesses, have thence hastily concluded that all devotion was akin to enthusiasm; and separating religion totally from the heart and affections, have reduced it to a frigid observance of what they call the rules of virtue. This is the extreme which I purpose at present to combat, by showing you, first, That true devotion is rational, and well-founded; next, That it is of the highest importance to every other part of religion and virtue; and, lastly, That it is most conducive to our happiness.

In the first place, True devotion is rational, and well-founded. It takes its life from affections, which are essential to the human frame. We are formed by Nature, to admire what is great, and to love what is amiable. Even inanimate objects have power to excite those emotions. The magnificent prospects of the natural world, fill the mind with reverential awe. Its beautiful scenes create delight. When we survey the actions and behaviour of our fellow-creatures, the affections glow with greater ardour; and, if to be unmoved, in the former case, argues a defect of sensibility in our powers, it discovers, in the latter, an odious hardness and depravity in the heart. The tenderness of an affectionate parent, the generosity of a forgiving enemy, the public spirit of a patriot or a hero, often fill the eyes with tears, and swell the breast with emotions too big for utterance. The object of those affections is frequently raised above us, in condition and rank. Let us suppose him raised also above us, in nature. Let us imagine, that an Angel, or any being of superior order, had condescended to be our friend, our guide, and patron; no person, sure, would hold the exaltation of his benefactor's character, to be an argument why he should love and revere him less.—Strange! that the attachment and veneration, the warmth and overflowing of heart, which excellence and goodness on every other occasion command, should begin to be accounted irrational, as soon as the Supreme Being becomes their object. For what reason must human sensibility be extinct towards him alone? Are all benefits entitled to gratitude, except the highest and the best? Shall goodness cease to be amiable, only because it is perfect?

It will, perhaps, be said, that an unknown and invisible being is not qualified to raise affection in the human heart. Wrapt up in the mysterious obscurity of his nature, he escapes our search, and affords no determinate object to our love or desire. *We go forward, but he is not there; and backward, but we cannot perceive him; on the left hand, where he worketh, but we cannot behold him: He hideth himself on the right hand, that we cannot see him* *.————Notwithstanding this obscurity, is there any being in the universe more real and certain, than the Creator of the world, and the Supporter of all existence? Is he, in whom we live and move, too distant from us to excite devotion? His form and essence, indeed, we cannot see; but to be unseen, and imperfectly known, in many other instances, precludes neither gratitude nor love. It is not the sight, so much as the strong conception, or deep impression, of an object, which affects the passions. We glow with admiration of personages, who have lived in a distant age. Whole nations have been transported with zeal and affection, for the generous hero, or public deliverer, whom they knew only by fame. Nay, properly speaking, the direct object of our love is, in every case, invisible. For that on which affection is placed, is the mind, the soul, the internal character of our fellow-creatures; which,

* *Job*, xxxiii. 8, 9.   surely,

surely, is no less concealed, than the Divine Nature itself is, from the view of sense. From actions, we can only infer the dispositions of men; from what we see of their behaviour, we collect what is invisible; but the conjecture which we form is, at best, imperfect; and when their actions excite our love, much of their heart remains still unknown. I ask, then, in what respect God is less qualified than any other being to be an object of affection? Convinced that he exists, beholding his goodness spread abroad in his works, exerted in the government of the world, displayed in some measure to sense, in the actions of his Son Jesus Christ; are we not furnished with every essential requisite which the heart demands, in order to indulge the most warm, and at the same time the most rational emotions?

If these considerations justify the reasonableness of devotion, as expressed in veneration, love, and gratitude, the same train of thought will equally justify it when appearing in the forms of desire, delight, or resignation. The latter are, indeed, the consequence of the former. For we cannot but desire some communication with what we love; and will naturally resign ourselves to one, on whom we have placed the full confidence of affection. The aspirations of a devout man after the favour of God, are the effects of that earnest wish for happiness which glows in every breast. All men have somewhat that may be called the object of their devotion; reputation, pleasure, learning, riches, or whatever apparent good has strongly attached their heart. This becomes the centre of attraction, which draws them towards it; which quickens and regulates all their motions. While the men of the world are thus influenced by the objects which they severally worship, shall he only who directs all his devotion towards the Supreme Being, be excluded from a place in the system of rational conduct? or be censured for having passions, whose sensibility corresponds to the great cause which moves them?—Having vindicated the reasonableness of devotion, I come,

In the second place, to show its importance, and the high place which it possesses in the system of religion. I address myself now to those, who, though they reject not devotion as irrational, yet consider it as an unnecessary refinement; an attainment which may be safely left to recluse and sequestered persons, who aim at uncommon sanctity. The solid and material duties of a good life, they hold, to be in a great measure independent of devout affection; and think them sufficiently supported, by their necessary connection with our interest, both in this and in a future world. They insist much upon religion being a calm, a sober, and rational principle of conduct.———I admit that it is very laudable to have a rational religion. But I must admonish you, that

that it is both reproachful and criminal, to have an insensible heart. If we reduce religion into so cool a state, as not to admit love, affection, and desire, we shall leave it in possession of small influence over human life. Look abroad into the world, and observe how few act upon deliberate and rational views of their true interest. The bulk of mankind are impelled by their feelings. They are attracted by appearances of good. Taste and inclination rule their conduct. To direct their inclination and taste towards the highest objects; to form a relish within them, for virtuous and spiritual enjoyment; to introduce religion into the heart, is the province of devotion; and hence arises its importance to the interests of goodness.

Agreeably to this doctrine, the great Author of our religion, who well *knew what was in man*, laid the foundation of his whole system in the regeneration of the heart. The change which was to be accomplished on his followers, he did not purpose to effect, merely by regulating their external conduct; but by forming within them a new nature; by *taking away the heart of stone, and giving them a heart of flesh*, that is, a heart relenting and tender, yielding to the Divine impulse, and readily susceptible of devout impressions. *Thou shalt love the Lord thy God with all thy heart, and mind, and soul, and strength: This is the first and great commandment. My son, give me thy heart*, is the call of God to each of us: And, indeed, if the heart be withheld, it is not easy to conceive what other offering we can present, that will be acceptable to him.

Of what nature must that man's religion be, who professes to worship God, and to believe in Christ; and yet raises his thoughts towards God, and his Saviour, without any warmth of gratitude or love? I speak not of those occasional decays of pious affection, to which the best are subject, but of a total insensibility to this part of religion. Surely let the outward behaviour be ever so irreproachable, there must be some essential defect in a heart, which remains always unmoved at the view of infinite goodness. The affections cannot, in this case, be deemed to flow in their natural channel. Some concealed malignity must have tainted the inward frame. This is not the man whom you would chuse for your bosom-friend; or whose heart you could expect to answer, with reciprocal warmth, to yours. His virtue, if it deserves that name, is not of the most amiable sort; and may, with reason, receive the appellation (often injudiciously bestowed) of cold and dry morality. Such a person must, as yet, be *far from the kingdom of Heaven*.

As devotion is thus essential to religion in its priciple, so it enters into the proper discharge of all its duties. It diffuses an auspicious influence over the whole of virtue. The prevailing temper of the mind is formed by its most frequent employments. Intercourse with Supreme

preme perfection cannot, therefore, but ennoble and improve it. The pure love of God naturally connects itself with the love of man. Hence devotion has been often found a powerful instrument in humanizing the manners of men, and taming their unruly passions. It smooths what is rough, and softens what is fierce, in our nature. It is the great purifier of the affections. It inspires contempt of the low gratifications belonging to animal life. It promotes a humble and cheerful contentment with our lot; and subdues that eager desire of riches and of power, which has filled this unhappy world with crimes and misery. Finally, it bestows that enlargement of heart in the service of God, which is the great principle, both of perseverance, and of progress in virtue. He who, unacquainted with devout affections, sets himself to keep the Divine commandments, will advance in obedience with a slow and languid pace; like one who, carrying a heavy burden, toils to mount the hill. But he whose heart devotion has warmed, will proceed on his way, cheerful and rejoicing. The one performs his duty, only because it is commanded; the other because he loves it. The one is inclined to do no more than necessity requires; the other seeks to excel. The one looks for his reward in somewhat besides religion; the other finds it in religion itself: It is *his meat and drink to do the will of that heavenly Father*, whom he loves and adores. Which of these two are likely to make the greatest improvement in goodness, is easily discerned. Let us now consider,

In the third place, the influence of devotion on the happiness of life. Whatever promotes and strengthens virtue, whatever calms and regulates the temper, is a source of happiness. Devotion, as I have just now shown, produces those effects in a remarkable degree. It inspires composure of spirit, mildness, and benignity; weakens the painful, and cherishes the pleasing emotions; and, by these means, carries on the life of a pious man, in a smooth and placid tenour.

Besides exerting this habitual influence on the mind, devotion opens a field of enjoyments, to which the vicious are entire strangers; enjoyments the more valuable, as they peculiarly belong to retirement when the world leaves us, and to adversity when it becomes our foe. These are the two seasons, for which every wise man would most wish to provide some hidden store of comfort. For let him be placed in the most favourable situation which the human state admits, the world can neither always amuse him, nor always shield him from distress. There will be many hours of vacuity, and many of dejection, in his life. If he be a stranger to God, and to devotion, how dreary will the gloom of solitude often prove? With what oppressive weight will sickness, disappointment, or old age, fall upon his spirits? But, for those pensive periods, the pious man has a relief prepared. From the tiresome repetition of the common vanities of life, or from the painful corrosion of its cares and sorrows, devotion transports him into a new region; and surrounds him there with such objects, as are the most fitted to cheer the dejection, to calm the tumults, and to heal the wounds of his heart. If the world has been empty and delusive, it gladdens him with the prospect of a higher and better order of things, about to arise. If men have been ungrateful and base, it displays before him the faithfulness of that Supreme Being, who, though every other friend fail, will never forsake him. Consult your experience, and you will find, that the two greatest sources of inward joy are, the exercise of love directed towards a deserving object, and the exercise of hope terminating on some high and assured happiness. Both these are supplied by devotion; and therefore we have no reason to be surprised, if, on some occasions, it fill the hearts of good men with a satisfaction not to be expressed.

The refined pleasures of a pious mind are, in many respects, superiour to the coarse gratifications of sense. They are pleasures which belong to the highest powers, and best affections of the soul; whereas the gratifications of sense reside in the lowest region of our nature. To the one, the soul stoops below its native dignity. The other, raise it above itself. The one, leaves always a comfortless, often a mortifying, remembrance behind them. The other, are reviewed with applause and delight. The pleasures of sense resemble a foaming torrent, which after a disorderly course, speedily runs out, and leaves an empty and offensive channel. But the pleasures of devotion resemble the equable current of a pure river, which enlivens the fields through which it passes, and diffuses verdure and fertility along its banks. To thee, O Devotion! we owe the highest improvement of our nature, and much of the enjoyment of our life. Thou art the support of our virtue, and the rest of our souls, in this turbulent world. Thou composest the thoughts. Thou calmest the passions. Thou exaltest the heart. Thy communications, and thine only, are imparted to the low, no less than to the high; to the poor as well as to the rich. In thy presence, worldly distinctions cease; and under thy influence, worldly sorrows are forgotten. Thou art the balm of the wounded mind. Thy sanctuary is ever open to the miserable; inaccessible only to the unrighteous and impure. Thou beginnest on earth, the temper of heaven. In thee, the hosts of angels and blessed spirits eternally rejoice. It now remains,

III.

III. To endeavour to correct some errors, into which men are apt to fall concerning devotion. For it is but too obvious, that errors are often committed in this part of religion. These frequently disfigure its appearance before the world, and subject it to unjust reproach. Let us therefore attend deliberately to its nature, so as to distinguish pure and rational devotion, of which I have hitherto treated, from that which is, in any degree, spurious and adulterated.

In the first place, It is an error to place devotion in the mere performance of any external act of worship. Prayer and praise, together with the ordinances peculiar to the Christian religion, are the appointed means of raising the heart towards the Supreme Being. They are the instituted signs of devotion; the language in which it naturally expresses itself. But let us remember, that they are signs and expressions only; and we all know, that in various cases, these may not correspond to the thing signified. It is in the disposition of the heart, not in the motion of the lips, or in the posture of the body, that devotion consists. The heart may pray or praise, when no words are uttered. But if the heart be unconcerned or ill affected, all the words we can utter, how properly framed soever, are no other than empty and unacceptable sounds in the ear of the Almighty.

In the second place, It is an error to conceive the pleasures and advantages of devotion, to be indiscriminately open to all. Devotion, like many parts of religion, may in some lights be considered as a privilege, and in others as a duty. It is the duty of all, to love God, and to resign themselves to his will. But it is the privilege of good men only; to rejoice in God, and to confide in his friendship. Hence a certain preparation is requisite, for the enjoyment of devotion in its whole extent. Not only must the life be reformed from gross enormities, but the heart must have undergone that change which the Gospel demands. A competent knowledge of God must be acquired. A proper foundation must be laid in faith and repentance, for intercourse with Heaven.

They who would rush all at once from the arms of the world, into the sacred retreat of devotion; they who imagine that retreat to stand always ready for the reception of such as betake themselves to it, for no reason, but because every other refuge excludes them, betray gross ignorance of this part of religion. They bring to it, faculties unqualified to taste its pleasures; and they grasp at hopes, to which they are not entitled. By incorporating with devotion the unnatural mixture of their unsanctified passions, they defile and corrupt it. Hence that gloom which has often spread over it. Hence those superstitious mortifications and austerities, by which the falsely devout hope to purchase

chase favour from God; haunted by the terrors of a guilty conscience, and vainly struggling to substitute a servile and cringing homage, in the room of the pure affections of a renewed heart. On such altars, the hollowed fire of true devotion cannot burn; nor can any incense ascend from them, that shall be grateful to Heaven. *Bring no more vain oblations. Wash ye, make you clean, put away the evil of your doings from before mine eyes, saith the Lord. Cease to do evil; learn to do well.* Then *draw nigh to God, and he will draw nigh to you.*———But though devotion requires a pure heart, and a virtuous life, and necessarily supposes the exercise of frequent retirement, I must observe,

In the third place, That it is an error to conceive it as requiring an entire retreat from the world. Devotion, like every other branch of religion, was intended to fit us for discharging the duties of life. We serve God, by being useful to one another. It is evident from the frame of our nature, and from our common necessities and wants, that we were designed by Providence for an active part on this earth. The Gospel of Christ, accordingly, considers us as engaged in the concerns of the world; and directs its exhortations to men, in all the various relations, characters, and employments of civil life. Abstraction from society, therefore, and total dedication of our time to devout exercises, cannot be the most proper method of acquiring the favour of God.

I mean not, however, to throw any blame on those, who having lost all relish for the ordinary pursuits of life, in consequence of severe wounds which they have received from affliction; who, being left to stand alone, and discerning their connections with the world to be in some measure broken off, choose to seek tranquility in a religious retirement, and to consecrate their days entirely to God. Situations sometimes occur, which both justify a great degree of retreat from the world, and entitle it to respect. But with regard to the bulk of mankind, Christian devotion neither requires nor implies any such sequestration from the affairs of men. Nay, for the most part, it will be cultivated with greater success, by those who mingle it with the active employments of life. For the mind, when entirely occupied by any one object, is in hazard of viewing it at last through a false medium. Objects, especially, so great and sublime as those of devotion, when we attempt to fix upon them unremitting attention, overstretch and disorder our feeble powers. The mind, by being relaxed, returns to them with more advantage. As none of our organs can bear intense sensations without injury; as the eye, when dazzled with overpowering light, beholds imaginary colours, and looses the real distinction of objects; so the mind, when overheated by perpetual contemplation of ce-

lestial

leſtial things, has been ſometimes found to miſtake the ſtrong impreſ-
ſions of fancy, for ſupernatural communications from above. To the
employments of devotion, as to all other things, there are due limits.
There is a certain temperate ſphere, within which it preſerves longeſt
its proper exertion, and moſt ſucceſsfully promotes the purpoſes for
which it was deſigned.

In the fourth place, It is an error to imagine, that devotion enjoins a total contempt of all the pleaſures and amuſements of human
ſociety. It checks, indeed, that ſpirit of diſſipation which is too prevalent. It not only prohibits pleaſures which are unlawful, but likewiſe that unlawful degree of attachment to pleaſures in themſelves
innocent, which withdraws the attention of man from what is ſerious and important. But it brings amuſement under due limitation,
without exterpating it. It forbids it as the buſineſs, but permits it
as the relaxation, of life. For there is nothing in the ſpirit of true
religion, which is hoſtile to a cheerful enjoyment of our ſituation in
the world.

They who look with a ſevere and indignant eye upon all the re-
creations by which the cares of men are relieved, and the union of
ſociety is cemented, are, in too reſpects, injurious to religion. Firſt,
they exhibit it to others under a forbidding form, by clothing it with
the garb of ſo much unneceſſary auſterity. And next, they deprive
the world of the benefit which their example might afford, in drawing the line between innocent and dangerous pleaſures. By a temperate participation of thoſe which are innocent, they might ſucceſsfully exert that authority, which a virtuous and reſpectable character always poſſeſſes, in reſtraining undue exceſs. They would ſhow
the young and unwary, at what point they ought to ſtop. They would
have it in their power to regulate, in ſome degree, the public manners; to check extravagance, to humble preſumption, and put vice
to the bluſh. But, through injudicious ſeverity, they fall ſhort of
the good they might perform. By an indiſcriminate cenſure of all
amuſement, they detract from the weight of their reproof, when
amuſement becomes undoubtedly ſinful. By totally withdrawing
themſelves from the circle of cheerful life, they deliver up the entertainments of ſociety, into the hands of the looſe and the corrupted;
and permit the blind power of faſhion, uncontrolled, to eſtabliſh its
own ſtandards, and to exerciſe its dangerous ſway over the world.

In the fifth place, It is an error to believe, that devotion nouriſhes
a ſpirit of ſeverity, in judging of the manners and characters of others.
Under this reproach, indeed, it has ſo long ſuffered in the world; that,

with

with too many, the appellation of devout, suggests no other character, but that of a sour recluse bigot, who delights in censure. But the reproach is unjust; for such a spirit is entirely opposite to the nature of true devotion. The very first traces which it imprints on the mind, are candour and humility. Its principles are liberal. Its genius is unassuming and mild. Severe only to itself, it makes every allowance for others which humanity can suggest. It claims no privilege of looking into their hearts, or of deciding with respect to their eternal state. —If your supposed devotion produce contrary effects; if it infuse harshness into your sentiments, and acrimony into your speech; you may conclude, that under a serious appearance, carnal passions lurk. And, if ever it shall so far lift you up with self-conceit as to make you establish your own opinions as an infallible standard for the whole Christian world, and lead you to consign to perdition, all who differ from you, either in some doctrinal tenets, or in the mode of expressing them; you may rest assured, that to much pride you have joined much ignorance, both of the nature of devotion, and of the Gospel of Christ. Finally,

In the sixth place, It is an error to think, that perpetual rapture and spiritual joy belong to devotion. Devout feelings admit very different degrees of warmth and exaltation. Some persons, by the frame of their minds, are much more susceptible than others of the tender emotions. They more readily relent at the view of divine goodness, glow with a warmer ardour or love, and, by consequence, rise to a higher elevation of joy and hope. But, in the midst of still and calm affections, devotion often dwells; and, though it produce no transports in the mind, diffuses over it a steady serenity. Devout sensations not only vary in their degree according to the frame of different tempers; but, even among the best disposed, suffer much interruption and decay. It were too much to expect, that, in the present state of human frailty, those happy feelings should be uniform and constant. Oppression of worldly cares, languor of spirits, and infirmities of health, frequently indispose us for the enjoyment of devout affections. Pious men, on these occasions, are in hazard of passing judgment on their own state with too much severity; as if, for some great iniquity, they were condemned by God to final hardness of heart. Hence arises that melancholy, which has been seen to overcloud them; and which has given occasion to many contemptuous scoffs of ungodly men. But it is a melancholy which deserves to be treated with tenderness, not with contempt. It is the excess of virtuous and pious sensibility. It is the overflowing of a heart affected, in an extreme degree, with the humble

ble fenfe of its own failings, and with ardent concern to attain the favour of God. A weaknefs however, we admit it to be, though not a crime; and hold it to be perfectly feparable from the effence of devotion. For contrition, though it may melt, ought not to fink or overpower the heart of a Chriftian. The tear of repentance brings its own relief. Religion is a fpring of confolation, not of terrour, to every well-informed mind, which, in a proper manner, refts its hope on the infinite goodnefs of God, and the all-fufficient merit of Chrift.

To conclude, Let us remove from devotion all thofe miftakes, to which the corruptions of men, or their ignorance and prejudices, have given rife. With us, let it be the worfhip of God, *in fpirit and in truth;* the elevation of the foul towards him in fimplicity and love. Let us purfue it as the principle of virtuous conduct, and of inward peace, by frequent and ferious meditation on the great objects of religion, let us lay ourfelves open to its influence. By means of the inftitutions of the Gofpel, let us cherifh its impreffions. And, above all, let us pray to God, that he may eftablifh its power in our heart. For here, if any where, his affiftance is requifite. The fpirit of devotion is his gift. From his infpiration it proceeds. Towards him it tends; and in his prefence hereafter, it fhall attain its full perfection.

SERMON

SERMON XI.

On the DUTIES of the YOUNG.

TITUS, ii. 6.

Young men likewise exhort, to be sober-minded.

SOBRIETY of mind is one of those virtues which the present condition of human life strongly inculcates. The uncertainty of its enjoyments checks presumption; the multiplicity of its dangers demands perpetual caution. Moderation, vigilance, and self-government, are duties incumbent on all; but especially on such as are beginning the journey of life. To them, therefore, the admonition in the Text is, with great propriety, directed; though there is reason to fear, that by them it is in hazard of being least regarded. Experience enforces the admonition on the most giddy, after they have advanced in years. But the whole state of youthful views and passions is adverse to sobriety of mind. The scenes which present themselves, at our entering upon the world, are commonly flattering. Whatever they be in themselves, the lively spirits of the young gild every opening prospect. The field of hope appears to stretch wide before them. Pleasure seems to put forth its blossoms on every side. Impelled by desire, forward they rush with inconsiderate ardour: Prompt to decide, and to choose; averse to hesitate, or to enquire; credulous, because untaught by experience; rash, because unacquainted with danger; headstrong, because unsubdued by disappointment. Hence arise the perils, of which it is my design at present to warn them. I shall take *sobriety of mind,* in its most comprehensive sense, as including the whole of that discipline which religion and virtue prescribe to youth. Though the words of the Text are directly addressed to *young men,* yet, as the same admonition is given in a preceding verse to the other sex, the instructions which arise from the Text are to be considered as common to both. I intend, first, to show them the importance of beginning early to give serious attention to their conduct; and, next, to point out those virtues which they ought chiefly to cultivate.

As

On the Duties

As soon as you are capable of reflection, you must perceive that there is a right and a wrong in human actions. You see, that those who are born with the same advantages of fortune, are not all equally prosperous in the course of life. While some of them, by wife and steady conduct, attain distinction in the world, and pass their days with comfort and honour; others of the same rank, by mean and vicious behaviour, forfeit the advantages of their birth, involve themselves in much misery; and end in being a disgrace to their friends, and a burden on society. Early, then, you may learn, that it is not on the external condition in which you find yourselves placed, but on the part which you are to act, that your welfare or unhappiness, your honour or infamy, depend. Now, when beginning to act that part, what can be of greater moment, than to regulate your plan of conduct with the most serious attention, before you have yet committed any fatal or irretrievable errors? If, instead of exerting reflection for this valuable purpose, you deliver yourselves up, at so critical a time, to sloth and pleasure; if you refuse to listen to any counsellor but humour, or to attend to any pursuit except that of amusement; if you allow yourselves to float loose and careless on the tide of life, ready to receive any direction which the current of fashion may chance to give you, what can you expect to follow from such beginnings? While so many around you are undergoing the sad consequences of a like indiscretion, for what reason shall not those consequences extend to you? Shall you attain success without that preparation, and escape dangers without that precaution, which is required of others? Shall happiness grow up to you, of its own accord, and solicit your acceptance, when, to the rest of mankind, it is the fruit of long cultivation, and the acquisition of labour and care?———Deceive not yourselves with such arrogant hopes. Whatever be your rank, Providence will not, for your sake, reverse its established order. The Author of your being hath enjoined you to *take heed to your ways: to ponder the paths of your feet; to remember your Creator in the days of your youth*. He hath decreed, that they only *who seek after wisdom, shall find it;* that *fools shall be afflicted, because of their transgressions;* and that *whoso refuseth instruction shall destroy his own soul*. By listening to these admonitions, and tempering the vivacity of youth with a proper mixture of serious thought, you may ensure cheerfulness for the rest of life; but by delivering yourselves up at present to giddiness and levity, you lay the foundation of lasting heaviness of heart.

When you look forward to those plans of life, which either your circumstances have suggested, or your friends have proposed, you will not hesitate to acknowledge, that in order to pursue them with advantage, some previous discipline is requisite. Be assured, that whatever is to be your profession, no education is more necessary to your success, than the acquirement of virtuous dispositions and habits. This is the universal preparation for every character, and every station in life. Bad as the world is, respect is always paid to virtue. In the usual course of human affairs, it will be found, that a plain understanding joined with acknowledged worth, contributes more to prosperity, than the brightest parts without probity or honour. Whether science, or business, or public life, be your aim, virtue still enters, for a principal share, into all those great departments of society. It is connected with eminence, in every liberal art; with reputation, in every branch of fair and useful business; with distinction, in every public station. The vigour which it gives the mind, and the weight which it adds to character; the generous sentiments which it breathes, the undaunted spirit which it inspires, the ardour of diligence which it quickens, the freedom which it procures from pernicious and dishonourable avocations, are the foundations of all that is high in fame, or great in success, among men.

Whatever ornamental or engaging endowments you now possess, virtue is a necessary requisite, in order to their shining with proper lustre. Feeble are the attractions of the fairest form, if it be suspected that nothing within corresponds to the pleasing appearance without. Short are the triumphs of wit, when it is supposed to be the vehicle of malice. By whatever arts you may at first attract the attention, you can hold the esteem, and secure the hearts of others, only by amiable dispositions, and the accomplishments of the mind. These are the qualities whose influence will last, when the lustre of all that once sparkled and dazzled has passed away.

Let not then the season of youth be barren of improvements so essential to your future felicity and honour. Now is the seed-time of life; and according to *what you sow, you shall reap*. Your character is now, under Divine assistance, of your own forming; your fate is, in some measure, put into your own hands. Your nature is as yet pliant and soft. Habits have not established their dominion. Prejudices have not pre-occupied your understanding. The world has not had time to contract and debase your affections. All your powers are more vigorous, disembarrassed, and free, than they will be at any future period. Whatever impulse you now give to your desires and passions, the direction is likely to continue. It will form the channel in which your life is to run; nay, it may determine its everlasting issue. Consider then the employment of this important period, as the highest trust which shall ever be committed to you; as, in a great measure, decisive of your happiness, in time, and in eternity. As in the succession of the seasons, each, by the invariable laws of Nature, affects the productions of what is next in course; so, in human life, every period of our age, according as it is well or ill spent, influences the happiness of that which is to follow. Virtuous youth gradually brings forward accomplished and flourishing manhood; and such manhood passes of itself, without uneasiness, into respectable and tranquil old age. But when nature is turned out of its regular course, disorder takes place in the moral, just as in the vegetable world. If the Spring put forth no blossoms, in Summer there will be no beauty, and in Autumn no fruit. So, if youth be trifled away without improvement, manhood will be contemptible, and old age miserable. If the beginnings of life have been *vanity*, its latter end can be no other than *vexation of spirit*.

Having thus shown the importance of beginning early to give serious attention to conduct, I come, next, to point out the virtues which are most necessary to be cultivated in youth. What I shall,

I. RECOMMEND, is piety to God. With this I begin, both as the foundation of good morals, and as a disposition particularly graceful and becoming in youth. To be void of it, argues a cold heart, destitute of some of the best affections which belong to that age. Youth is the season of warm and generous emotions. The heart should then, spontaneously, rise into the admiration of what is great, glow with the love of what is fair and excellent, and melt at the discovery of tenderness and goodness. Where can any object be found, so proper to kindle those affections, as the Father of the universe, and the Author of all felicity? Unmoved by veneration, can you contemplate that grandeur and majesty, which his works every where display? Untouched by gratitude, can you view that profusion of good, which, in this pleasing season of life, his beneficent hand pours around you? Happy in the love and affection of those with whom you are connected, look up to the Supreme Being, as the inspirer of all the friendship which has ever been shown you by others; himself, your best and your first friend; formerly, the supporter of your infancy, and the guide of your childhood; now, the guardian of your youth, and the hope of your coming years. View religious homage, as a natural expression of gratitude to him for all his goodness. Consider it as the service of the *God of your fathers*; of him, to whom your parents devoted you; of him, whom in former ages your ancestors honoured; and by whom they are now rewarded, and blessed in heaven. Connected with so many tender sensibilities of soul, let religion be with you, not the cold

and

and barren offspring of speculation, but the warm and vigorous dictate of the heart.

But though piety chiefly belongs to the heart, yet the aid of the understanding is requisite, to give a proper direction to the devout affections. You must endeavour, therefore, to acquire just views, both of the great principles of natural religion, and of the peculiar doctrines of the Gospel. For this end study the sacred scriptures. Consult the word of God, more than the systems of men, if you would know the truth in its native purity. When, upon rational and sober enquiery, you have established your principles, suffer them not to be shaken by the scoffs of the licentious, or the cavils of the sceptical. Remember, that in the examination of every great and comprehensive plan, such as that of Christianity, difficulties may be expected to occur; and that reasonable evidence is not to be rejected, because the nature of our present state allows us only to *know in part, and see through a glass, darkly.*

Impress your minds with reverence for all that is sacred. Let no wantonness of youthful spirits, no compliance with the intemperate mirth of others, ever betray you into prophane sallies. Besides the guilt which is there by incurred, nothing gives a more odious appearance of petulance and presumption to youth, than the affectation of treating religion with levity. Instead of being an evidence of superiour understanding, it discovers a pert and shallow mind; which, vain of the first smatterings of knowledge, presumes to make light of what the rest of mankind revere.

At the same time you are not to imagine, that when exhorted to be religious, you are called upon to become more formal and solemn in your manners than others of the same years, or to erect yourselves into supercilious reprovers of those around you. The spirit of true religion breaths gentleness and affability. It gives a native, unaffected ease to the behaviour. It is social, kind and cheerful; far removed from that gloomy and illiberal superstition which clouds the brow, sharpens the temper, dejects the spirit, and teaches men to fit themselves for another world, by neglecting the concerns of this. Let your religion on the contrary, connect preparation for heaven, with an honourable discharge of the duties of active life. Let it be associated in your imagination, with all that is manly and useful; *with whatsoever things are true, are just, are pure, are lovely, are of good report,* wherever there is *any virtue,* and wherever there is *any praise.* Of such religion discover, on every proper occasion, that you are not ashamed; but avoid making any unnecessary ostentation of it before the world.

II.

II. To piety, join modesty and docility, reverence of your parents, and submission to those who are your superiours in knowledge, in station, and in years. Dependence and obedience belong to youth. Modesty is one of its chief ornaments; and has ever been esteemed a presage of rising merit. When entering on the career of life, it is your part, not to assume the reins as yet into your hands; but to commit yourselves to the guidance of the more experienced, and to become wise by the wisdom of those who have gone before you.

Of all the follies incident to youth, there are none which either deform its present appearance, or blast the prospect of its future prosperity, more than self-conceit, presumption, and obstinacy. By checking its natural progress in improvement, they fix it in long immaturity; and frequently produce mischiefs, which can never be repaired. Yet these are vices too commonly found among the young. Big with enterprise, and elated by hope, they resolve to trust for success to none but themselves. Full of their own abilities, they deride the admonitions which are given them by their friends, as the timorous suggestions of age. Too wise to learn, too impatient to deliberate, too forward to be restrained, they plunge, with precipitant indiscretion, into the midst of all the dangers with which life abounds. *Seest thou a young man wise in his own conceit? There is more hope of a fool, than of him.*—Positive as you now are in your opinions, and confident in you assertions, be assured, that the time approaches when both men and things will appear to you in a different light. Many characters which you now admire, will, by and bye, sink in your esteem; and many opinions, of which you are at present most tenacious, will alter as you advance in years. Distrust, therefore, that glare of youthful presumption, which dazzles your eyes. Abound not in your own sense. Put not yourselves forward with too much eagerness; nor imagine, that by the impetuosity of juvenile ardour, you can overturn systems which have been long established, and change the face of the world. *Learn not to think more highly of yourselves than you ought to think, but to think soberly.* By patient and gradual progression in improvement, you may, in due time, command lasting esteem. But by assuming, at present, a tone of superiority, to which you have no title, you will disgust those whose approbation it is most important to gain. Forward vivacity may fit you to be the companions of an idle hour. More solid qualities must recommend you to the wise, and mark you out for importance and consideration in subsequent life.

III. It is necessary to recommend to you, sincerity and truth. This is the basis of every virtue. That darkness of character, where we can see no heart; those foldings of art, through which no native affection is allowed to penetrate, present an object, unamiable in every season of life, but particularly odious in youth. If, at an age when the heart is warm, when the emotions are strong, and when nature is expected to shew itself free and open, you can already smile and deceive, what are we to look for when you shall be longer hackneyed in the ways of men; when interest shall have completed the obduration of your heart, and experience shall have improved you in all the arts of guile? Dissimulation in youth, is the fore-runner of perfidy in old age. Its first appearance, is the fatal omen of growing depravity, and future shame. It degrades parts and learning; obscures the lustre of every accomplishment; and sinks you into contempt with God and man.

As you value, therefore, the approbation of Heaven, or the esteem of the world, cultivate the love of truth. In all your proceedings, be direct and consistant. Ingenuity and candour possess the most powerful charm; they bespeak universal favour, and carry an apology for almost every failing. *The lip of truth, shall be established for ever; but a lying tongue, is but for a moment* *. The path of truth, is a plain and a safe path; that of falsehood, is a perplexing maze. After the first departure from sincerity, it is not in your power to stop. One artifice unavoidably leads on to another; till, as the intricacy of the labyrinth increases, you are left entangled in your own snare. Deceit discovers a little mind, which stops at temporary expedients, without rising to comprehensive views of conduct. It betrays, at the same time, a dastardly spirit. It is the resource of one who wants courage to avow his designs, or to rest upon himself. Whereas openness of character displays that generous boldness which ought to distinguish youth. To set out in the world with no other principle than a crafty attention to interest, betokens one who is destined for creeping through the inferior walks of life. But to give an early preference to honour above gain, when they stand in competition; to despise every advantage, which cannot be attained without dishonest arts; to brook no meanness, and to stoop to no dissimulation; are the indications of a great mind, the presages of future eminence and distinction in life.

At the same time, this virtuous sincerity is perfectly consistent with the most prudent vigilance and caution. It is opposed to cunning, not to true wisdom. It is not the simplicity of a weak and improvident, but the candour of an enlarged and noble mind; of one who scorns deceit, because he accounts it both base and unprofitable; and who seeks no disguise, because he needs none to hide him. *Lord! who shall abide in thy tabernacle? Who shall ascend into thy holy hill? He that walketh uprightly, and worketh righteousness, and speaketh the truth in his heart.* * Prov. xii. 19. IV.

IV. YOUTH is the proper season of cultivating the benevolent and humane affections. As a great part of your happiness is to depend on the connections which you form with others, it is of high importance that you acquire, betimes, the temper and the manners which will render such connections comfortable. Let a sense of justice be the foundation of all your social qualities. In your most early intercourse with the world, and even in your youthful amusements, let no unfairness be found. Engrave on your mind that sacred rule, of *doing all things to others, according as you wish that they should do unto you.* For this end, impress yourselves with a deep sense of the original and natural equality of men. Whatever advantages of birth or fortune you possess, never display them with an ostentatious superiority. Leave the subordinations of rank, to regulate the intercourse of more advanced years. At present, it becomes you to act among your companions, as man with man. Remember how unknown to you are the vicissitudes of the world; and how often they, on whom ignorant and contemptuous young men once look down with scorn, have risen to be their superiours in future years.

Compassion is an emotion of which you ought never to be ashamed. Graceful in youth is the tear of sympathy, and the heart that melts at the tale of woe. Let not ease and indulgence contract your affections, and wrap you up in selfish enjoyment. But go sometimes to the *house of mourning,* as well as *to the house of feasting.* Accustom yourselves to think of the distresses of human life; of the solitary cottage, the dying parent, and the weeping orphan. *Thou shalt not harden thy heart, nor shut thy hand from thy poor brother: but thou shalt surely give unto him in the day of his need: And thine heart shall not be grieved when thou givest unto him; because that for this thing, the Lord thy God shall bless thee in all thy works*.* Never sport with pain and distress, in any of your amusements; nor treat even the meanest insect with wanton cruelty.

In young minds, there is commonly a strong propensity to particular intimacies and friendships. Youth, indeed, is the season when friendships are sometimes formed, which not only continue through succeeding life, but which glow to the last, with a tenderness unknown to the connections begun in cooler years. The propensity therefore is not to be discouraged; though at the same time it must be regulated with much circumspection and care. Too many of the pretended friendships of youth, are mere combinations in pleasure. They are often founded in capricious likings; suddenly contracted, and as suddenly dissolved. Sometimes they are the effect of interested complaisance and flattery on the one side, and of credulous fondness on the other. Beware of such rash and dangerous connections, which may

* *Deut.* xv. 7, 10. afterwards

afterwards load you with dishonour. Remember, that by the character of those whom you choose for your friends, your own is likely to be formed, and will certainly be judged of by the world. Be slow, therefore, and cautious in contracting intimacy; but when a virtuous friendship is once established, consider it as a sacred engagement. Expose not yourselves to the reproach of lightness and inconstancy, which always bespeak, either a trifling, or a base mind. Reveal none of the secrets of your friend. Be faithful to his interests. Forsake him not in danger. Abhor the thought of acquiring any advantage by his prejudice or hurt. *There is a friend that loveth at all times, and a brother that is born for adversity. Thine own friend, and thy father's friend, forsake not* *.

Finally, on this head; in order to render yourselves amiable in society, correct every appearance of harshness in behaviour. Let that courtesy distinguish your demeanour, which springs, not so much from studied politeness, as from a mild and gentle heart. Follow the customs of the world in matters indifferent; but stop when they become sinful. Let your manners be simple and natural; and of course they will be engaging. Affectation is certain deformity. By forming themselves on fantastic models, and vying with one another in every reigning folly, the young begin with being ridiculous, and end in being vicious and immoral.

V. Let me particularly exhort youth to temperance in pleasure: Let me admonish them, to beware of that rock on which thousands, from race to race, continue to split. The love of pleasure, natural to man in every period of his life, glows at this age with excessive ardour. Novelty adds fresh charms, as yet, to every gratification. The world appears to spread a continued feast; and health, vigour, and high spirits, invite them to partake of it without restraint. In vain we warn them of latent dangers. Religion is accused of insufferable severity, in prohibiting enjoyment: and the old, when they offer their admonitions, are upbraided with having forgot that they once were young. —And yet, my friends, to what do the restraints of religion, and the counsels of age, with respect to pleasure, amount? They may all be comprized in few words, not to hurt yourselves, and not to hurt others, by your pursuit of pleasure. Within these bounds, pleasure is lawful; beyond them, it becomes criminal, because it is ruinous. Are these restraints any other, than what a wise man would choose to impose on himself? We call you not to renounce pleasure, but to enjoy it in safety. Instead of abridging it, we exhort you to pursue it on an extensive plan. We propose measures for securing its possession, and for prolonging its duration.

* *Prov.* xvii. 17.—xxvii. 10. Consult

Confult your whole nature. Confider yourfelves not only as fenfitive, but as rational beings; not only as rational, but focial; not only as focial, but immortal. Whatever violates your nature in any of thefe refpects, cannot afford true pleafure; any more than that which undermines an effential part of the vital fyftem can promote health. For the truth of this conclufion, we appeal, not merely to the authority of religion, nor to the teftimony of the aged, but to yourfelves and your own experience. We afk, Whether you have not found, that in a courfe of criminal excefs, your pleafure was more than compenfated by fucceeding pain? Whether, if not from every particular inftance, yet from every habit, at leaft, of unlawful gratification, there did not fpring fome thorn to wound you, there did not arife fome confequence to make you repent of it in the iffue? *How long then, ye fimple ones! will ye love fimplicity?* How long repeat the fame round of pernicious folly, and tamely expofe yourfelves to be caught in the fame fnare? If you have any confideration, or any firmnefs left, avoid temptations, for which you have found yourfelves unequal, with as much care, as you would fhun peftilential infection. Break off all connections with the loofe and profligate. *When finners entice thee, confent thou not. Look not on the wine when it is red, when it giveth its colour in the cup; for at the laft, it biteth like a ferpent, and ftingeth like an adder. Remove thy way from the ftrange woman, and come not near the door of her houfe. Let not thine heart decline to her ways; for her houfe is the way to hell. Thou goeft after her as a bird hafteth to the fnare, and knoweth not that it is for his life.*

By thefe unhappy exceffes of irregular pleafure in youth, how many amiable difpofitions are corrupted or deftroyed! How many rifing capacities and powers are fuppreffed! How many flattering hopes of parents and friends are totally extinguifhed! Who but muft drop a tear over human nature, when he beholds that morning which arofe fo bright, overcaft with fuch untimely darknefs; that good humour which once captivated all hearts, that vivacity which fparkled in every company, thofe abilities which were fitted for adorning the higheft ftation, all facrificed at the fhrine of low fenfuality; and one who was formed for running the fair career of life in the midft of public efteem, cut off by his vices at the beginning of his courfe, or funk, for the whole of it, into infignificancy and contempt!—Thefe, O finful Pleafure! are thy trophies. It is thus that, co-operating with the foe of God and man, thou degradeft human honour, and blafteft the opening profpects of human felicity.

VI.

VI. DILIGENCE, industry, and proper improvement of time, are material duties of the young. To no purpose are they endowed with the best abilities, if they want activity for exerting them. Unavailing, in this case, will be every direction that can be given them, either for their temporal or spiritual welfare. In youth the habits of industry are most easily acquired. In youth, the incentives to it are strongest, from ambition and from duty, from emulation and hope, from all the prospects which the beginning of life affords. If, dead to these calls, you already languish in slothful inaction, what will be able to quicken the more sluggish current of advancing years?

Industry is not only the instrument of improvement, but the foundation of pleasure. Nothing is so opposite to the true enjoyment of life, as the relaxed and feeble state of an indolent mind. He who is a stranger to industry, may possess, but he cannot enjoy. For it is labour only which gives the relish to pleasure. It is the appointed vehicle of every good to man. It is the indispensable condition of our possessing a sound mind in a sound body. Sloth is so inconsistent with both, that it is hard to determine whether it be a greater foe to virtue, or to health and happiness. Inactive as it is in itself, its effects are fatally powerful. Though it appear a slowly flowing stream, yet it undermines all that is stable and flourishing. It not only saps the foundation of every virtue, but pours upon you a deluge of crimes and evils. It is like water which first putrifies by stagnation, and then sends up noxious vapours, and fills the atmosphere with death.

Fly, therefore, from idleness, as the certain parent both of guilt and of ruin. And under idleness I include, not mere inaction only, but all that circle of trifling occupations, in which too many saunter away their youth; perpetually engaged in frivolous society or public amusements, in the labours of dress, or the ostentation of their persons.—Is this the foundation which you lay for future usefulness and esteem? By such accomplishments, do you hope to recommend yourselves to the thinking part of the world, and to answer the expectations of your friends, and your country?———Amusements, youth requires. It were vain, it were cruel to prohibit them. But though allowable as the relaxation, they are most culpable as the business, of the young. For they then become the gulf of time, and the poison of the mind. They foment bad passions. They weaken the manly powers. They sink the native vigour of youth, into contemptible effeminacy.

Redeeming your time from such dangerous waste, seek to fill it
with

with employments which you may review with satisfaction. The acquisition of knowledge is one of the most honourable occupations of youth. The desire of it discovers a liberal mind, and is connected with many accomplishments, and many virtues. But though your train of life should not lead you to study, the course of education always furnishes proper employments to a well-disposed mind. Whatever you pursue, be emulous to excel. Generous ambition, and sensibility to praise, are, especially at your age, among the marks of virtue. Think not, that any affluence of fortune, or any elevation of rank, exempts you from the duties of application and industry. Industry is the law of our being; it is the demand of Nature, of Reason, and of God. Remember always, that the years which now pass over your heads, leave permanent memorials behind them. From your thoughtless minds they may escape; but they remain in the remembrance of God. They form an important part of the register of your life. They will hereafter bear testimony, either for or against you, at that day, when, for all your actions, but particularly for the employments of youth, you must give an account to God.

THUS I have set before you some of the chief qualifications which belong to that *sober mind*, that virtuous and religious character, which the Apostle in my Text recommends to youth; piety, modesty, truth, benevolence, temperance, and industry. Whether your future course is destined to be long or short, after this manner it should commence; and, if it continue to be thus conducted, its conclusion, at what time soever it arrives, will not be inglorious or unhappy. For *honourable age is not that which standeth in length of time, or that which is measured by number of years. But wisdom is the grey hair to man, and an unspotted life is old age.*

LET me finish the subject, with recalling your attention to that dependence on the blessing of Heaven, which, amidst all your endeavours after improvement, you ought continually to preserve. It is too common with the young, even when they resolve to tread the path of virtue and honour, to set out with presumptuous confidence in themselves. Trusting to their own abilities for carrying them successfully through life, they are careless of applying to God, or of deriving any assistance from what they are apt to reckon the gloomy discipline of religion. Alas! how little do they know the dangers which await them? Neither human wisdom, nor human virtue, unsupported by religion, are equal for the trying situations which often occur in life. By the shock of temptation, how frequently have the most virtuous intentions been overthrown? Under the pressure of disaster, how often has the greatest constancy sunk? *Every good, and every perfect gift, is from above.* Wisdom and virtue, as well as *riches and honour, come from God.* Destitute of his favour, you are in no better situation, with all your boasted abilities, than orphans left to wander in a trackless desert, without any guide to conduct them, or any shelter to cover them from the gathering storm. Correct, then, this ill-founded arrogance. Expect not, that your happiness can be independent of him who made you. By faith and repentance, apply to the Redeemer of the world. By piety and prayer, seek the protection of the God of heaven. I conclude with the solemn words, in which a great Prince delivered his dying charge to his son; words which every young person ought to consider as addressed to himself, and to engrave deeply on his heart: *Thou, Solomon, my son, know thou the God of thy fathers; and serve him with a perfect heart, and with a willing mind. For the Lord searcheth all hearts, and understandeth all the imaginations of the thoughts. If thou seek him, he will be found of thee; but if thou forsake him, he will cast thee off for ever*.*

* 1 Chron. xxviii. 9.

SERMON

SERMON XII.

On the DUTIES and CONSOLATIONS of the AGED.

PROV. xvi. 31.

The hoary head is a crown of glory, if it be found in the way of righteousness.

TO *fear God, and to keep his commandments,* is the rule of our duty, in every period of life. But, as the light which guides our steps, varies with the progress of the day, so the rule of religious conduct is diversified in its application, by the different stages of our present existence. To every age, there belongs a distinct propriety of behaviour. There arises from it, a series of duties peculiar to itself.

Of those which are incumbent on youth, I have treated in the preceding discourse. As we advance from youth to middle age, a new field of action opens, and a different character is required. The flow of gay and impetuous spirits begins to subside. Life gradually assumes a graver cast; the mind a more sedate and thoughtful turn. The attention is now transferred from pleasure to interest; that is, to pleasure diffused over a wider extent, and measured by a larger scale. Formerly, the enjoyment of the present moment occupied the whole attention. Now, no action terminates ultimately in itself, but refers to some more distant aim. Wealth and power, the instruments of lasting gratification, are now coveted more than any single pleasure. Prudence and foresight lay their plans. Industry carries on its patient efforts. Activity pushes forward; address winds around. Here, an enemy is to be overcome; there, a rival to be displaced. Competitions warm; and the strife of the world thickens on every side. To guide men through this busy period, without loss of integrity; to guard them against the temptations which arise from mistaken or interfering interests; to call them from worldly pursuits to serious thoughts of their spiritual concerns, is the great office of religion.

But as this includes, in a great measure, the whole compass of moral duty, as the general strain of religious exhortation is addressed to

those

those who are in this season of life; a delineation of the virtues properly belonging to middle age, may appear unneceffary, and would lead us into too wide a field. Let us therefore turn our view to a bounded profpect; and contemplate a period of life, the duties of which are circumfcribed within narrower limits. Old age is a ftage of the human courfe, which every one hopes to reach; and therefore the confideration of it interefts us all. It is a period juftly entitled to general refpect. Even its failings ought to be touched with a gentle hand; and though the petulant, and the vain, may defpife the *hoary head;* yet the wifeft of men has afferted in the Text, that when *found in the way of righteoufnefs, it is a crown of glory.* I fhall firft offer fome counfels, concerning the errors which are moft incident to the aged. Secondly, I fhall fuggeft the peculiar duties they ought to practife; and, thirdly, point out the confolations they may enjoy.

I. As the follies and vices of youth are chiefly derived from inexperience and prefumption; fo almoft all the errors of age may be traced up to the feeblenefs and diftreffes peculiar to that time of life. Though, in every part of life, vexations occur, yet, in former years, either bufinefs, or pleafure, ferved to obliterate their impreffion, by fupplying occupation to the mind. Old age begins its advances, with difqualifying men for relifhing the one, and for taking an active part in the other. While it withdraws their accuftomed fupports, it impofes, at the fame time, the additional burden of growing infirmities. In the former ftages of their journey, hope continued to flatter them with many a fair and enticing profpect. But in proportion as old age increafes, thofe pleafing illufions vanifh. Life is contracted within a narrow and barren circle. Year after year fteals fomewhat away from their ftore of comfort, deprives them of fome of their ancient friends, blunts fome of their powers of fenfation, or incapacitates them for fome function of life.

Though, in the plan of Providence, it is wifely ordered, that before we are called away from the world, our attachment to it fhould be gradually loofened; though it be fit in itfelf, that as in the day of human life, there is a morning and a noon, fo there fhould be an evening alfo, when the lengthening fhadows fhall admonifh us of approaching night; yet we have no reafon to be furprifed, if they who are arrived at this dejecting feafon, feel and lament the change which they fuffer. The complaints, therefore, of the aged, fhould meet with tendernefs rather than cenfure. The burden under which they labour, ought to be viewed with fympathy, by thofe who muft bear it in their turn, and who, perhaps, hereafter, may complain of it as bitterly. At the fame time, the old fhould confider, that all the feafons of life have

their

their several trials allotted to them; and that to bear the infirmities of age with becoming patience, is as much their duty, as it is that of the young to refill the temptations of youthful pleasure. By calmly enduring, for the short time that remains, what Providence is pleased to inflict, they both express a resignation most acceptable to God, and recommend themselves to the esteem and assistance of all who are around them.

But though the querulous temper imputed to old age, is to be considered as a natural infirmity, rather than as a vice; the same apology cannot be made for that peevish disgust at the manners, and that malignant censure of the enjoyments, of the young, which is sometimes found to accompany declining years. Nothing can be more unjust, than to take offence at others, on account of their partaking of pleasures, which it is past your time to enjoy. By indulging this fretful temper, you both aggravate the uneasiness of age, and you alienate those on whose affection much of your comfort depends. In order to make the two extremes of life unite in amicable society, it is greatly to be wished, that the young would look forward, and consider that they shall one day be old; and that the old would look back, and, remembering that they once were young, make proper allowances for the temper and the manners of youth.

But instead of this, it is too common to find the aged at declared enmity with the whole system of present customs and manners; perpetually complaining of the growing depravity of the world, and of the astonishing vices and follies of the rising generation. All things, according to them, are rushing fast into ruin. Decency and good order have become extinct, ever since that happy discipline, under which they spent their youth, has passed away.———Part, at least, of this displeasure, you may fairly impute to the infirmity of age, which throws its own gloom on every surrounding object. Similar lamentations were, in the days of your youth, poured forth by your fathers; and they who are now young, shall, when it comes to their turn, inveigh, in the like strain, against those who succeed them. Great has been the corruption of the world in every age. Sufficient ground there is for the complaints made by serious observers, at all times, of abounding iniquity and folly. But though particular modes of vice prevail in one age, more than in others, it does not follow, that on that age all iniquity is accumulated. It is the form, perhaps, more than the quantity of corruption, which makes the distinction. In the worst of times, God has assured us, that there shall be always a seed who shall serve him *. Say not thou, *What is the cause that the former days were better than these? for thou dost not enquire wisely concerning this. Be not righteous overmuch; neither make thyself overwise* ‡.

* *Psal.* xii. 30.   ‡ *Ecclef.* vii. 10, 16.   Former

Former follies pass away, and are forgotten. Those which are present, strike observation, and sharpen censure. Had the depravation of the world continued to increase in proportion to those gloomy calculations which, for so many centuries past, have estimated each race as worse than the preceding; by this time, not one ray of good sense, nor one spark of piety and virtue, must have remained unextinguished among mankind.

One of the vices of old age, which appears the most unaccountable, is that covetous attachment to worldly interest, with which it is often charged. But this too, can naturally be deduced from the sense of its feebleness and decay. In proportion as the vigour both of body and mind declines, timidity may be expected to increase. With anxious and fearful eye, the aged look forward to the evils which threaten them, and to the changes which may befal. Hence, they are sometimes apt to overvalue riches, as the instrument of their defence against these dangers, and as the most certain means of securing them against solitude and disrespect. But though their apprehensions may justify a cautious frugality, they can by no means excuse a sordid avarice. It is no less absurd, than it is culpable, in the old, from the dread of uncertain futurity, to deny themselves the enjoyment of the present; and to increase in anxiety about their journey, in proportion as it draws nearer to its close. There are more effectual methods of commanding respect from the world, than the mere possession of wealth. Let them be charitable, and do good. Let them mix beneficence to their friends, with a cheerful enjoyment of the comforts which befit their state. They will then receive the returns of real respect and love. Whereas, by their riches, they procure no more than pretended demonstrations of regard; while their ill-judged parsimony occasions many secret wishes for their death.

As increasing years debilitate the body, so they weaken the force, and diminish the warmth of the affections. Chilled by the hand of time, the heart loses that tender sensibility, with which it once entered into the concerns and sorrows of others. It is, in truth, a merciful appointment of Providence, that as they who see many days, must behold many a sad scene, the impressions of grief upon their heart should be blunted by being often repeated; and that, in proportion as their power of advancing the prosperity of others decreases, their participation of the misfortunes of others should also lessen. However, as in every period of life, humanity and friendship contribute to happiness, it is both the duty and the interest of the aged, to cherish the remains of the kind affections; and, from the days of former years, to recal such impressions as may tend to soften their hearts. Let them not from having suffered much in the course of their long pilgrimage,

mage, become callous to the sufferings of others. But, remembering that they still are men, let them study to keep their heart open to the sense of human woe. Practised in the ways of men, they are apt to be suspicious of design and fraud; for the knowledge and the distrust of mankind too often go together. Let not, however, that wary caution, which is the fruit of their experience, degenerate into craft. Experience ought also to have taught them, that amidst all the falsehood of men, integrity is the best defence; and that he who continueth to the end to *walk uprightly*, shall continue to *walk surely*. Having thus offered some admonitions concerning the errors most incident to age, I proceed,

II. To point out the duties which peculiarly belong to it.

The first which I shall mention, is a timely retreat from the world. In every part of life, we are in hazard of being too deeply immersed in its cares. But during its vigorous periods, the impulse of active spirit, the necessary business of our station, and the allowable endeavours to advance our fortune by fair industry, render it difficult to observe due moderation. In old age, all the motives of eager pursuit deminish. The voice of Nature then calls you to leave to others the bustle and contest of the world; and gradually to disengage yourselves from a burden, which begins to exceed your strength. Having borne your share of the heat and labour of the day, let the evening of life be passed in the cool and quiet shade. It is only in the shade, that the virtues of old age can flourish. There, its duties are discharged with more success; and there, its comforts are enjoyed with greatest satisfaction.

By the retreat of old age, however, I do not mean a total cessation from every worldly employment. There is an error in this, as well as in the opposite extreme. Persons who have been long harrassed with business and care, sometimes imagine, that when life declines, they cannot make their retirement from the world too complete. But where they expected a delicious enjoyment of leisure and ease, they have often found a melancholy solitude. Few are able, in any period of their days, to bear a total abstraction from the world. There remains a vacancy which they cannot fill up. Incapable of being always employed in the exercises of religion, and often little qualified for the entertainments of the understanding, they are in hazard of becoming a burden to themselves, and to all with whom they are connected. It is, therefore, the duty of the aged, not so much to withdraw entirely from worldly business, as to contract its circle; not so

Y

much to break off, as to loosen their communication with active life. Continuing that train of occupation to which they have been most accustomed, let them pursue it with less intenseness; relaxing their efforts, as their powers decline; retiring more and more from public observation, to domestic scenes, and serious thoughts; till as the decays of life advance, the world shall of itself withdraw to a greater distance from their view; its objects shall gradually yield their place to others of more importance; and its tumults shall sound in their ears, only like a noise which is heard from afar.

If it be the duty of the old, to retreat betimes from the fatigue of worldly care, it is still more incumbent on them to quit the pursuit of such pleasures as are unsuitable to their years. Cheerfulness, in old age, is graceful. It is the natural concomitant of virtue. But the cheerfulness of age is widely different from the levity of youth. Many things are allowable in that early period, which, in maturer years, would deserve censure; but which, in old age, become both ridiculous and criminal. By awkwardly affecting to imitate the manners, and to mingle in the vanities of the young, as the aged depart from the dignity, so they forfeit the privileges of grey hairs. But if, by follies of this kind, they are degraded, they are exposed to much deeper blame, by descending to vicious pleasure, and continuing to hover round those sinful gratifications to which they were once addicted. Amusement and relaxation the aged require, and may enjoy. But let them consider well, that by every intemperate indulgence, they accelerate decay; instead of enlivening, they oppress, and precipitate their declining-state. Ease, safety, and respect, are the proper enjoyments of age. Within these bounds let it remain, and not vainly attempt to break through that barrier, by which nature has separated the pleasures of youth, from the comforts left to the concluding years of life.

A material part of the duty of the aged, consists, in studying to be useful to the race who are to succeed them. Here opens to them an extensive field, in which they may so employ themselves, as considerably to advance the interest of religion, and the happiness of mankind. To them it belongs, to impart to the young the fruit of their long experience; to instruct them in the proper conduct, and to warn them of the various dangers, of life; by wise counsel, to temper their precipitate ardour; and, both by precept and example, to form them to piety and virtue.

It is not by rigorous discipline, and unrelaxing austerity, that they
can

can maintain an afcendant over youthful minds. The conftraint which their prefence will impofe, and the averfion which their manners will create, if the one be conftantly awful, and the other fevere, tend to fruftrate the effect of all their wifdom. They muft affume the fpirit of the companion, and the friend; and mix, with the authority of age, a proper degree of indulgence to the manners of the young. Inftead of leffening the refpect due to their years by fuch condefcenfion, they take the fureft method to increafe it. Old age never appears with greater dignity than, when tempered with mildnefs, and enlivened with good humour, it acts as the guide and the patron of youth. Religion, difplayed in fuch a character, ftrikes the beholders, as at once amiable and venerable. They revere its power, when they fee it adding fo much grace to the decays of nature, and fhedding fo pleafing a luftre over the evening of life. The young wifh to tread in the fame fteps, and to arrive at the clofe of their days with equal honour. They liften with attention to counfels which are mingled with tendernefs and rendered refpectable by grey hairs. For notwithftanding all its prefumption, youth naturally bends before fuperiour knowledge and years. Aged wifdom, when joined with acknowledged virtue, exerts an authority over the human mind, greater even than that which arifes from power and ftation. It can check the moft forward, abafh the moft profligate, and ftrike with awe the moft giddy and unthinking.

In the midft of their endeavours to be ufeful to others, let not the aged forget thofe religious employments which their own ftate particularly requires. The firft of thefe, is, reflection on their paft behaviour, with a view to difcover the errors which they have committed; and as far as remaining life allows, to apply themfelves to repentance and amendment.———Long has the world bewildered you in its maze, and impofed upon you by its arts. The time is now come, when this great feducer fhould miflead you no more. From the calm ftation at which you are arrived, fequeftered from the crowd of the deceiving and the deceived, review your conduct with the eye of Chriftians and immortal beings. After all the tumult of life is over, what now remains to afford you folid fatisfaction? Have you ferved God with fidelity, and difcharged your part to your fellow-creatures with integrity and a good confcience? Can you look forward without terrour to that day which is to diffolve your connexion with this world, and to bring you into the prefence of him who made you in order to give account of your actions?—The retrofpect of life is feldom wholly unattended by uneafinefs and fhame. Though, to the good and the bad, it prefents a very different fcene; yet, to all men, it recalls much guilt incurred, and much time mif-fpent. It too much

resembles

resembles the review which a traveller takes from some eminence, of a barren country, through which he has passed, where the heath and the desert form the chief prospect; diversified only by a few scattered spots of imperfect cultivation.

Turn then your thoughts to the proper methods of making your peace with God through Jesus Christ; and implore, from Divine grace, that *new heart* and *right spirit*, which will fit you for a better world. Let devotion fill up many of those hours which are now vacant from worldly business and care. Let your affections dwell among divine and immortal objects. In silent and thoughtful meditation, walk as on the shore of that vast ocean, upon which you are soon to embark. Summon up all the considerations, which should reconcile you to your departure from life; and which may prepare you for going through its last scene, with firmness and decency. Often let your thanksgivings ascend to God, for that watchful care with which he hath hitherto conducted you, through the long journey of life. Often let your prayers be heard, that in what remains of your pilgrimage, he may not forsake you; and, that when you enter into the *valley of the shadow of death*, he may there support you with *his staff*, and defend you with *his rod*.—Amidst such thoughts and cares, let old age find you employed; betaking yourselves to a prudent and timely retreat; disengaged both from the oppressive load of business, and from the unseasonable pursuit of pleasure; applying yourselves to form the succeeding race, by your counsels, to virtue and wisdom; reviewing seriously your past life; by repentance and devotion, preparing yourselves for a better; and, with humble and manly composure, expecting that hour, which Nature cannot now long delay. It remains,

III. To suggest the consolations which belong to old age, when thus *found in the way of righteousness*.

I must introduce them with observing, That nothing is more reasonable in itself, than to submit patiently to those infirmities of Nature which are brought on by the increase of years. You knew beforehand what you had to expect, when you numbered the successive Summers and Winters which were passing over your heads. Old age did not attack you by surprise, nor was it forced upon you against your choice. Often, and earnestly, did you wish to *see long life and many days*. When arrived at the desired period, have you any just cause to complain, on account of enduring what the constitution of our being imposes on all? Did you expect, that, for your sake, Providence was to alter its established order? Throughout the whole vegetable,

getable, sensible, and rational world, whatever makes progress towards maturity, as soon as it has passed that point, begins to verge towards decay. It is as natural for old age to be frail, as for the stalk to bend under the ripened ear, or for the autumnal leaf to change its hue. To this law, all who went before you, have submitted; and all who shall come after you, must yield. After they have flourished for a season, they shall fade, like you, when the period of decline arrives, and bow under the pressure of years.

During the whole progress of the human course, the principal materials of our comfort, or uneasiness, lie within ourselves. Every age will prove burdensome to those who have no fund of happiness in their own breast. Preserve them, if you could, from all infirmity of frame; bestow upon them, if it were possible, perpetual youth; still they would be restless and miserable, through the influence of illgoverned passions. It is not surprising, that such persons are peevish, and querulous, when old. Unjustly they impute to their time of life, that misery with which their vices and follies embitter every age. Whereas, to good men, no period of life is unsupportable, because they draw their chief happiness from sources which are independent of age or time. Wisdom, piety, and virtue, grow not old with our bodies. They suffer no decay from length of days. To them only belongs unalterable and unfading youth. *Those that be planted in the house of the Lord, shall flourish in the courts of our God. They shall still bring forth fruit in old age; they shall be fat and flourishing* *.

You can now, it is true, no longer relish many of those pleasures which once amused you. Your sensations are less quick than formerly; your days more languishing. But if you have quitted the region of pleasure, in return, you possess that of tranquillity and repose. If you are strangers to the vivacity of enjoyment, you are free, at the same time, from the pain of violent and often disappointed desire. Much fatigue, much vexation, as well as vanity, attend that turbulence of life, in which the younger part of mankind are engaged. Amidst those keen pursuits, and seeming pleasures, for which you envy them, often they feel their own misery, and look forward with a wishful eye to the season of calmness and retreat. For on all sides of human life, the balance of happiness is adjusted with more equality than at first appears; and if old age throws some new distresses into the scale, it lightens also the weight of others. Many passions, which formerly disturbed your tranquillity, have now subsided. Many competitions, which long filled your days with disquiet and strife, are

* *Psalm.* xcii. 13, 14.

are now at an end. Many afflictions, which once rent your hearts with violent anguish, are now softened into a tender emotion, on the remembrance of past woe. In the beginnings of life, there was room for much apprehension concerning what might befal in its progress. Your security was never untroubled. Your hopes were interrupted by many anxieties and fears. Having finished the career of labour and danger, your anxiety ought of course to lessen. Ready to enter into the harbour, you can look back, as from a secure station, upon the perils you have escaped, upon the tempest by which you was tossed, and upon the multitudes who are still engaged in conflicting with the storm.

If you have acted your part with integrity and honour, you are justly entitled to respect, and you will generally receive it. For rarely, or never, is old age contemned, unless when, by vice or folly, it renders itself contemptible. Though length of time may have worn off superficial ornaments, yet what old age loses in grace, it often gains in dignity. The veneration, as was before observed, which grey hairs command, puts it in the power of the aged, to maintain a very important place in human society. They are so far from being insignificant in the world, that families long held together by their authority, and societies accustomed to be guided by their counsels, have frequently had cause to regret their loss, more than that of the most vigorous and young. To success of every kind, the head which directs, is no less essential than the hand which executes. Vain, nay often dangerous, were youthful enterprise, if not conducted by aged prudence. *I said, Days should speak, and multitude of years should teach wisdom**. *Therefore, thou shalt rise up before the hoary head, and honour the face of the old man, and fear thy God* †.

Though, in old age, the circle of your pleasures is more contracted than it has formerly been; yet, within its limits, many of those enjoyments remain, which are most grateful to human nature. Temperate mirth is not extinguished by advanced years. The mild pleasures of domestic life still cheer the heart. The entertainments of conversation, and social intercourse, continue unimpaired. The desire of knowledge is not abated by the frailty of the body; and the leisure of old age affords many opportunities of gratifying that desire. The sphere of your observation and reflection is so much enlarged by long acquaintance with the world, as to supply, within itself, a wide range of improving thought. To recall the various revolutions which have occurred since you began to act your part in life; to compare the characters

* *Job*, xxiii. 7. † *Lev.* xix. 32.

characters of paſt and preſent times; to trace the hand of Providence, in all the incidents of your own lot; to contemplate with thoughtful eye, the ſucceſſive new appearances which the world has aſſumed around you, in government, education, opinions, cuſtoms, and modes of living; theſe are employments, no leſs entertaining than inſtructive to the mind.

While you are engaged in ſuch employments, you are, perhaps, ſurrounded with your families, who treat you with attention and reſpect; you are honoured by your friends; your character is eſtabliſhed; you are placed beyond the reach of clamour, and *the ſtrife of tongues;* and, free from diſtracting cares, you can attend calmly to your eternal intereſts. For ſuch comforts as theſe, have you not cauſe moſt thankfully to acknowledge the goodneſs of heaven? Do they not afford you ground to paſs the remainder of your days in reſignation and peace; diſpoſing yourſelves to riſe in due time, like ſatisfied gueſts, from the banquet that has been ſet before you; and to praiſe and bleſs, when you depart, the great Maſter of the feaſt? *To a man that is good in his ſight,* whether he be young or old, *God giveth wiſdom, and knowledge, and joy.* For every ſeaſon of life, the benignity of his providence hath prepared its own ſatisfactions, while his wiſdom hath appointed its peculiar trials. No age is doomed to total infelicity; provided that we attempt not to do violence to Nature, by ſeeking to extort from one age, the pleaſures of another; and to gather, in the Winter of life, thoſe flowers which were deſtined to bloſſom only in its Summer, or its Spring.

But perhaps it will be ſaid, That I have conſidered old age only in its firſt ſtages, and in its moſt favourable point of light; before the faculties are as yet much impaired, and when diſeaſe or affliction has laid no additional load on the burden of years. Let us then view it with all its aggravations of diſtreſs. Let us ſuppoſe it arrived at its utmoſt verge, worn out with infirmities, and bowed down by ſickneſs and ſorrow. Still there remains this conſolation, that it is not long ere *the weary ſhall be at reſt.* Having paſſed through ſo many of the toils of life, you may now ſurely, when your pilgrimage touches on its cloſe, bear, without extreme impatience, the hardſhips of its concluding ſtage. From the ineſtimable promiſes of the Goſpel, and from the gracious preſence of God, the afflictions of old age cannot ſeclude you. Though *your heart ſhould begin to faint, and your fleſh to fail,* there is One, who can be *the ſtrength of your heart, and your portion for ever.* Even *to your old age, ſaith the Lord, I am He; and even to*

hoary

hoary hairs will I carry you. I have made, and I will bear; even I will carry, and will deliver you*. *Leave thy fatherless children; I will preserve them alive; and let thy widows trust in me †.*

There is undoubtedly a period, when there ought to be a satiety of life, as there is of all other things; and when death should be viewed, as your merciful difmission from a long warfare. *To come to the grave in a full age, like as a shock of corn cometh in, in its season ‡,* is the natural termination of the human course. Amidst multiplying infirmities, to prolong life beyond its usual bounds, and to draw out your existence here to the last and foulest dregs, ought not to be the wish of any wife man. Is it desireable, to continue lingering on the borders of the grave, after every tie which connects you with life is broken; and to be left a solitary individual, in the midst of a new generation, whose faces you hardly know? The shades of your departed friends rise up before you, and warn you, that it is time to depart. Nature and providence summon you, to be *gathered to your fathers.* Reason admonishes you, that as your predecessors made way for you, it is just that you should yield your place to those who have arisen to succeed you on this busy stage; who, for a while, shall fill it with their actions and their sufferings, their virtues and their crimes; and then shall, in their turn, withdraw, and be joined to the forgotten multitudes of former ages.

Could death, indeed, be considered in no other view than as the close of life, it would afford only a melancholy retreat. The total extinction of being, is a thought, which human nature, in its most distressed circumstances, cannot bear without dejection. But, blessed be God! far other prospects revive the spirits of the aged, who have spent their life in piety and virtue. To them, death is not the extinction, but the renovation of the living principle; its removal from *the earthly house of this tabernacle, to the house not made with hands, eternal in the heavens. Having fought the good fight; having finished their course, and kept the faith; there is laid up for them the crown of righteousness.* The Saviour of the world hath not only *brought immortality to light,* but placed it within the reach of their hope and trust. By making atonement for their guilt, he hath prepared their way *within the veil;* and secured to them, the possession of *an inheritance, incorruptible and undefiled, reserved in the heavens.*——Such are the hopes and prospects which cheer the sorrows of old age, and surmount the fear of death. Faith and piety are the only adequate supports of human nature, in all its great emergencies. After they have guided us through the various trials of life, they uphold us, at

* *Isa.* xlvi. 4.   † *Jer.* xlix. 11.   ‡ *Job,* v. 26.   last,

Consolations of the aged.

last, amidst the ruins of this falling frame; and when the *silver cord is just ready to be loosed, and the golden bowl to be broken; when the pitcher is broken at the fountain, and the wheel broken at the cistern;* they enable us to say, *O Death! where is thy sting? O Grave! where is thy victory?*

SERMON

SERMON XIII.

On the POWER of CONSCIENCE.

GENESIS, xlii. 21, 22.

And they said one to another, We are verily guilty concerning our brother, in that we saw the anguish of his soul, when he besought us: and we would not hear: Therefore is this distress come upon us. And Ruben answered them, saying, Speak I not unto you, saying, Do not sin against the child; and ye would not hear? Therefore, behold also his blood is required.

THIS book of Genesis displays a more singular and interesting scene, than was ever presented to the world by any other historical record. It carries us back to the beginning of time, and exhibits mankind in their infant and rising state. It shows us human manners in their primitive simplicity, before the arts of refinement had polished the behaviour, or disguised the characters of men; when they gave vent to their passions without dissimulation, and spoke their sentiments without reserve. Few great societies were, as yet, formed on the earth. Men lived in scattered tribes. The transactions of families made the chief materials of history; and they are related in this book, with that beautiful simplicity, which, in the highest degree, both delights the imagination, and affects the heart.

Of all the patriarchal histories, that of Joseph and his brethren is the most remarkable, for the characters of the actors, the instructive nature of the events, and the surprising revolutions of worldly fortune. As far as relates to the Text, and is necessary for explaining it, the story is to the following purpose :———Joseph, the youngest, except one, of the sons of Jacob, was distinguished by his father with such marks of peculiar affection, as excited the envy of his brethren. Having related to them, in the openness of his heart, certain dreams which portended his future advancement above them, their jealousy rose to such a height, that they unnaturally conspired his destruction. Seizing the opportunity of his being at a distance from home, they first threw him into a pit, and afterwards sold him for a slave; imposing

posing on their father by a false relation of his death. When they had thus gratified their resentment, they lost all remembrance of their crime. The family of Jacob was rich and powerful; and several years passed away, during which they lived in prosperity; without being touched, as far as appears, with the least remorse for the cruel deed which they had committed.

Meanwhile, Joseph was safely conducted, by the hand of Providence, through a variety of dangers, until, from the lowest condition, he rose at last to be chief favourite of the King of Egypt, the most powerful monarch at that time in the world. While he possessed this high dignity, a general famine distressed all the neighbouring countries In Egypt alone, by means of his foresight and prudent administration, plenty still reigned. Compelled to have recourse to that kingdom for supply of food, the brethren of Joseph, upon this occasion, appeared in his presence, and made their humble application to him, for liberty to purchase corn; little suspecting the Governour of the land, before whom they *bowed down their faces to the earth*, to be him, whom, long ago, they had sold as a slave to the Ishmaelites. But Joseph no sooner saw, than he knew his brethren; and, at this unexpected meeting, his heart melted within him. Fraternal tenderness arose in all its warmth, and totally effaced from his generous breast the impression of their ancient cruelty. Though, from that moment, he began to prepare for them a surprise of joy; yet he so far constrained himself, as to assume an appearance of great severity. By this he intended, both to oblige them to bring into Egypt his youngest and most beloved brother, whose presence he instantly required; and also, to awaken within them a due sense of the crime which they had formerly perpetrated. Accordingly, his behaviour produced the designed effect. For while they were in this situation, strangers in a foreign land, where they had fallen, as they conceived, into extreme distress; where they were thrown into prison by the Governour, and treated with rigour, for which they could assign no cause; the reflection mentioned in the Text arose in their minds. Conscience brought to remembrance their former sins. It recalled, in particular, their long forgotten cruelty to Joseph; and, without hesitation, they interpreted their present distress to be a judgment, for this crime, inflicted by Heaven. *They said one to another, We are verily guilty concerning our brother, in that we saw the anguish of his soul when he besought us, and we would not hear: therefore is this distress come upon us.——Behold also his blood is required.*

From this instructive passage of history, the following observations naturally arise. I. That a sense of right and wrong in conduct, or

of

of moral good and evil, belongs to human nature. II. That it produces an apprehension of merited punishment, when we have committed evil. III. That although this inward sentiment be stifled during the season of prosperity, yet in adversity it will revive. And, IV. That, when it revives, it determines us to consider every distress which we suffer, from what cause soever it has arisen, as an actual infliction of punishment by Heaven. The consideration of these particulars will lead us to a very serious view of the nature of man, and of the government of God.

I. THERE belongs to human nature, a sense of moral good and evil, or a faculty which distinguishes right from wrong, in action and conduct. *They said one to another, We are verily guilty.*——In an age, when the law was not yet given, when no external revelation of the Divine will subsisted, except what had been handed down among the Patriarchs, from one generation to another; the brethren of Joseph reasoned concerning their conduct, upon the same moral principles, and were affected by the same feelings, of which we are conscious at this day. Such sentiments are coeval with human nature; for they are the remains of a law which was originally *written in our heart*. In the darkest regions of the earth, and among the rudest tribes of men, a distinction has ever been made between just and unjust, between a duty and a crime. Throughout all the intercourse of human beings these distinctions are supposed. They are the foundation of the mutual trust which the transactions of life require; nay, the very entertainments of society constantly appeal to them. The Historian, who studies to magnify his hero, by representing him as just and generous; the Poet, who seeks to interest the world in his fictions, by engaging the heart in behalf of distressed virtue; are sufficient to confute the sceptic, who denies any natural perception of a distinction in actions.

But though a sense of moral good and evil be deeply impressed on the heart of man, yet it is not of sufficient power to regulate his life. In his present corrupted state, it is both too general to afford him full direction in conduct, and too feeble to withstand the opposition of contrary principles in his nature. It is often perverted by ignorance and superstition; it is too easily overcome by passion and desire. Hence, the importance of that Divine revelation, which communicates both light and strength: which, by the instructive discoveries it makes, and by the powerful assistance it supplies, raises man to a station infinitely superior to that which he possesses under the mere light of Nature.

It is of consequence, however, to remark, That this revelation necessarily

sarily suppofes an antecedent fenfe of right and wrong to take place in the human mind. It addreffes itfelf to men, as poffeffed of fuch a faculty; and, when it commands them, in general terms, to purfue *whatfoever things are true, whatfoever things are honeft, whatfoever things are juft, pure, lovely, or of good report, if there be any virtue, and if there be any praife,* it plainly appeals to the native dictates of their heart. Nay, unlefs men were endowed by Nature with fome fenfe of duty, or of moral obligation, they could reap no benefit from revelation; they would remain incapable of all religion whatever. For, in vain were a fyftem of duty prefcribed to them by the word of God; allegiance were in vain required towards their Creator, or love and gratitude enjoined towards their Redeemer; if, previoufly, there was no principle in their nature, which made them feel the obligations of duty, of allegiance, and of gratitude. They could have no ideas correfponding to fuch terms; nor any conviction, that, independently of fear or intereft, they were bound to regard, either him who made, or him who redeemed them.—This, therefore, is to be held as a principle fundamental to all religion, That there is in human nature, an approving or condemning fenfe of conduct; by means of which, *they who have not the law, are a law unto themfelves* *. They who, from a miftaken zeal for the honour of Divine revelation, either deny the exiftence, or vilify the authority of natural religion, are not aware, that by difallowing the fenfe of obligation, they undermine the foundation, on which revelation builds its power of commanding the heart.

The Text leads us to obferve, That one of the cafes in which the natural fenfe of good and evil opperates moft forcibly, is when men have been guilty of injuftice or inhumanity. *We faw the anguifh of our brother's foul when he befought us, and we would not hear.* An inward principle prompts us to do good to others; but with much greater authority, it checks and condemns us, when we have done them injuries. This part of the human conftitution deferves to be remarked as a fignal proof of the wifdom of its Author, and of the gracious provifion which he has made for the welfare of mankind. We are all committed, in fome meafure, to the care and affiftance of one another. But our mutual influence reaches much farther with refpect to the evils, than with refpect to the enjoyments, of thofe around us. To advance their profperity, is often beyond our ability; but to inflict injuries, is almoft always within our power: And, at the fame time, felf-intereft very frequently tempts us to commit them. With the utmoft propriety, therefore, we are fo framed, that the influence of the moral principle fhould be moft authoritative, in cafes where its aid is moft needed; that to promote the happinefs of others, fhould appear to us as

* *Rom.* ii. 14. praifeworthy,

praiseworthy, indeed and generous; but that, to abstain from injuring them, should be felt as matter of the strictest duty.—Amidst the distress which the Patriarchs suffered in Egypt, had only this suggestion occurred, " We saw our brother beginning to prosper, and we contributed not to his advancement," their minds would have been more easily quieted. But, when their reflection was, *We saw his anguish when he besought us, and we would not hear*, then compunction turned upon them its sharpest edge. I proceed to observe,

II. THAT our natural sense of right and wrong, produces an apprehension of merited punishment when we have committed a crime. When it is employed in surveying the behaviour of others, it distinguishes some actions, as laudable and excellent; and disapproves of others, as evil and base. But when it is directed upon our own conduct, it assumes a higher office, and exercises the authority of a judge. It is then properly termed Conscience; and the sentiments which it awakens, upon the perpetration of a crime, are styled, Remorse. *Therefore*, said the brethren of Joseph, *is this distress come upon us; behold also his blood is required*. They acknowledged, not only that they had committed a wrong, but a wrong for which they were justly doomed to suffer.

Did not conscience suggest this natural relation between guilt and punishment, the mere principle of approbation, or disapprobation, with respect to moral conduct, would prove of small efficacy. For disapprobation attends, in some degree, every conviction of impropriety or folly. When one has acted unsuitably to his interest, or has trespassed against the rules of prudence or decorum, he reflects upon his conduct with pain, and acknowledges that he deserves blame. But the difference between the sense of misconduct, and the sense of guilt, consists in this, that the latter penetrates much deeper into the heart. It makes the criminal feel, that he is not only blamable, but justly punishable, for the part which he has acted. With reference to this office of conscience, the inspired writers frequently speak of it, in terms borrowed from the awful solemnities of judicial procedure; as, *bearing witness for or against us; accusing or excusing, judging and condemning*. It will be found, that in the language of most nations, terms of the same import are applied to the operations of conscience; expressing the sense, which all mankind have, of its passing sentence upon them, and pronouncing rewards or punishments to be due to their actions.

The sense of punishment merited, you are further to observe, can never be separated from the dread, that, at some time or other, punishment

nishment shall be actually inflicted. This dread is not confined to the vengeance of man. For let the sinner's evil deeds be ever so thoroughly concealed from the knowledge of the world, his inward alarms are not quieted by that consideration. Now, punishment is the sanction of a law. Every law supposes a rightful superior: And therefore, when conscience threatens punishment to secret crimes, it manifestly recognises a supreme Governour, from whom nothing is hidden. The belief of our being accountable to him, is what the most hardened wickedness has never been able to eradicate. It is a belief which arises, not merely from reasoning, but from internal sentiment. Conscience is felt to act as the delegate of an invisible ruler; both anticipating his sentence, and foreboding its execution.

Hence arise the terrours, which so often haunt guilt, and rise in proportion to its atrocity. In the history of all nations, the tyrant and the oppressor, the bloody and the flagitious, have been ever pointed out, as fearful, unquiet, and restless; subject to alarms and apprehensions of an unaccountable kind. And surely, to live under such disquietude, from the dread of merited punishment, is already to undergo one of the most severe punishments which human nature can suffer. When the world threatens us with any of its evils, we know the extent, and discern the limits of the danger. We see the quarter, on which we are exposed to its attack. We measure our own strength with that of our adversary; and can take precautions, either for making resistance, or for contriving escape. But when an awakened conscience places before the sinner the just vengeance of the Almighty, the prospect is confounding, because the danger is boundless. It is a dark unknown which threatens him. The arm that is stretched over him, he can neither see nor resist. On every side he dreads it; and on every object which surrounds him, he looks with terrour, because he is conscious that every object can be employed against him as an instrument of wrath. No wonder that the lonesome solitude, or the midnight hour, should strike him with horror. His troubled mind beholds forms, which other men see not; and hears voices, which sound only in the ear of guilt. A hand appears to come forth, and to write upon the wall over against him, as it did of old, in the sight of an impious monarch. *He shall find no ease, nor rest. For the Lord shall give him a trembling heart, and failing of eyes, and sorrow of mind: And his life shall hang in doubt before him; and he shall fear day and night, and have none assurance of his life. In the morning he shall say, Would to God it were even; and at even he shall say, Would to God it were morning, for the fear of his heart wherewith he shall fear, and for the sight which his eyes shall see. His life*

life shall be grievous unto him *.—Adverfity! how blunt are all the arrows of thy quiver, in comparifon with thofe of guilt!—But if fuch be the power of confcience, whence, it may be afked, comes it to pafs, that its influence is not more general, either in reftraining men from the commiffion of fin, or in leading them to a timely repentance? This brings me to obferve,

III. THAT, during a courfe of profperity, the operations of confcience are often fufpended; and that adverfity is the feafon which reftors them to their proper force. At the time when crimes are committed, the mind is too much heated by paffion, and engroffed by the object of its purfuit, to be capable of proper reflection. After this tumult of fpirits has fubfided, if a train of new paffions be at hand to employ its activity, or a fucceffion of pleafurable objects occur to engage its attention, it may for a while remain, though not entirely free from inward mifgivings, yet unconfcious of the degree of its guilt. Diffipated among the amufements of life, the finner efcapes, in fome meafure, from his own view. If he reflects upon himfelf at all, the continuance of profperity feems to him a ftrong juftification of his conduct. For it will be found, that in the hearts of all men, there is a natural propenfity to judge of the favour of the Supreme Being, from the courfe of external events. When they are borne with a fmooth gale along the ftream of life, and behold every thing proceeding according to their wifh, hardly can they be brought to believe, that Providence is their enemy. Bafking in the fun-fhine of profperity, they fuppofe themfelves to enjoy the fmile of indulgent Heaven; and fondly conclude, that they are on terms of friendfhip, with all above, and with all below. Eafy they find it, then, to fpread over the groffeft crimes a covering, thin, indeed, and flight, yet fufficient to conceal them from a fuperficial view.

Of this we have a very remarkable inftance, in thofe brethren of Jofeph, whofe hiftory we now confider. Not only from the filence of the infpired writer, we have ground to believe that their remorfe was ftifled, while their profperity remained; but we are able to trace fome of the pretences, by which, during that period, they quieted their minds. For when they were contriving the deftruction of Jofeph, we find Judah faying to his brethren, *What profit is it, if we flay our brother, and conceal his blood? Let us fell him to the Ifhmaelites; and let not our hand be upon him; for he is our brother, and our flefh: And his brethren were content* ‡. Here you behold them juftifying their crime,

* *Deut.* xxviii. 65, 66, 67. *Ifa.* xv. 4. by
‡ *Gen.* xxxvii. 26, 27.

by a fort of pretended humanity; and making light of felling their brother for a flave, becaufe they did not take away his life. How ftrangely are the opinions of men altered, by a change in their condition! How different is this fentiment of the Patriarchs, from that which they afterwards entertained of the fame action, when, as you fee in the Text, the remembrance of it wrung their hearts with anguifh?

But men, in truth, differ as much from themfelves, in profperity, and in adverfity, as if they were different creatures. In profperity, every thing tends to flatter and deceive. In adverfity, the illufions of life vanifh. Its avocations, and its pleafures, no longer afford the finner that fhelter he was wont to find from confcience. Formerly he made a part of the crowd. He now feels himfelf a folitary individual, left alone with God, and with his own mind. His fpirits are not fupported, as before, by fallacious views of the favour of Heaven. The *candle of the Lord* fhines not on his head; his pride is humbled; and his affections are foftened for receiving every ferious impreffion. In this fituation, a man's *iniquity is fure to find him out.* Whatever has been notoriously criminal in his former conduct, rifes as a fpectre, and places itfelf before him. The increafed fenfibility of his mind renders him alive to feelings which lately were faint; and wounds which had been ill healed bleed afrefh. When *men take the timbrel and the harp, and rejoice at the found of the organ, they fay, What is the Almighty that we fhould ferve him?* But when *they are holden in the cords of affliction, then he fheweth them their work, and their tranfgreffion, that they have exceeded. He openeth alfo their ears to difcipline; and commandeth, that they return from iniquity.*

Hence, we may perceive the great ufefulnefs and propriety of that interchange of conditions, which takes place in human life. By profperity, God gives fcope to our paffions, and makes trial of our difpofitions. By adverfity, he revives the ferious principle within. Neither the one, nor the other, could be borne entire and unmixed. Man, always profperous, would be giddy and infolent; always afflicted, would be fullen and defpondent. Hopes and fears, joy and forrow, are, therefore, fo blended in his life, as both to give room for worldly purfuits, and to recall, from time to time, the admonitions of confcience. Of the proportion in which they fhould be mixed for this purpofe, we are very incompetent judges. From our ignorance of the degree of difcipline, which the fpiritual ftate of others requires, we often cenfure Providence unjuftly, for its feverity towards them: And, from the vanity and rafhnefs of our wifhes, we complain, without reason, of its rigour to ourselves. While we consult nothing but our ease, God attends to our spiritual improvement. When we seek what is pleasing, he sends what is useful. When, by drinking too deep of worldly prosperity, we draw in a secret poison, he mercifully infuses a medicine, at the time that he troubles and embitters the waters. It remains now to observe,

IV. THAT when conscience is thoroughly awakened, it determines the sinner to consider every calamity which he suffers, as a positive infliction of punishment by Heaven. As it had before alarmed him with threatenings of Divine displeasure, it tells him, when he falls under distress, that the threatened day of account is come. Afflictions, on some occasions, rise directly out of our sins. Thus diseases are brought on by intemperance; poverty springs from idleness; and disgrace from presumption. In such cases, the punishment is so closely connected with the crime, that it is impossible to avoid discerning the relation which the one bears to the other. But the appointment of Providence, which we now consider, reaches farther than this. God has framed us so, that distresses, which have no perceivable connection with our former crimes, are nevertheless interpreted by conscience, to be inflicted on their account. They force themselves upon our apprehension, under this view. They are made to carry, not only that degree of pain which properly belongs to themselves, but that additional torment also, which arises from the belief of their being the vengeance of the Almighty.

Let a man fall unexpectedly into some deep calamity. Let that calamity be brought upon him, either by means which the world calls fortuitous; or by a train of incidents, in which his own misconduct, or guilt, has apparently had no part; yet one of the first questions, which, in such a situation, he puts to himself, is, What have I done to deserve this? His reflection is, almost instinctively, drawn back upon his former life; and if, in the course of that retrospect, any flagrant guilty deed occur to smite his conscience, on this he cannot avoid resting with anxiety and terrour, and connecting it in his imagination with what he now suffers. He sees, or thinks that he sees, a Divine arm lifted up; and what, in other circumstances, he would have called a reverse of fortune, he now views as a judgment of Heaven.

When the brethren of Joseph, confined in the Egyptian prison, were bewailing the distress into which they had fallen, there was no circumstance which pointed out any relation between their present misfortune, and their former cruelty to their brother. A long course of years had intervened, during which they flourished in wealth and ease. They were now far from the scene of their crime; in a foreign land, where they believed themselves utterly unknown, and where they had done nothing to offend. But conscience formed a connexion between events, which, according to the ordinary apprehension of men, were entirely independent of each other. It made them recollect, that they, who once had been deaf to the supplications of a brother, were now left friendless and forlorn, imploring pity in vain from an unrelenting Governour; and that they who had first conspired to kill their brother, and afterwards sold him for a slave, were themselves deprived of liberty, and threatened with an ignominious death. How undeservedly soever these evils befell them on the part of men, they confessed them to be just on the part of Providence. They concluded the hour of retribution to be arrived; and, in the person of the Governour of Egypt, they beheld the Ruler of the world calling them to account for guilt. *Therefore is this distress come upon us. Behold also his blood is required.*

Similar sentiments on like occasions, will be found not uncommon among mankind. Pious men, there is no doubt, are at all times disposed to look up to God, and to acknowledge his hand in every event of life. But what I now observe is, That where no habitual acknowledgment of God takes place; nay where a daring contempt of his authority has prevailed, conscience, nevertheless, constrains men, in the day of their distress, to recognize God, under the most awful of all characters, The avenger of past guilt.

Herein the wisdom of God appears in such a light, as justly to claim our highest admiration. The ordinary course of his Providence is carried on by human means. He has settled a train of events, which proceed in a regular succession of causes and effects, without his appearing to interpose, or to act. But these, on proper occasions, are made to affect the human mind, in the same manner as if he were beheld descending from his throne, to punish the sinner with his own hand. Were God to suspend the laws of Nature, on occasion of every great crime that was committed on earth, and to govern the world by frequent interpositions of a miraculous kind, the whole order of human affairs would be unhinged; no plans of action could be formed; and no scope would be given for the probation and trial of men. On the other hand, were the operation of second causes allowed to conceal a Divine hand totally from view, all sense of superior government would be lost; the world would seem to be void of God; the sinner would perceive nothing but chance and fortune

tune in the diftreffes which he fuffered. Whereas, by its being fo ordered, that feveral incidents of life fhall carry the fame force, and ftrike the mind with the fame impreffion, as if they were fupernatural interpofitions, the fear of God is kept alive among men, and the order of human affairs is, at the fame time, preferved unbroken. The finner fees his diftrefs to be the immediate effect of human violence or oppreffion; and is obliged, at the fame moment, to confider it as a Divine judgment. His confcience gives to an ordinary misfortune, all the edge and the fting of a vifitation from Heaven.

FROM the train of thought which the Text has fuggefted, feveral inferences naturally follow. But I fhall confine myfelf to two, which claim your particular attention.

The firft is, the clear evidence which the preceding obfervations afford, of a Divine government now exercifed over mankind. This moft important and awful of all truths, cannot be too often prefented to our view, or too ftrongly impreffed on our mind. To the imperfect conviction of it, which obtains in the world, muft be afcribed, in a great meafure, the prevalence of fin. Did men firmly believe that the Almighty Being, who formed them, is carrying on a fyftem of adminiftration which will not leave guilt unpunifhed, it is impoffible that they could remain fo inattentive, as we often behold them, to their moral conduct. But the bulk of mankind are giddy and thoughtlefs. Struck by the fuperficial appearances of pleafure, which accompany licentioufnefs, they inquire no farther; and deliver themfelves up to their fenfes and their paffions. Whereas, were they to reflect, but for a moment, upon that view which has now been given of human nature, they might foon be fatisfied, that the moral government of God is no matter of doubtful difcuffion. It is a fact, no lefs obvious and inconteftable, than the government exercifed by thofe earthly rulers, whom we behold with the enfigns of their office before our eyes.

To govern, is to require a certain courfe of action, or, to prefcribe a law; and to enforce that law by a fuitable diftribution of rewards and punifhments. Now, God has not only invefted confcience, as we have feen, with authority to promulgate, but endowed it alfo with power to enforce, his law. By placing inward approbation and peace on the fide of virtue, he gave it the fanction of reward. But this was not enough. Pain is a more powerful principle than pleafure. To efcape mifery is a ftronger motive for action, than to obtain good. God, therefore, fo framed human nature, that the

painful

painful sense of ill-desert should attend the commission of crimes; that this sense of ill-desert should necessarily produce the dread of punishment; and that this dread should so operate on the mind, in the time of distress, as to make the sinner conceive Providence to be engaged against him, and to be concerned in inflicting the punishment which he suffers. All these impressions he hath stamped upon the heart with his own hand. He hath made them constituent parts of our frame; on purpose, that by the union of so many strong and pungent sentiments, he might enforce repentance and reformation, and publish to the human race his detestation of sin. Were he to speak to us from the clouds, his voice could not be more decisive. What we discern to be interwoven with the contexture of human nature, and to pervade the whole course of human affairs, carries an evidence not to be resisted. We might, with as much reason, doubt whether the sun was intended to enlighten the earth, or the rain to fertilize it; as whether he who has framed the human mind, intended to announce righteousness to mankind, as his law.

THE second inference which I make from the foregoing discourse, respects the intimate connexion, which those operations of conscience have, with the peculiar and distinguishing doctrines of the Gospel of Christ. They will be found to accord with them so remarkably, as to furnish an answer to some of those objections, which superficial reasoners are apt to raise against the Christian revelation. In particular, they coincide with that awful view which the Gospel gives us, of the future consequences of guilt. If the sinner is now constrained by conscience, to view the Almighty as pursuing him with evil for long-forgotten crimes, how naturally must he conclude that, in a subsequent period of existence, the Divine administration will proceed upon the same plan, and complete what has been left imperfect here? If, during this life, which is only the time of trial, the displeasure of Providence at sin is displayed by tokens so manifest, what may be apprehended to follow, when justice, which at present only begins to be executed, shall be carried to its consummation? What conscience forebodes, revelation verifies; assuring us that a day is appointed, when *God will render to every man according to his works; to them, who by patient continuance in well-doing, seek for glory, honour, and immortality; eternal life: But unto them that are contentious, and obey not the truth, but obey unrighteousness; indignation and wrath, tribulation and anguish, upon every soul of man that doth evil, of the Jew first, and also of the Gentile. For there is no respect of persons with God. For as many*

as

as have sinned without the law, shall also perish without the law; and as many as have sinned in the law, shall be judged by the law *.

While the threatenings of conscience thus strengthen the evidence of the scripture doctrine concerning future punishments, they likewise pave the way for the belief of what is revealed concerning the method of our deliverance by Christ. They suggest to the sinner, some deep and dark malignity contained in guilt, which has drawn upon his head such high displeasure from Heaven. They call forth his most anxious efforts, to avert the effects of that displeasure; and to propitiate his offended Judge. Some atonement, he is conscious, must be made; and the voice of Nature has, in every age, loudly demanded suffering, as the proper atonement for guilt. Hence mankind have constantly fled for refuge to such substitutions, as they could devise to place in the room of the offender; and, as by general consent, victims have every where been slain, and expiatory sacrifices have been offered up on innumerable altars. *Wherewith shall I come before the Lord, and bow myself before the most high God? Shall I come before him with burnt offerings, and calves of a year old? Will the Lord be pleased with thousands of rams, or with ten thousands of rivers of oil? Or, shall I give my first-born for my transgression; the fruit of my body, for the sin of my soul* † ? These perplexities and agitations of a guilty conscience, may be termed preludes, in some measure, to the Gospel of Christ. They are the pointings of unenlightened Nature, towards that method of relief, which the grace of God has provided. Nature felt its inability to extricate itself from the consequences of guilt: The Gospel reveals the plan of Divine interposition and aid. Nature confessed some atonement to be necessary: The Gospel discovers, that the necessary atonement is made. The remedy is no sooner presented, than its suitableness to the disease appears; and the great mystery of redemption, though it reaches, in its full extent, beyond our comprehension, yet, as far as it is revealed, holds a visible congruity with the sentiments of Conscience, and of Nature.

Natural and revealed religion proceed from the same Author; and, of course, are analogous and consistent. They are part of the same plan of Providence. They are connected measures of the same system of government. The serious belief of the one, is the best preparation for the reception of the other. Both concur in impressing our mind with a deep sense of one most important truth, which is the result of this whole discourse, That as *we sow now we must reap;* that under the government of God, no one shall be permitted, with impunity, to gratify his criminal passions, and to make light of the great duties of life.

* *Rom.* ii. 7—13. † *Micah,* vi. 6, 7.   SERMON

SERMON XIV.

On the Mixture of JOY and FEAR in RELIGION.

PSALM ii. 11.

Rejoice with trembling.

JOY and Fear, are two great springs of human action. The mixed condition of this world, gives scope for both; and, according as the one or the other predominates, it influences the general tenour of our conduct. Each of them possesses a proper place in religion. To *serve the Lord with gladness*, is the exhortation of the Psalmist David [*]. To *serve him with reverence and godly fear*, is the admonition of the Apostle Paul [†]. But, under the present imperfection of human nature, each of these principles may be carried to a dangerous extreme. When the whole of religion is placed in joy, it is in hazard of rising into unwarrantable rapture. When it rests altogether on fear, it degenerates into superstitious servility. The Text enjoins a due mixture of both; and inculcates this important maxim, That joy, tempered with fear, is the proper disposition of a good man. In discoursing of this subject, I shall endeavour to show, first, That joy is essential to religion; and next, That, for various reasons, this joy ought to be mixed with fear; whence we shall be able to ascertain the nature of that steady and composed spirit, which is most suitable to our present condition, and most acceptable to God.

I. JOY is essential to religion, in two respects; as religion inspires joy, and as it requires it. In other words; To rejoice is both the privilege, and the duty, of good men.

IN the first place, Religion inspires joy. It affords just ground of gladness, to all who firmly believe its doctrines, and sincerely study to obey its laws. For it confers on them the two most material requisites of joy; a favourable situation of things without, and a proper disposition of mind within, to relish that favourable situation.

When they examine their situation without, they behold themselves placed in a world which is full of the influence of a gracious

* *Psalm.* c. 2.   † *Heb.* xii. 28.   Providence;

On the Mixture of -

Providence; where beauty and good are every where predominant; where various comforts are bestowed; and where, if any be withheld, they have reason to believe that they are with-held by parental wisdom. Among the crowd that encompass them, they may be at a loss to discern, who are their friends, and who their enemies. But it is sufficient to know, that they are under the protection of an invisible Guardian, whose power can keep them from every evil. All the steps of his conduct, they may be unable to trace. Events may befal them, of which they can give no account. But as long as they are satisfied, that the system of Divine government is founded on mercy, no present occurrences are able to destroy their peace. *For he who spared not his own Son, but delivered him up for them, how shall he not with him freely give them all things?* If their nature is frail, Divine assistance is promised to strengthen it. If their virtue is imperfect, a dispensation is opened, which gives them the hope of pardon. If their external circumstances be in any respect unfavourable, it is because a higher interest is consulted. *All things,* they are assured, *shall work together for their good.* On their prosperity rests, the blessing; on their adversity, the sanctifying Spirit of the Almighty. Old age may advance, and life decay; but beyond those boundaries of Nature, faith opens the prospect of their lasting felicity. Without anxiety, they pass through the different periods of their present existence, because they know it to be no more than an introduction to immortality.

As such a situation of things without, lays a solid foundation for joy; so the disposition which religion forms within, promotes the relish of it. It is indeed from within, that the chief sources of enjoyment or trouble rise. The minds of bad men are always disorderly; and hence their lives are so generally uneasy. In vain *they take the timbrel and the harp, and endeavour to rejoice at the sound of the organ.* Spleen and disgust pursue them, through all the haunts of amusement. Pride and ill humour torment them. Oppressed with discontent, their spirits flag; and their worn-out pleasures afford them entertainment no more. But religion subdues those malignant passions, which are the troublers of human repose; which either overcast the mind with the gloom of peevishness, or disquiet it by the violence of agitation. It infuses, in their room, those mild and gentle dispositions, whose natural effect is to smooth the tenour of the soul. Benevolence and candour, moderation and temperance, wherever they reign, produce cheerfulness and serenity. The consciousness of integrity gives ease and freedom to the mind. It enables good men to extract from every

every object, the whole satisfaction which it is capable of yielding; and adds the flavour of innocence, to all their external pleasures.

In the second place, As religion naturally inspires joy; so, what it inspires, it commands us to cherish. As a necessary proof of our sincerity, it requires cheerfulness in the performance of our duty; because, if this be wanting, our religion discovers itself not to be genuine in principle, and in practice it cannot be stable.

Religious obedience, destitute of joy, is not genuine in its principle. For, did either faith or hope, the love of God, or the love of goodness, rule the heart, they could not fail to produce satisfaction in piety and virtue. All those causes of joy which I have mentioned would then operate; and their native effect on the mind, would follow. The prospects which religion opens, would gladden, and the affections which it inspires, would sooth the heart. We serve, with pleasure, the benefactor whom we love. We rejoice in every study and pursuit, to which we are sincerely attached. If we serve not God with pleasure, it is because we know him not, or love him not. If we rejoice not in virtue, it is because our affection is alienated from it, and our inclinations are depraved. We give too evident proof, that either we believe not the principles of religion, or that we feel not their power. Exclude joy from religion; and you leave no other motives to it, except compulsion and interest. But are these suitable grounds, on which to rest the whole of our obedience to the Supreme Being? *My son, give me thy heart,* is the call of God. Surely if there be no pleasure in fulfilling his commands, the heart is not given him; and, in that case, *the multitude of sacrifices and burnt offerings* is brought to his altar in vain.

As religion, destitute of joy, is imperfect in its principle; so, in practice, it must be unstable. In vain you endeavour to fix any man to the regular performance of that, in which he finds no pleasure. Bind him ever so fast by interest or fear, he will contrive some method of eluding the obligation. Ingenuity is never so fertile of evasions, as where pleasure is all on the one side, and mere precept on the other. He may study to save appearances. He may dissemble and constrain himself. But his heart revolts in secret; and the weight of inclination will, in the end, draw the practice after it. If perseverance is not to be expected, still less can zeal be looked for from him, who, in his religious duties, trembles without rejoicing. Every attempt towards virtue which he forms will be feeble and awkward. He applies to it as a task; he dreads the task-master; but he will labour no more than necessity enjoins. To escape from punishment is his sole aim. He bargains for immunity, by every duty which he performs; and all beyond, he esteems superfluous toil.—Such religion as this, can neither purify the heart, nor prepare for heavenly bliss. It is the refuge of an abject mind. It may form the ritual of the monk, or prescribe the penance of the idolater; but has no concern with the homage of him, who *worships the Father in spirit and in truth.* His character is, that the *joy of the Lord is his strength**. It attaches his heart to religion. It inspires his zeal. It supports his constancy; and accelerates his progress.

There is no man but has some object to which he cleaves for enjoyment; somewhat that flatters him with distant hope, or affords him present pleasure. Joy is the end towards which all rational beings tend. For the sake of it, they live; it resembles the air they breathe, which is necessary for the motion of the heart, and all the vital functions. But as the breathing of infected air proves fatal to life; in the same manner joy, drawn from a corrupted source, is destructive, both of virtue and of true happiness. When you have no pleasure in goodness, you may with certainty conclude the reason to be, that your pleasure is all derived from an opposite quarter. You have exhausted your affection upon the world. You have drunk too much of its poisoned waters, to have any relish for a pure spring.

Estimate, therefore, the genuineness of your religious principles; estimate the degree of your stability in religious practice, by the degree of your satisfaction in piety and virtue. Be assured, that where your treasure is, there will your delight be also. The worldly man rejoices in his possessions; the voluptuous in his pleasures; the social in his friends and companions. The truly good man rejoices in *doing justly, loving mercy, and walking humbly with the Lord his God.* He is happy, when employed in the regular discharge of the great duties of life. Spontaneous they flow from the affections of a pure heart. Not only from the keeping of the divine commandments he expects, but *in the keeping of them*, he enjoys *a great reward.*—Accordingly, in the sentiments of holy men recorded in scripture, we find this spirit every-where prevalent. Their language was; *Thy statutes have I taken as mine heritage for ever; for they are the rejoicing of my heart. They are my songs in the house of my pilgrimage. They are sweeter than honey, and the honey-comb. Whom have I in heaven but thee? And there is none upon earth that I desire besides thee.* They did not receive the spirit of bondage, but the spirit of adoption. They were filled

* Neh. viii. 10.

with

Joy and Fear in Religion.

with peace and joy in believing. They rejoiced in hope of the glory of God. As soon as the Æthiopian eunuch received from Philip the light of the Gospel, that light revived and cheered his heart. A new sun seemed to arise; a new glory to shine around him. Every object brightened; *and he went on his way rejoicing* *. After the same manner should every good man proceed in his journey through life, with a serene and cheerful spirit. Consternation and dejection let him leave to the slaves of guilt; who have every thing to dread, both from this world and the next. If he appear before others with a dispirited aspect, he dishonours religion; and affords ground for suspicion, that he is either ignorant of its nature or a stranger to its power.

Thus I have shown joy to be essential to religion. It is the spirit which it inspires, and which it requires, in good men. But in our present state, the best principles may be carried to a dangerous excess; and joy, like other things, has its due limits. To serve God with unmixed delight, belongs to more advanced spirits in a happier world. In this region of imperfection, some infusions from a different cup, must of necessity tincture our joy. Let us then,

II. TURN to the other side of the argument, and consider the reasons which render it proper, that when we rejoice, we should *rejoice with trembling*.

In the first place, because all the objects of religion, which afford ground for joy, tend to inspire, at the same time, reverence and fear. We serve a Benefactor, it is true, in whom we have reason to delight; whose purposes are gracious; whose law is the plan of our happiness. But this Benefactor, is the King *eternal, immortal, and invisible;* at whose presence the mountains shake, and Nature trembles. *Every good, and every perfect gift, come down from him.* But the hand which confers them, we cannot see. Mysterious obscurity rests upon his essence. He dwelleth *in the secret place of thunder;* and clouds and darkness surround him. He is the *Hearer of prayer;* but we lift our voice to him from afar. Into his immediate presence no access is permitted. Our warmest devotion admits no familiarity with him. *God is in heaven, and thou upon earth; therefore, let thy words be few.* If his omniscience administers comfort in our secret distress, it likewise fills with awe the heart that is conscious of guilt. For, if he *knows our frame, and remembers we are dust; our iniquities,* also, *are ever before him: our secret sins, in the light of his countenance.*

Throughout all his dispensations, greatness, in conjunction with goodness, strikes our view; and wherever we behold the Parent, we

* *Acts,* viii. 39. behold

behold the Legiflator alfo. The death of Chrift, in behalf of a guilty world, is the chief ground of religious hope and joy. But it is no lefs the ground of reverence; when, in this high tranfaction, we contemplate God, as at once ftrict in juftice, and great in mercy. *I the Lord keep mercy for thoufands of them that fear me. I forgive their iniquity, tranfgreffion, and fin; but I will by no means clear the guilty.* When we open the book of the Law, we find promifes and threatenings mingled in the fame page. On the one fide, we fee Heaven difplayed in all its glory: On the other, Hell opening its terrours. In fhort, in whatever light we view religion, it appears folemn and venerable. It is a temple full of majefty, to which the worfhippers may approach with comfort, in the hope of *obtaining grace, and finding mercy;* but where they cannot enter, without being impreffed with awe. If we may be permitted to compare fpiritual with natural things, religion refembles not thofe fcenes of natural beauty, where every object fmiles. It cannot be likened to the gay landfcape, or the flowery field. It refembles more the auguft and fublime appearances of Nature; the lofty mountain, the expanded ocean, and the ftarry firmament; at the fight of which, the mind is at once overawed and delighted; and, from the union of grandeur with beauty, derives a pleafing, but a ferious, emotion.

In the fecond place, As joy, tempered by fear, fuits the nature of religion, fo it is requifite for the proper regulation of the conduct of man. Let his joy flow from the beft and pureft fource; yet, if it remain long unmixed, it is apt to become dangerous to virtue. As waters which are never ftirred, nor troubled, gather a fediment, which putrifies them; fo the undifturbed continuance of placid fenfations engenders diforders in the human foul. It is wifely ordered in our prefent ftate, that joy and fear, hope and grief, fhould act alternately, as checks and balances upon each other, in order to prevent an excefs in any of them, which our nature could not bear. If we were fubject to no alarms of danger, the wifeft would foon become improvident; and the moft humble, prefumptuous. Man is a pilgrim on earth. Were his path to be always fmooth and flowery, he would be tempted to relinquifh his guide, and to forget the purpofe of his journey. Caution and fear are the fhields of happinefs. Unguarded joy begets indolence; indolence produces fecurity; fecurity leads to rafhnefs; and rafhnefs ends in ruin. In order to rejoice long, it is neceffary that we *rejoice with trembling.* Had our firft parents obferved this rule, man might have been ftill in paradife. He who faith

in

in his heart, *My mountain stands strong; I shall never be moved;* may be assured, that his state already begins to totter. Religion, therefore, performs a kind office, in giving us the admonition of the Text. It inspires cheerfulness in the service of God. It proposes joy, as our chief spring of action. But it supports joy, by guarding it with fear; not suppressing, but regulating its indulgence; requiring us to rejoice, like persons who have obtained a treasure, which, through want of vigilance, they are exposed to lose. Dependent beings are formed for submission; and to submit, is to stand in awe. *Because the Lord reigneth, let the earth be glad.* We are the subjects of God; and therefore may justly rejoice. But still we are subjects; and, therefore, trembling must mix itself with our joy.

In the third place, The unstable condition of all human things, naturally inspires fear in the midst of joy. The spirit to which religion forms us, must undoubtedly correspond to the state in which we are placed, and to the part which is assigned us to act. Now, the first view under which our present state appears, is that of fallen creatures, who are undergoing in this world, probation and trial for their recovery; and are commanded to *work out their salvation with fear and trembling.* This view of our condition infers not habitual dejection of mind. It requires not melancholy abstraction from the affairs, or total contempt of the amusements of life. But it inspires humility. It enforces dependence on divine aid; and calls forth the voice of supplication to Heaven. In a situation so critical, and where interests so important are at stake, every reasonable person must confess, that seriousness ought to temper rejoicing.

Were there in human life any fixed point of stability and rest, attainable by man; could we, at any one moment, assure ourselves, that there remained no latent source of danger, either to our temporal, or our spiritual state; then I admit we might lay trembling aside, and rejoice in full security. But, alas! no such safe station, no such moment of confidence, is allowed to man during his warfare on earth. Vicissitudes of good and evil, of trials and consolations, fill up his life. The best intentioned are sometimes betrayed into crimes; the most prudent, overwhelmed with misfortunes. The world is like a wheel incessantly revolving, on which human things alternately rise and fall. What is past of our life has been a chequered scene. On its remaining periods, uncertainty and darkness rest. Futurity is an unknown region, into which no man can look forward without awe, because he cannot tell what forms of danger or trial may meet him there. This we know well, that in every period of our life, the path of happiness

shall

shall be found steep and arduous; but swift and easy the descent to ruin. What, with much exertion of care and vigilance, we had built up, one unwary action may, in an evil hour, overthrow. The props of human confidence are, in general, insecure. The sphere of human pleasures is narrow. While we form schemes for strengthening the one, and for enlarging the other, death, mean-while, advances. Life, with a swift, though insensible course, glides away; and, like a river which undermines its banks, gradually impairs our state. Year after year steals something from us; till the decaying fabric totter of itself, and crumble at length into dust. So that, whether we consider life or death, time or eternity, all things appear to concur in giving to man the admonition of the text, *Rejoice with trembling*.

I HAVE now shown, in what respects religion both promotes joy, and inspires seriousness. It places us in the most favourable situation, which human life affords, for joy; and it gives us every assistance, for relishing that joy. It renders it our duty to cultivate the satisfaction which it yields. It demands a cheerful spirit, in order to ascertain the sincerity of our principles, and to confirm us in good practice. At the same time the joy which it inspires, is tempered with fear by the genius of religion itself; by the danger to which unguarded joy would expose us; and by the impropriety of indulging it, in a situation so mixed as the present. The *trembling* which is here enjoined, is not to be understood as signifying a pusillanimous dejection. It imports no more than that caution and sobriety, which prudence dictates, as belonging to our state. By connecting such trembling with our joy, religion means to recommend to us, a cheerful, but a composed, spirit, equally remote from the humiliating depression of fear, and the exulting levity of joy. Always to rejoice, is to be a fool. Always to tremble, is to be a slave. It is a modest cheerfulness, a chastened joy, a manly seriousness, which becomes the servant of God.

BUT is this, it may perhaps be said, the whole amount of that boasted satisfaction which religion bestows? Is this all the compensation which it makes, for those sacrifices it exacts? Are not the terms which vice holds out far more enticing, when it permits us to gratify every desire; and, in return for our surmounting the timorous scruples of conscience, promises us a life of gaiety, festivity, and unrestrained joy?———Such promises vice may indeed make; but, how far it fulfils them, we may safely refer to the determination of the greatest sensualist, when he has finished his carreer, and looks back on what

he

he has enjoyed. Afk him, Whether he would recommend to his children, and his friends, to hold the fame courfe; and whether, with his dying breath, he dare affure them, that the gratifications of licentioufnefs afford the greatelt enjoyment of life? Whatever hopes vice may at the beginning infpire, yet, after the trial is made, it has been always found that criminal pleafures are the bane of happinefs, the poifon, not the cordial, of our prefent ftate. They are pleafures compenfated by an infinite overbalance of pain; moments of delight, fucceeded by years of regret; purchafed at the expence of injured reputation, broken health, and ruined peace. Even abftracting from their pernicious confequences, they are, for moft part, in themfelves treacherous pleafures; unfound and difturbed in the moments of enjoyment. *In the midft of fuch laughter, the heart is forrowful.* Often is the fmile of gaiety affumed, while the heart akes within: And though folly may laugh, guilt will fting. Correcting this pernicious phrenzy of pleafure, and reducing it to a more fober and regulated ftate, religion is, in truth, no other than wifdom; introducing peace and order into the life of man.

While religion condemns fuch pleafures as are immoral, it is chargeable with no improper aufterity, in refpect of thofe which are of an innocent kind. Think not, that by the cautious difcipline which it prefcribes, it excludes you from all gay enjoyment of life. Within the compafs of that fedate fpirit, to which it forms you, all that is innocently pleafing will be found to lie. It is a miftake to imagine, that in conftant affufions of giddy mirth, or in that flutter of fpirits which is excited by a round of diverfions, the chief enjoyment of our ftate confifts. Were this the cafe, the vain and the frivolous would be on better terms for happinefs, than the wife, the great, and the good. To arrange the plans of amufement, or to prefide in the haunts of jollity, would be more defirable than to exert the higheft effort of mental powers for the benefit of nations. A confequence fo abfurd, is fufficient to explode the principle from which it flows. To the amufements and leffer joys of the world, religion affigns their proper place. It admits of them, as relaxations from care, as inftruments of promoting the union of men, and of enlivening their focial intercourfe. But though, as long as they are kept within due bounds, it does not cenfure nor condemn them; neither does it propofe them as rewards to the virtuous, or as the principal objects of their purfuit. To fuch, it points out nobler ends of action. Their felicity it engages them to feek, in the difcharge of an ufeful, an upright, and honourable,

nourable part in life; and, as the habitual tenour of their mind, it promotes cheerfulness, and discourages levity.

Between these two there is a wide distinction; and the mind which is most open to levity, is frequently a stranger to cheerfulness. It has been remarked, that transports of intemperate mirth, are often no more than flashes from the dark cloud; and that in proportion to the violence of the effulgence, is the succeeding gloom. Levity may be the forced production of folly or vice; cheerfulness is the natural offspring of wisdom and virtue only. The one is an occasional agitation; the other a permanent habit. The one degrades the character; the other is perfectly consistent with the dignity of reason, and the steady and manly spirit of religion. To aim at a constant succession of high and vivid sensations of pleasure, is an idea of happiness altogether chimerical. Calm and temperate enjoyment, is the utmost that is allotted to man. Beyond this, we struggle in vain to raise our state; and, in fact, depress our joys, by endeavouring to heighten them. Instead of those fallacious hopes of perpetual festivity, with which the world would allure us, religion confers upon us a cheerful tranquility. Instead of dazzling us with meteors of joy, which sparkle and expire, it sheds around us a calm and steady light. By mixing *trembling* with our joy, it renders that joy more solid, more equal, and more lasting.

In this spirit, then, let us serve God, and hold our course through life. Let us approach to the Divine Being, as to a sovereign of whom we stand in awe, and to a father in whom we trust. In our conduct, let us be cautious and humble, as those who have ground to fear; well pleased and cheerful, as those who have cause to rejoice. Let us show the world, that a religious temper, is a temper sedate, not sad; that a religious behaviour, is a behaviour regulated, not stiff and formal. Thus we shall *use the world, as not abusing it;* we shall pass through its various changes, with the least discompofure; and we shall vindicate religion from the reproaches of those who would attribute to it either enthusiastic joys or slavish terrours. We shall show, that it is a rational rule of life, worthy of the perfection of God, and suited to the nature and state of man.

SERMON

SERMON XV.

On the Motives to CONSTANCY in VIRTUE.

GALAT. vi. 9.

And let us not be weary in well-doing; for in due season we shall reap, if we faint not.

DISCONTENT is the moſt general of all the evils which trouble the life of man. It is a diſeaſe, which every where finds materials to feed itſelf; for if real diſtreſſes be wanting, it ſubſtitutes ſuch as are imaginary in their place. It converts even the good things of the world, when they have been long enjoyed, into occaſions of diſguſt. In the midſt of proſperity, it diſpoſes us to complain; and renders tranquility tireſome, only becauſe it is uniform. There is no wonder that this ſpirit of reſtleſſneſs and diſſatisfaction, which corrupts every terreſtrial enjoyment, ſhould have ſometimes penetrated into the region of virtue. Good men are not without their frailties; and the perverſeneſs incident to human nature, too readily leads us, who become weary of all other things, to *be weary, alſo, in well-doing.*

Let me put a caſe, which, perhaps, will be found not unfrequent in ordinary life. Suppoſe a perſon, after much commerce with the world, to be convinced of its vanity. He has ſeen its moſt flattering hopes to be fallacious. He has felt its moſt boaſted pleaſures to be unſatisfactory. He reſolves, therefore, to place his happineſs in virtue; and, diſregarding all temptations from intereſt, to adhere to what is right and honourable in conduct. He cultivates acquaintance with religion. He performs, with ſerioufneſs, the offices of devotion. He lays down to himſelf, a rational and uſeful plan of life; and, with ſatisfaction, holds on for a while in this reformed courſe. But, by degrees, diſcouragements ariſe. The peace which he hoped to enjoy, is interrupted, either by his own frailties, or by the vices of others. Paſſions, which had not been thoroughly ſubdued, ſtruggle for their accuſtomed gratification. The pleaſure which he expected to to find in devotion, sometimes fails him; and the injustice of the world often sours and frets him. Friends prove ungrateful; enemies misrepresent, rivals supplant him: And part, at least, of the mortifications which he suffers, he begins to ascribe to virtue.——Is this all the reward of my serving God, and renouncing the pleasures of sin? *Verily, in vain I have cleansed my heart, and washed my hands in innocency. Behold, the ungodly prosper in the world, and have more than heart can wish; while, all the day long, I am plagued and chastened every morning.*—To such persons as these, and to all who are in hazard of being infected with their spirit, I now address myself. In reply to their complaints, I propose to show, That in no state they can chuse on earth, by no plan of conduct they can form, it is possible for them to escape uneasiness and disappointment; that in a life of virtue, they will suffer less uneasiness, and fewer disappointments, than in a course of vice; they will possess much higher resources and advantages; and they will be assured of complete reward at the end. From these considerations, I hope to make it appear, that there is no sufficient reason for our being *weary in well-doing;* and that, taking human life upon the whole, Virtue is far the most eligible portion of man.

I. UNEASINESS and disappointment are inseparable, in some degree, from every state on earth. Were it in the power of the world, to render those who attach themselves to it, satisfied and happy, you might then, I admit, have some title to complain, if you found yourselves placed upon worse terms in the service of God. But this is so far from being the case, that among the multitudes who devote themselves to earthly pleasure, you will not find a single person who has completely attained his aim. Enquire into the condition of the high and the low, of the gay and the serious, of the men of business and the men of pleasure, and you shall behold them all occupied in supplying some want, or in removing some distress. No man is pleased with being precisely what he is. Everywhere there is a void; generally, even in the most prosperous life, there is some corner possessed by sorrow. He who is engaged in business, pines for leisure. He who enjoys leisure, languishes for want of employment. In a single state, we envy the comforts of a family. In conjugal life, we are chagrined with domestic cares. In a safe station, we regret the want of objects for enterprise. In an enterprising life, we lament the want of safety. It is the doom of man, that his sky should never be free from all clouds. He is, at

present,

present, in an exiled and fallen state. The objects which surround him, are beneath his native dignity. God has tinged them all with vanity, on purpose to make him feel, that this is not his rest; that here he is not in his proper place, nor arrived at his true home.

If, therefore, you aim at a condition which shall be exempted from every disquiet, you pursue a phantom; you increase the vanity and vexation of life, by engaging in a chase so fruitless. If you complain of virtue, because there is incident to it a portion of that uneasiness which is found in every other state, your complaint is most unreasonable. You claim an immunity from evil, which belongs not to the lot of man. Reconcile yourselves, then, to your condition; and, instead of looking for perfect happiness any where on earth, gladly embrace that state which contains the fewest sorrows.

II. THOUGH no condition of human life is free from uneasiness, I contend, That the uneasiness belonging to a sinful course, is far greater than what attends a course of well-doing. If you be weary of the labours of virtue, be assured, that the world, whenever you try the exchange, will lay upon you a much heavier load. It is the outside, only, of a licentious life, which is gay and smiling. Within, it conceals toil, and trouble, and deadly sorrow. For vice poisons human happiness in the spring, by introducing disorder into the heart. Those passions which it seems to indulge, it only feeds with imperfect gratifications; and thereby strengthens them for preying, in the end, on their unhappy victims.

It is a great mistake to imagine, that the pain of self-denial is confined to virtue. He who follows the world as much as he who follows Christ, must *take up his cross;* and to him, assuredly, it will prove a more oppressive burden. Vice allows all our passions to range uncontrolled; and where each claims to be superiour, it is impossible to gratify all. The predominant desire can only be indulged at the expence of its rival. No mortifications which virtue exacts, are more severe than those, which ambition imposes upon the love of ease, pride upon interest, and covetousness upon vanity. Self-denial, therefore, belongs, in common, to vice and virtue; but with this remarkable difference, that the passions which virtue requires us to mortify, it tends to weaken; whereas, those which vice obliges us to deny, it, at the same time, strengthens. The one diminishes the pain of self-denial, by moderating the demand of passion; the other increases it, by rendering those demands imperious and violent. What distresses, that occur in the calm life of virtue, can be compared ed to those tortures, which remorse of conscience inflicts on the wicked; to those severe humiliations, arising from guilt combined with misfortunes, which sink them to the dust; to those violent agitations of shame and disappointment, which sometimes drive them to the most fatal extremities, and make them abhor their existence? How often, in the midst of those disastrous situations, into which their crimes have brought them, have they cursed the seductions of vice; and, with bitter regret, looked back to the day on which they first forsook the path of innocence!

But, perhaps, you imagine, that to such miseries as these, great criminals only are exposed; and that, by a wary and cautious management, it is possible to avoid them. Take vice and virtue, then, in the most general point of view. Compare God and the world as two masters, the one or other of whom you must obey; and consider fairly, in whose service there will be reason for your being weary soonest, and repenting most frequently. The world is both a hard and a capricious master. To submit to a long servitude, in the view of a recompence from which they are excluded in the end, is known to be often the fate of those, who are devoted to the world. They sacrifice their present ease to their future prospects. They court the great, and flatter the multitude. They prostitute their conscience, and dishonour their character: And, after all their efforts, how uncertain is their success! Competitors justle, and outstrip them. The more artful deceive, the more violent overthrow them. Fair prospects once smiled; but clouds soon gather; the sky is darkened; the scene changes; and that fickle world, which, a moment before, had flattered, the next moment forgets them.

God is never mistaken in the character of his servants; for *he seeth their hearts, and judgeth according to the truth.* But the world is often deceived in those who court its favour; and, of course, is unjust in the distribution of its rewards. Flattery gains the ear of power. Fraud supplants innocence; and the pretending and assuming occupy the place of the worthy and the modest. In vain you claim any merit with the world, on account of your good intentions. The world knows them not; regards them not. It judges of you solely by your actions; and, what is worse, by the success of your actions, which often depends not on yourselves. But, in the sight of the Supreme Being, good intentions supply the place of good deeds, which you had not the opportunity of performing. The well-meant

endeavours

endeavours of the poor find the same acceptance with him, as the generous actions of the rich. The *widow's mite* is, in his eye, a costly offering; and even he *who giveth to a disciple a cup of cold water, when he can give him no more, goeth not without his reward.*

As the world is unjust in its judgments, so it is ungrateful in its requitals. Time speedily effaces the memory of the greatest services; and when we can repeat them no more, we are neglected, and thrown aside. It was the saying of a noted great man of the world, on the fall of his fortunes, "Had I served God as faithfully "as I have done my King, he would not have cast me off in my old "age." Unfaithfulness, and ingratitude, are unknown to God. With him no new favourites arise, to usurp the place, or to bear off the rewards, of his ancient servants. *Even to your old age, I am He; and even to hoary hairs, I will carry you. I have made, and I will bear; even I will carry, and will deliver you, saith the Lord Almighty.**—Since, then, in our several departments, we must labour, What comparison is there, between labouring for God, and for the world? How unjust are they, who become weary so much sooner in the service of God, than they do in that of the most severe and imperious of all masters!

III. THE resources of virtue are much greater than those of the world; the compensations which it makes for our distresses, far more valuable. Perpetual success belongs neither to the one, nor the other. But under disappointments, when they occur, virtue bears us up; the world allows us to sink. When the mind of a good man is hurt by misfortunes, religion administers the cordial, and infuses the balm. Whereas the world inflicts wounds, and then leaves them to fester. It brings sorrows, but it provides no consolation. Consolation is entirely the province of religion. Supposing religion to be inferiour to vice in external advantages, it must be allowed to possess internal peace in a much higher degree. This is so certain, that almost all men, at some period or other of their life, look forward to it, as to a desirable retreat. When the ends of their present pursuit shall be accomplished, they propose to themselves much satisfaction, in an honourable discharge of the duties of their station, amidst those moderate passions, and temperate pleasures, which innocence allows. That which all men agree in holding to be second in importance to the pursuit which they follow, may be safely esteemed to be the first in real worth; and it may be concluded, that if they were not blinded by some prevailing passion, they would discern and adopt it as such.

* *Isa.* xlvi. 4.

It is the peculiar effect of virtue, to make a man's chief happiness arise from himself and his own conduct. A bad man is wholly the creature of the world. He hangs upon its favour, lives by its smiles, and is happy or miserable, in proportion to his success. But to a virtuous man, success in worldly undertakings is but a secondary object. To discharge his own part with integrity and honour, is his chief aim. If he has done properly what was incumbent on him to do, his mind is at rest; to Providence he leaves the event. *His witness is in heaven, and his record is on high.* Satisfied with the approbation of God, and the testimony of a good conscience, he enjoys himself, and despises the triumphs of guilt. In proportion as such manly principles rule your heart, you will become independent of the world; and will forbear complaining of its discouragements. It is the imperfection of your virtue, which occasions you to *be weary in well-doing.* It is because your hearts remain divided between God and the world, that you are so often discontented; partly wishing to discharge your duty, and partly seeking your happiness from somewhat that is repugnant to your duty. Study to be more consistent in principle, and more uniform in practice, and your peace will be more unbroken.

Though virtue may appear at first sight to contract the bounds of enjoyment, you will find, upon reflection, that, in truth, it enlarges them. If it restrains the excess of some pleasures, it favours and increases others. It precludes you from none, but such as are either fantastic and imaginary, or pernicious and destructive. Whatever is truly valuable in human enjoyment, it allows to a good man, no less than to others. It not only allows him such pleasures, but heightens them, by that grateful relish which a good conscience gives to every pleasure. It not only heightens them, but adds to them, also, the peculiar satisfactions which flow from virtuous sentiments, from devout affections, and religious hopes. On how much worse terms is the sinner placed, in the midst of his boasted gratifications? His portion is confined to this world. His good things are all of one sort only; he has neither knowledge, nor relish, of any thing beyond them. His enjoyment, therefore, rests on a much narrower basis, than that of the servants of God. Enlarge, as much as you please, the circle of worldly gratifications; yet, if nothing of the mind and the heart, nothing of a refined and moral nature, enter into that circle, and vary the enjoyment, languor and weariness soon succeed. Among whom do you hear more peevish expressions of discontent, or more frequent complaints of low spirits, than among the professed votaries of worldly pleasure?

Vice and virtue, in their progress, as in every other respect, hold an opposite course. The beginnings of vice are enticing. The first steps of worldly advancement, are flattering and pleasing. But the continuance of success blunts enjoyment, and flattens desire. Whereas the beginnings of virtue are laborious. But, by perseverance, its labours diminish, and its pleasures increase. As it ripens into confirmed habit, it becomes both smoother in practice, and more complete in its reward. In a worldly life, the termination of our hopes always meets our view. We see a boundary before us, beyond which we cannot reach. But the prospects of virtue are growing and endless. *The righteous shall hold on in his way; and he that hath clean hands, shall wax stronger and stronger. The path of the just is as the shining light, that shineth more and more unto the perfect day.* This brings me to consider,

IV. THE assured hope, which good men enjoy, of a full reward at last. I have endeavoured by several considerations, to correct your impatience under the present discouragements of virtue. I have shown many high advantages, which it already possesses. But now, laying all these aside; supposing virtue to have brought you no advantage, but to have only engaged you in perpetual struggles with an evil world; the Text suggests what is sufficient to answer every objection, and to silence every complaint; *In due season you shall reap, if you faint not.* It is not a loose encouragement, or a dubious hope, which is held forth to us. A direct and explicit declaration is made by the Spirit of God, that piety and virtue, how discouraged soever, or oppressed, they may be for a while, shall not be frustrated of their reward; but that *in due season*, when the period which is fixed by the Divine decree shall come, all who have not been *weary in well-doing*, though they may *have sown in tears, shall reap in joy*. As this great principle of faith is so essential to our present argument, and is indeed the foundation of all religion, it will be proper that we now take a view of the grounds on which it rests. By fixing our attention, both on the proofs which reason suggests, and on the discoveries which revelation has made, of a state of future retribution, we shall take an effectual method of confirming our adherence to religion, and of baffling those temptations which might lead us to *be weary in well-doing*.

THE first, and most obvious presumption, which reason affords in behalf of future rewards to the righteous, arises from the imperfect distribution of good and evil in our present state. Notwithstanding what I have advanced concerning the pleasures and advantages of virtue, it cannot be denied, that the happiness of good men is often left incomplete. The vicious possess advantages, to which they have no right; while the conscientious suffer for the sake of virtue, and groan under distresses which they have not merited from the world. Indeed, were the distribution of good and evil in this life, altogether promiscuous; could it be said, with truth, that the moral condition of men had no influence whatever upon their happiness or misery; I admit, that from such a state of things, no presumption would arise of any future retribution being intended. They who delight to aggravate the miseries of life, and the distresses of virtue, do no service to the argument in behalf of Providence. For, if total disorder be found to prevail now, suspicions may, too justly, arise, of its prevailing for ever. If he who rules the universe, entirely neglects virtue here, the probability must be small, of his rewarding it hereafter. But this is far from being the true state of the fact. What human life presents to the view of an impartial observer, is by no means a scene of entire confusion; but a state of order, begun and carried on a certain length. Virtue is so far from being neglected by the Governour of the world, that from many evident marks it appears to be a chief object of his care. In the constitution of human nature, a foundation is laid, for comfort to the righteous, and for internal punishment to the wicked. Throughout the course of Divine government, tendencies towards the happiness of the one, and the misery of the other, constantly appear. They are so conspicuous, as not to have escaped the notice of the rudest nations. Over the whole earth, they have diffused the belief, that Providence is propitious to virtue, and averse to guilt. Yet these tendencies are, sometimes, disappointed of their effect; and that which Providence visibly favours, is left, at present, without an adequate reward.

From such an imperfect distribution of happiness, what are we to conclude, but that this system is the beginning, not the whole of things; the opening only of a more extensive plan, whose consummation reaches into a future world? If God has already *set his throne for judgment;* if he has visibly begun to reward and to punish, in some degree on earth, he cannot mean to leave the exercise of government

vernment incomplete. Having laid a foundation of a great and noble structure, he will in due time rear it up to perfection. The unfinished parts of the fabric evidently show, that a future building is intended. All his other works are constructed according to the most full and exact proportion. In the natural world, nothing is deficient, nothing redundant. It is in the moral world, only, that we discover irregularity and defect. It falls short of that order and perfection which appear in the rest of the creation. It exhibits not, in its present state, the same features of complete wisdom, justice, or goodness. But can we believe, that, under the government of the Supreme Being, those apparent disorders shall not be rectified at the last? or, that from his conduct towards his rational creatures, the chief of his works, the sole objection against his perfection shall be allowed to rise, and shall continue unremoved for ever?

On the supposition of future rewards and punishments, a satisfying account can be given, of all the disorders which at present take place on earth. Christianity explains their origin, and traces them to their issue. Man, fallen from his primæval felicity, is now undergoing probation and discipline for his final state. Divine justice remains, for a season, concealed; and allows men to act their parts with freedom on this theatre, that their characters may be formed and ascertained. Amidst discouragements and afflictions, the righteous give proof of their fidelity, and acquire the habits of virtue. But, if you suppose the events of this life to have no reference to another, the whole state of man becomes not only inexplicable, but contradictory and inconsistent. The powers of the inferior animals are perfectly suited to their station. They know nothing higher than their present condition. In gratifying their appetites, they fulfil their destiny, and pass away. Man, alone, comes forth to act a part, which carries no meaning, and tends to no end. Endowed with capacities, which extend far beyond his present sphere; fitted by his rational nature for running the race of immortality, he is stopped short in the very entrance of his course. He squanders his activity on pursuits, which he discerns to be vain. He languishes for knowledge, which is placed beyond his reach. He thirsts after a happiness, which he is doomed never to enjoy. He sees and laments the disasters of his state; and yet, upon this supposition, can find nothing to remedy them.—Has the eternal God any pleasure in sporting himself with such a scene of misery and folly, as this life, if it had no connexion with another, must exhibit to his eye? Did he call into existence this magnificent universe,

universe, adorn it with so much beauty and splendour, and surround it with those glorious luminaries which we behold in the heavens, only that some generations of mortal men might arise to behold these wonders, and then disappear for ever? How unsuitable, in this case, were the habitation to the wretched inhabitant! How inconsistent the commencement of his being, and the mighty preparation of his powers and faculties, with his despicable end! How contradictory, in fine, were every thing which concerns the state of man, to the wisdom and perfection of his Maker!

Throughout all ages, and among all nations, the persuasion of a future life has prevailed. It sprung not from the refinements of science, or the speculations of philosophy; but from a deeper and stronger root, the natural sentiments of the human heart. Hence it is common to the philosopher and the savage; and is found in the most barbarous, as well as in the most civilized regions. Even the belief of the being of a God, is not more general on the earth, than the belief of immortality. Dark, indeed, and confused, were the notions which men entertained concerning a future state. Yet still, in that state, they looked for retribution, both to the good and the bad? and in the perfection of such pleasures, as they knew best and valued most highly, they placed the rewards of the virtuous. So universal a consent seems plainly to indicate an original determination given to the soul by its Creator. It shows this great truth to be native and congenial to man.

When we look into our own breasts, we find various anticipations and presages of future existence. Most of our great and high passions extend beyond the limits of this life. The ambitious and the self-denied, the great, the good, and the wicked, all take interest in what is to happen after they shall have left the earth. That passion for fame, which inspires so much of the activity of mankind, plainly is animated by the persuasion, that consciousness is to survive the dissolution of the body. The virtuous are supported by the hope, the guilty tormented with the dread, of what is to take place after death. As death approaches, the hopes of the one, and the fears of the other, are found to redouble. The soul, when issuing hence, seems more clearly to discern its future abode. All the operations of conscience proceed upon the belief of immortality. The whole moral conduct of men refers to it. All legislators have supposed it. All religions are built upon it. It is so essential to the order of society, that were it erased, human laws would prove

ineffectual

ineffectual reſtraints from evil, and a deluge of crimes and miſeries would overflow the earth. To ſuppoſe this univerſal and powerful belief to be without foundation in truth, is to ſuppoſe, that a principle of deluſion was interwoven with the nature of man; is to ſuppoſe, that his Creator was reduced to the neceſſity of impreſſing his heart with a falſehood, in order to make him anſwer the purpoſes of his being.

BUT though theſe arguments be ſtrong, yet all arguments are liable to objection. Perhaps this general belief, of which I have ſpoken, has been owing to inclination and deſire, more than to evidence. Perhaps, in our reaſonings on this ſubject from the Divine perfections, we flatter ourſelves with being of more conſequence, than we truly are, in the ſyſtem of the univerſe. Hence the great importance of a diſcovery proceeding from God himſelf, which gives full authority to all that reaſon had ſuggeſted, and places this capital truth beyond the reach of ſuſpicion or diſtruſt.

The method which Chriſtianity has taken, to convey to us the evidence of a future ſtate, highly deſerves our atteution. Had the Goſpel been addreſſed, like a ſyſtem of philoſophy, ſolely to the underſtanding of men; had it aimed only at enlightening the ſtudious and reflecting, it would have confined itſelf to abſtract truth; it would have ſimply informed us, that the righteous are hereafter to be rewarded, and ſinners to be puniſhed. Such a declaration as that contained in the Text, would have been ſufficient: *Be not weary in well-doing, for in due ſeaſon you ſhall reap, if you faint not*. But the Goſpel has not ſtopped, at barely announcing life and immortality to mankind. It was calculated for popular edification. It was intended to be the religion not merely of the few, whoſe underſtanding was to be informed; but of the many, alſo, whoſe imagination was to be impreſſed, and whoſe paſſions were to be awakened, in order to give the truth its due influence over them. Upon this account it not only reveals the certainty of a future ſtate, but, in the perſon of the great Founder of our religion, exhibits a ſeries of facts relating to it; by means of which, our ſenſes, our imagination, and paſſions, all become intereſted in this great object.

The reſurrection of Chriſt from the grave, was deſigned to be a ſenſible evidence, that death infers not a final extinction of the living principle. He roſe, in order to ſhew, that, in our name, he had conquered death, and was *become the firſt-fruits of them that ſleep*. Nor did he only riſe from the grave, but, by aſcending to heaven in a viſible form, before many witneſſes, gave an ocular ſpecimen of the transition from this world into the region of the blessed. The employments which now occupy him there, are fully declared. *As our forerunner, he hath entered within the veil. He appears in the presence of God for us. He maketh perpetual intercession for his people. I go,* saith he, *to my Father and your Father, to my God and your God. In my Father's house are many mansions. I go to prepare a place for you. I will come again, and receive you to myself, that where I am, there ye may be also.* The circumstances of his coming again, are distinctly foretold. The sounding of the last trumpet, the resurrection of the dead, the appearance of the Judge, and the solemnity with which he shall discriminate the good from the bad, are all described. The very words in which he shall pronounce the final sentence, are recited in our hearing: *Come, ye blessed of my Father! inherit the Kingdom prepared for you from the foundation of the world.* Then shall the holy and the just be *caught up in the clouds, to meet the Lord in the air.* They shall enter with him into the *city of the living God.* They shall possess the *new earth and new heavens, wherein dwelleth righteousness. God shall wipe away all tears from their eyes. They shall behold his face in righteousness, and be satisfied with his likeness for ever.*— By recording such a train of striking circumstances and facts, the Gospel familiarizes us in some measure with a future state. By accommodating this great discovery, in so useful a manner, to the conceptions of men, it furnishes a strong intrinsic evidence of its divine origin.

Thus, upon the whole, whether you consult your reason, or listen to the discoveries of revelation, you behold our argument confirmed; you behold a life of piety and virtue issuing in immortal felicity. Of what worldly pursuit can it be pronounced, that its reward is certain? Look every where around you, and you shall see, that *the race is far from being always to the swift, or the battle to the strong.* The most diligent, the most wise, the most accomplished, may, after all their labours, be disappointed in the end; and be left to suffer the regret, of having *spent their strength for nought.* But for the righteous is *laid up the crown of life.* Their final happiness is prepared in the eternal plan of Providence, and secured by the labours and sufferings of the Saviour of the world.

Cease then, from your unjust complaints against virtue and religion. Leave discontent, and peevishness, to worldly men. In no period of distress, in no moment of disappointment, allow yourselves to suspect, that piety and integrity are fruitless. In every state of being, they

they lead to happiness. If you enjoy not at present their full rewards, it is because the season of recompense is not yet come. For, *in due season you shall reap.* There is a time which is proper for reward; and there is a period which belongs to trial. How long the one should last, and when the other should arrive, belongs not to you to determine. It is fixed by the wise, though unknown decree of the Almighty. But, be assured, that *He that cometh, shall come, and will not tarry.* He shall come *in due season*, to restore perfect order among his works; to bring rest to the weary, comfort to the afflicted, and just retribution to all men. Behold, saith the faithful and true Witness, *I come quickly, and my reward is with me. To him that overcometh, will I give to eat of the tree of life, which is in the midst of the paradise of God. I will give him the morning star. I will make him a pillar in my temple. He shall be clothed in white raiment; and shall sit down with me, on my throne.**

* *Rev.* xxii. 12.—ii. 7. 28.—iii. 12. 5. 21.

SERMON

SERMON XVI.

On the IMPORTANCE of ORDER in CONDUCT.

1 CORINTH. xiv. 40.

Let all things be done—in order.

RELIGION, like every regular and well-connected system, is composed of a variety of parts; each of which possesses its separate importance, and contributes to the perfection of the whole. Some graces are essential to it; such as faith and repentance, the love of God, and the love of our neighbour; which, for that reason, must be often inculcated on men. There are other dispositions and habits, which, though they hold not so high a rank, yet are necessary to the introduction and support of the former; and therefore, in religious exhortations, these also justly claim a place. Of this nature is that regard to order, method, and regularity, which the apostle enjoins us in the text to carry through the whole of life. Whether you consider it as, in itself, a moral duty, or not, yet I hope soon to convince you that it is essential to the proper discharge of almost all duties, and merits, upon that account, a greater degree of attention than is commonly paid to it in a religious view.

If you look abroad into the world, you may be satisfied at the first glance, that a vicious and libertine life is always a life of confusion. Thence it is natural to infer, that order is friendly to religion. As the neglect of it coincides with vice, so the preservation of it must assist virtue. By the appointment of Providence, it is indispensably requisite to worldly prosperity. Thence arises a presumption, that it is connected also with spiritual improvement. When you behold a man's affairs, through negligence and misconduct, involved in disorder, you naturally conclude that his ruin approaches. You may at the same time justly suspect, that the causes which affect his temporal welfare, operate also to the prejudice of his moral interests. The apostle teaches us in this chapter, that *God is not the author of confusion.* *

fufion.* He is a lover of order : and all his works are full of order. But *where confufion is, there is,* its close attendant, *every evil work.*† In the sequel of this discourse I shall point out some of those parts of conduct wherein it is most material to virtue that order take place; and then shall conclude with shewing the high advantages which attend it. Allow me to recommend to you order in the conduct of your affairs; order in the distribution of your time; order in the management of your fortune; order in the regulation of your amusements; order in the arrangement of your society. Thus *let all things be done in order.*

I. MAINTAIN order in the conduct of your worldly affairs. Every man, in every station of life, has some concerns, private, domestic, or public, which require succeslive attention; he is placed in some sphere of active duty. Let the employments which belong to that sphere be so arranged, that each may keep its place without justling another; and that which regards the world may not interfere with what is due to God. In proportion to the multiplicity of affairs, the observance of order becomes more indispensable. But scarcely is there any train of life so simple and uniform but what will suffer through the neglect of it. I speak not now of suffering in point of worldly interest. I call upon you to attend to higher interests; to remember that the orderly conduct of your temporal affairs forms a great part of your duty as Christians.

Many, indeed, can hardly be persuaded of this truth. A strong propensity has, in every age, appeared among men, to sequestrate religion from the commerce of the world. Seasons of retreat and devotion they are willing to appropriate to God. But the world they consider as their own province. They carry on a sort of separate interest there. Nay, by the respect which, on particular occasions, they pay to religion, they too often imagine that they have acquired the liberty of acting in worldly matters, according to what plan they chuse. How entirely do such persons mistake the design of Christianity!—In this world you were placed by Providence as on a great field of trial. By the necessities of your nature you are called forth to different employments. By many ties you are connected with human society. From superiours and inferiours, from neighbours and equals, from friends and enemies, demands arise, and obligations circulate through all the ranks of life. This active scene was contrived by the wisdom of Heaven, on purpose that it might

bring

* *Ver.* 33. † *James* iii. 16.

bring into exercife all the virtues of the Chriftian character; your juftice, candour and veracity, in dealing with one another; your fidelity to every truft, and your confcientious difcharge of every office, which is committed to you; your affection for your friends; your forgivenefs of enemies; your charity to the diftreffed; your attention to the interefts of your family. It is by fulfilling all thefe obligations, in proper fucceffion, that you fhew *your converfation to be fuch as becometh the gofpel of Chrift.* It is thus you make *your light fo to fhine before men, that they may fee your good works, and glorify your Father which is in heaven.* It is thus you are rendered *meet for the inheritance of the faints in light.*—But how can thofe various duties be difcharged by perfons who are ever in that hurry and perplexity which diforder creates? You wifh, perhaps, to perform what your character and ftation require. But from the confufion in which you have allowed yourfelves to be involved, you find it to have become impoffible. What was neglected to be done in its proper place, thrufts itfelf forward at an inconvenient feafon. A multitude of affairs crowd upon you together. Different obligations diftract you: and this diftraction is fometimes the caufe, fometimes the pretence, of equally neglecting them all, or, at leaft, of facrificing the greater to the leffer.

Hence arife fo many inconfiftent characters, and fuch frequent inftances of partial and divided goodnefs, as we find in the world; appearances of generofity without juftice, honour without truth, probity to men without reverence of God. He who conducts his affairs with method and regularity, meets every duty in its proper place, and affigns it its due rank. But where there is no order in conduct, there can be no uniformity in character. The natural connection and arrangement of duties are loft. If virtue appear at all, it will be only in fits and ftarts. The authority of confcience may occafionally operate, when our fituation affords it room for exertion. But in other circumftances of equal importance, every moral fentiment will be overpowered by the tumultuous buftle of worldly affairs. Fretfulnefs of temper, too, will generally characterize thofe who are negligent of order. The hurry in which they live, and the embarraffments with which they are furrounded, keep their fpirits in perpetual ferment. Conflicting with difficulties which they are unable to overcome, confcious of their own mifconduct, but afhamed to confefs it, they are engaged in many a fecret ftruggle; and the uneafinefs which they fuffer within, recoils in bad humour on all who are around them. Hence the wretched refources to which, at laft, they

are

are obliged to fly, in order to quiet their cares. In defpair of being able to unravel what they have fuffered to become fo perplexed, they fometimes fink into fupine indolence, fometimes throw themfelves into the arms of intemperance and loofe pleafure; by either of which they aggravate their guilt, and accellerate their ruin. To the end that order may be maintained in your affairs, it is necellary,

II. THAT you attend to order in the diftribution of your time. Time you ought to confider as a facred truft committed to you by God, of which you are now the depofitaries, and are to render account at the laft. That portion of it which he has allotted you is intended partly for the concerns of this world, partly for thofe of the next. Let each of thefe occupy, in the diftribution of your time, that fpace which properly belongs to it. Let not the hours of hofpitality and pleafure interfere with the difcharge of your necellary affairs; and let not what you call necellary affairs encroach upon the time which is due to devotion. *To every thing there is a feafon, and a time for every purpofe under the heaven* *. If you delay till to-morrow what ought to be done to day, you over-charge the morrow with a burden which belongs not to it. You load the wheels of time, and prevent it from carrying you along fmoothly. He who every morning plans the tranfactions of the day, and follows out that plan, carries on a thread which will guide him through the labyrinth of the moft bufy life. The orderly arrangement of his time is like a ray of light which darts itfelf through all his affairs. But where no plan is laid, where the difpofal of time is furrendered merely to the chance of incidents, all things lie huddled together in one chaos, which admits neither of diftribution nor review.

The firft requifite for introducing order into the management of time, is to be impreffed with a juft fenfe of its value. Confider well how much depends upon it, and how faft it flies away. The bulk of men are in nothing more capricious and inconfiftent than in their appretiation of time. When they think of it as the meafure of their continuance on earth, they highly prize it, and with the greateft anxiety feek to lengthen it out. But when they view it in feparate parcels, they appear to hold it in contempt, and fquander it with inconfiderate profufion. While they complain that life is fhort, they are often wifhing its different periods at an end. Covetous of every other poffeffion, of time only they are prodigal. They allow every idle man to be mafter of this property, and make every frivolous occupation

* *Ecclef* iii. 1.

cupation welcome that can help them to confume it. Among thofe who are fo carelefs of time, it is not to be expected that order fhould be obferved in its diftribution. But, by this fatal neglect, how many materials of fevere and lafting regret are they laying up in ftore for themfelves! The time which they fuffer to pafs away in the midft of confufion, bitter repentance feeks afterwards in vain to recal. What was omitted to be done at its proper moment, arifes to be the torment of fome future feafon. Manhood is difgraced by the confequences of neglected youth. Old age, oppreffed by cares that belonged to a former period, labours under a burden not its own. At the clofe of life, the dying man beholds with anguifh that his days are finifhing, when his preparation for eternity is hardly commenced. Such are the effects of a diforderly wafte of time, through not attending to its value. Every thing in the life of fuch perfons is mifplaced. Nothing is performed aright, from not being performed in due feafon.

But he who is orderly in the diftribution of his time, takes the proper method of efcaping thofe manifold evils. He is juftly faid to *redeem the time*. By proper management he prolongs it. He lives much in little fpace; more in a few years than others do in many. He can live to God and his own foul, and at the fame time attend to all the lawful interefts of the prefent world. He looks back on the paft, and provides for the future. He catches and arrefts the hours as they fly. They are marked down for ufeful purpofes, and their memory remains. Whereas thofe hours fleet by the man of confufion like a fhadow. His days and years are either blanks of which he has no remembrance, or they are filled up with fuch a confufed and irregular fucceffion of unfinifhed tranfactions, that though he remembers he has been bufy, yet he can give no account of the bufinefs which has employed him. Of him, more than of any other, it may with juftice be pronounced, that *he walketh in a vain fhew; he is difquieted in vain.*

III. INTRODUCE order into the management of your fortune. Whatever it be, let the adminiftration of it proceed with method and œconomy. From time to time examine your fituation; and proportion your expence to your growing or diminifhing revenue. Provide what is neceffary, before you indulge in what is fuperfluous. Study to do juftice to all with whom you deal, before you affect the praife of liberality. In a word, fix fuch a plan of living as you find that your circumftances will fairly admit, and adhere to it invariably againft every temptation to improper excefs.

No admonition refpecting morals is more neceffary than this to the age

age in which we live; an age manifestly diftinguished by a propenfity to thoughtlefs profusion; wherein all the different ranks of men are obferved to prefs with forward vanity on thofe who are above them; to vie with their fuperiours in every mode of luxury and oftentation; and to feek no farther argument for juftifying extravagance, than the fafhion of the times, and the fuppofed neceffity of living like others around them. This turn of mind begets contempt for fober and orderly plans of life. It overthrows all regard to domeftic concerns and duties. It pufhes men on to hazardous and vifionary fchemes of gain; and unfortunately unites the two extremes, of grafping with rapaciousnefs, and of fquandering with profusion. In the midft of fuch diforder, no profperity can be of long continuance. While confufion grows upon men's affairs, and prodigality at the fame time waftes their fubftance, poverty makes its advances *like an armed man*. They tremble at the view of the approaching evil; but have loft the force of mind to make provifion againft it. Accuftomed to move in a round of fociety and pleafures difproportioned to their condition, they are unable to break through the enchantments of habit; and with their eyes open fink into the gulph which is before them. Poverty enforces dependance; and dependance increafes corruption. Neceffity firft betrays them into mean compliances; next, impels them to open crimes; and beginning with oftentation and extravagance, they end in infamy and guilt. Such are the confequences of neglecting order in our worldly circumftances. Such is the circle in which the profufe and the diffolute daily run.——To what caufe, fo much as to the want of order, can we attribute thofe fcenes of diftrefs which fo frequently excite our pity; families that once were flourifhing reduced to ruin; and the melancholy widow and neglected orphan thrown forth, friendlefs, upon the world? What caufe has been more fruitful in engendering thofe atrocious crimes which fill fociety with difquiet and terrour; in training the gamefter to fraud, the robber to violence, and even the affaffin to blood?

Be affured, then, that order, frugality, and œconomy, are the neceffary fupports of every perfonal and private virtue. How humble foever thefe qualities may appear to fome, they are, neverthelefs, the bafis on which liberty, independence, and true honour, muft rife He who has the fteadinefs to arrange his affairs with method and regularity, and to conduct his train of life agreeably to his circumftances, can be mafter of himfelf in every fituation into which he may be thrown. He is under no neceffity to flatter or to lie, to ftoop to what is mean, or to commit what is criminal. But he who wants that firmness of mind which the observance of order requires, is held in bondage to the world; he can neither act his part with courage as a man, nor with fidelity as a Christian. From the moment you have allowed yourselves to pass the line of œconomy, and to live beyond your fortune, you have entered on the path of danger. Precipices surround you on all sides. Every step which you take may lead to mischiefs, that, as yet, lie hidden; and to crimes that will end in your everlasting perdition.

IV. OBSERVE order in your amusements; that is, allow them no more than their proper place; study to keep them within due bounds; mingle them in a temperate succession with serious duties, and the higher business of life. Human life cannot proceed to advantage without some measure of relaxation and entertainment. We require relief from care. We are not formed for a perpetual stretch of serious thought. By too intense and continued application, our feeble powers would soon be worn out. At the same time, from our propensity to ease and pleasure, amusement proves, among all ranks of men, the most dangerous foe to order. For it tends incessantly to usurp and encroach, to widen its territories, to thrust itself into the place of more important concerns, and thereby to disturb and counteract the natural course of things. One frivolous amusement indulged out of season, will often carry perplexity and confusion through a long succession of affairs.

Amusements, therefore, though they be of an innocent kind, require steady government, to keep them within a due and limited province. But such as are of an irregular and vicious nature, are not to be governed, but to be banished from every orderly society. As soon as a man seeks his happiness from the gaming-table, the midnight revel, and the other haunts of licentiousness, confusion seizes upon him as its own. There will no longer be order in his family, nor order in his affairs, nor order in his time. The most important concerns of life are abandoned. Even the order of nature is by such persons inverted; night is changed into day, and day into night. Character, honour, and interest itself, are trampled under foot. You may with certainty prognosticate the ruin of these men to be just at hand. Disorder, arisen to its height, has nearly accomplished its work. The spots of death are upon them. Let every one who would escape the pestilential contagion fly with haste from their company.

V.

V. PRESERVE order in the arrangement of your fociety; that is, entangle not yourfelves in a perpetual and promifcuous crowd; felect with prudence and propriety thofe with whom you chufe to affociate; let company and retreat fucceed each other at meafured intervals. There can be no order in his life who allots not a due fhare of his time to retirement and reflection. He can neither prudently arrange his temporal affairs, nor properly attend to his fpiritual interefts. He lives not to himfelf, but to the world. By continual diffipation, he is rendered giddy and thoughtlefs. He unavoidably contracts from the world that fpirit of diforder and confufion which is fo prevalent in it.

It is not a fufficient prefervative againft this evil, that the circles of fociety in which you are engaged are not of a libertine and vicious kind. If they withdraw you from that attention to yourfelves, and your domeftic concerns, which becomes a good man, they are fubverfive of order, and inconfiftent with duty. What is innocent in itfelf, degenerates into guilt from being carried to excefs; and idle, trifling fociety is near a-kin to fuch as is corrupting: One of the firft principles of order is, to learn to be happy at home. It is in domeftic retreat that every wife and virtuous man finds his chief fatisfaction. It is there he forms the plans which regulate his public conduct. He who knows not how to enjoy himfelf when alone, can never be long happy abroad. To his vacant mind, company may afford a temporary relief; but when forced to return to himfelf, he will be fo much more oppreffed and languid. Whereas, by a due mixture of public and private life, we keep free from the fnares of both, and enjoy each to greater advantage.

WHEN we review thofe different parts of behaviour to which I have fhewn that order is effential, it muft neceffarily occur to you, that they are all mutually connected, and hang upon each other. Throughout your affairs, your time, your expence, your amufements, your fociety, the principle of order muft be equally carried, if you expect to reap any of its happy fruits. For if into any one of thofe great departments of life you fuffer diforder to enter, it will fpread through all the reft. In vain, for inftance, you purpofe to be orderly in the conduct of your affairs, if you be irregular in the diftribution of your time. In vain you attempt to regulate your expence, if into your amufements, or your fociety, diforder has crept. You have admitted a principle of confufion which will defeat all your plans; and perplex and entangle what you fought to arrange. Uniformity is

above

above all things neceſſary to order. If you defire that any thing ſhould proceed according to method and rule, let *all things*, as the text exhorts, *be done in order.*

I muſt alſo admoniſh you, that in ſmall, as well as in great affairs, a due regard to order is requiſite. I mean not that you ought to look on thoſe minute attentions which are apt to occupy frivolous minds, as connected either with virtue or wiſdom. But I exhort you to remember, that diſorder, like other immoralities, frequently takes riſe from inconſiderable beginnings. They who, in the leſſer tranſactions of life, are totally negligent of rule, will be in hazard of extending that negligence, by degrees, to ſuch affairs and duties as will render them criminal. Remiſſneſs grows on all who ſtudy not to guard againſt it; and it is only by frequent exerciſe that the habits of order and punctuality can be thoroughly confirmed.

From what has been ſaid, the great importance of this principle to moral and religious conduct muſt already be evident. Let us, however, conclude, with taking a ſummary view of the advantages which attend it.

Firſt, the obſervance of order ſerves to correct that negligence which makes you omit ſome duties, and that hurry and precipitancy which makes you perform other imperfectly. Your attention is thereby directed to its proper objects. You follow the ſtraight path which Providence has pointed out to man; in the courſe of which all the different buſineſs of life preſents itſelf regularly to him on every ſide. God and man, time and eternity, poſſeſs their proper ſtations, ariſe in ſucceſſion to his view, and attract his care. Whereas he who runs on in a diſorderly courſe, ſpeedily involves himſelf in a labyrinth, where he is ſurrounded with intricacy and darkneſs. The crooked paths into which he ſtrikes, turn him aſide from the proper line of human purſuit; hide from his ſight the objects which he ought chiefly to regard, and bring others under his view, which ſerve no purpoſe but to diſtract and miſlead him.

Next, by attending to order, you avoid idleneſs, that moſt fruitful ſource of crimes and evils. Acting upon a plan, meeting every thing in its own place, you conſtantly find innocent and uſeful employment for time. You are never at a loſs how to diſpoſe of your hours, or to fill up life agreeably. In the courſe of human action, there are two extremes equally dangerous to virtue; the multiplicity of affairs, and the total want of them. The man of order ſtands in the middle between theſe two extremes, and ſuffers from neither. He is occupied ed but not oppreffed. Whereas the d forderly, overloading one part of time, and leaving another vacant, are at one period overwhelmed with bufinefs, and at another, either idle through want of employment, or indolent through perplexity. Thofe feafons of indolence and idlenefs, which recur fo often in their life, are their moft dangerous moments. The mind, unhappy in its fituation, and clinging to every object which can occupy or amufe it, is then apteft to throw itfelf into the arms of every vice and every folly.

Farther, by the prefervation of order, you check inconftancy and levity. Fickle by nature is the human heart. It is fond of change; and perpetually tends to ftart afide from the ftraight line of conduct. Hence arifes the propriety of bringing ourfelves under fubjection to method and rule; which, though at firft it may prove conftraining, yet by degrees, and from the experience of its happy effects, becomes natural and agreeable. It rectifies thofe irregularities of temper and manners to which we give the name of caprice; and which are diftinguifhing characteriftics of a diforderly mind. It is the parent of fteadinefs of conduct. It forms confiftency of character. It is the ground of all the confidence we repofe in one another. For, the diforderly we know not where to find. In him only can we place any truft who is uniform and regular; who lives by principle, not by humour; who acts upon a plan, and not by defultory motions.

The advantages of order hitherto mentioned belong to rectitude of conduct. Confider alfo how important it is to your felf-enjoyment and felicity. Order is the fource of peace; and peace is the higheft of all temporal bleffings. Order is indeed the only region in which tranquillity dwells. The very mention of confufion imports difturbance and vexation. Is it poffible for that man to be happy, who cannot look into the ftate of his affairs, or the tenor of his conduct, without difcerning all to be embroiled; who is either in the midft of remorfe for what he has neglected to do, or in the midft of hurry to overtake what he finds, too late, was neceffary to have been done? Such as live according to order may be compared to the celeftial bodies which move in regular courfes, and by ftated laws; whofe influence is beneficent; whofe operations are quiet and tranquil. The diforderly refemble thofe tumultuous elements on earth, which, by fudden and violent irruptions, difturb the courfe of nature. By mifmanagement of affairs, by excefs in expence, by irregularity in the indulgence of company and amufement, they are perpetually creating moleftation both to themfelves and others. They depart from their road to feek pleafure; and inftead of it, they every where raife up forrows,

rows. Being always found out of their proper place, they of courſe interfere and jar with others. The diſorders which they raiſe never fail to ſpread beyond their own line, and to involve many in confuſion and diſtreſs; whence they neceſſarily become the authors of tumult and contention, of diſcord and enmity. Whereas order is the foundation of union. It allows every man to carry on his own affairs without diſturbing his neighbour. It is the golden chain, which holds together the ſocieties of men in friendſhip and peace.

In fine, the man of order is connected with all the higher powers and principles in the univerſe. He is the follower of God. He walks with him, and acts upon his plan. His character is formed on the ſpirit which religion breaths. For religion in general, and the religion of Chriſt in particular, may be called the great diſcipline of order. To *walk ſinfully*, and to *walk diſorderly*, are ſynonymous terms in Scripture. From *ſuch as walk diſorderly* we are commanded, *in the name of the Lord Jeſus Chriſt*, to *withdraw ourſelves**. The kingdom of Satan is the reign of diſorder and darkneſs. To reſtore order among the works of God, was the end for which the Son of God deſcended to the earth. He requires order to be obſerved in his church. His undertaking is to be conſummated in that perfect order which he ſhall introduce at the laſt day. In *the new earth and the new heavens*, undiſturbed order ſhall for ever prevail among the *ſpirits of the juſt made perfect*; and whatever farther preparation may be requiſite for our being admitted to join their ſociety, it is certain that we ſhall never ſhare in it, unleſs we make it now our ſtudy to *do all things decently, and in order*.

* 2 *Theſſ.* iii. 6.

SERMON

SERMON XVII.

On the GOVERNMENT of the HEART.

PROVERBS, iv. 23.

Keep thy heart with all diligence: for out of it are the issues of life.

AMONG the many wise counsels given by this inspired writer, there is none which deserves greater regard than that contained in the text. Its importance, however, is too seldom perceived by the generality of men. They are apt to consider the regulation of external conduct as the chief object of religion. If they can act their part with decency, and maintain a fair character, they conceive their duty to be fulfilled. What passes in the mean time within their mind, they suppose to be of no great consequence, either to themselves, or to the world. In opposition to this dangerous plan of morality, the wise man exhorts us *to keep the heart;* that is, to attend not only to our actions, but to our thoughts and desires; and *to keep the heart with all diligence,* that is, with sedulous and unremitting care; for which he assigns this reason, that, *out of the heart are the issues of life.*—In discoursing on this subject I purpose to consider, separately, the government of the thoughts, of the passions, and of the temper. But before entering on any of these, let us begin with enquiring, in what sense *the issues of life* are said to be *out of the heart;* that we may discern the force of the argument which the text suggests, to recommend this great duty of *keeping the heart.*

The issues of life are justly said to be out of the heart, because the state of the heart is what determines our moral character, and what forms our chief happiness or misery.

First, It is the state of the heart which determines our moral character. The tenor of our actions will always correspond to the dispositions that prevail within. To dissemble, or to suppress them, is a fruitless attempt. In spite of our efforts, they will perpetually break forth in our behaviour. On whatever side the weight of inclination hangs, it will draw the practice after it. In vain therefore you study to preserve your hands clean, unless you resolve at the same time

F f

time to keep your heart pure. *Make the tree good*, as our Saviour directs, *and then its fruits will be good also*. For *out of the heart proceed not only evil thoughts, but murders, adulteries, fornications, theft, false witness, blasphemies* *. If that fountain be once poisoned, you can never expect that salubrious streams will flow from it. Throughout the whole of their course, they will carry the taint of the parent spring.

But it is not merely from its influence on external action that the importance of the heart to our moral character arises. Independent of all action, it is, in truth, the state of the heart itself which forms our character in the sight of God. With our fellow-creatures, actions must ever hold the chief rank; because, by these only we can judge of one another; by these we effect each other's welfare; and therefore to these alone the regulation of human law extends. But in the eye of that Supreme Being, to whom our whole internal frame is uncovered, dispositions hold the place of actions; and it is not so much what we perform, as the motive which moves us to performance, that constitutes us good or evil in his sight. Even among men, the morality of actions is estimated by the principle from which they are judged to proceed; and such as the principle is, such is the man accounted to be. One, for instance, may spend much of his fortune in charitable actions; and yet, if he is believed to be influenced by mere ostentation, he is deemed not charitable, but vain. He may labour unweariedly to serve the public; but if he is prompted by the desire of rising into power, he is held not public spirited, but ambitious: And if he bestows a benefit, purely that he may receive a greater in return, no man would reckon him generous, but selfish and interested. If reason thus clearly teaches us to estimate the value of actions by the dispositions which give them birth, it is an obvious conclusion, that, according to those dispositions, we are all ranked and classed by him who seeth into every heart. The rectification of our principles of action is the primary object of religious discipline; and, in proportion as this is more or less advanced, we are more or less religious. Accordingly the regeneration of the heart is every where represented in the Gospel as the most essential requisite in the character of a Christian.

SECONDLY, The state of the heart not only determines our moral character, but forms our principal happiness or misery. External situations of fortune are no farther of consequence, than as they operate on the heart; and their operation there is far from corresponding to

* *Matth*. xv. 18.

of the Heart.

the degree of worldly profperity or adverfity. If, from any internal caufe, a man's peace of mind be difturbed, in vain you load him with all the honours or riches which the world can beftow. They remain without, like things at a diftance from him. They reach not the fource of enjoyment. Difcompofed thoughts, agitated paffions, and a ruffled temper, poifon every ingredient of pleafure which the world holds out; and overcaft every object which prefents itfelf, with a melancholy gloom. In order to acquire a capacity of happinefs, it muft be our firft ftudy to rectify fuch inward diforders. Whatever difcipline tends to accomplifh this purpofe, is of greater importance to man, than the acquifition of the advantages of fortune. Thefe are precarious and doubtful in their effect; internal tranquillity is a certain good. Thefe are only means; but that is the end. Thefe are no more than inftruments of fatisfaction; that, is fatisfaction itfelf.

Juftly is it faid by the Wife Man, that *he who hath no rule over his fpirit, is like a city that is broken down and without walls**. All is wafte; all is in diforder and ruins within him. He poffeffes no defence againft dangers of any fort. He lies open to every infurrection of ill-humour, and every invafion of diftrefs. Whereas he who is employed in regulating his mind, is making provifion againft all the accidents of life. He is erecting a fortrefs into which, in the day of danger, he can retreat with fafety. And hence, amidft thofe endeavours to fecure happinefs which inceffantly employ the life of man, the careful regulation, or the improvident neglect of the inward frame, forms the chief diftinction between wifdom and folly.

THUS it appears with how much propriety the *iffues of life* are faid to be *out of the heart*. Here rife thofe great fprings of human conduct whence the main currents flow of our virtue, or our vice; of our happinefs, or our mifery. Befides this powerful argument for *keeping the heart with all diligence*, I muft mention another important confideration taken from the prefent ftate of human nature. Think what your heart now is, and what muft be the confequence of remitting your vigilance in watching over it. With too much juftice it is faid in fcripture, to be *deceitful above all things, and defperately wicked*. Its bias of innate corruption gives it a perpetual tendency downwards into vice and diforder. To direct and impel it upwards, requires a conftant effort. Experience may convince you, that almoft every defire has a propenfity to wander into an improper direction; that every paffion tends to excefs; and that around your imagination there perpetually crowds a whole fwarm of vain and corrupting thoughts.

* *Prov.* xxv. 28.

thoughts. After all the care that can be bestowed by the best men on the regulation of the heart, it frequently baffles their efforts to keep it under proper discipline. Into what universal tumult then must it rise, if no vigilance be employed, and no government be exercised over it? Inattention and remissness is all that the great adversary of mankind desires, in order to gain full advantage. While you *sleep, he sows his tares in the field.* The house which he finds vacant and unguarded, he presently *garnishes with evil spirits.*

Add to this, that the human temper is to be considered as a system, the parts of which have a mutual dependence on each other. Introduce disorder into any one part, and you derange the whole. Suffer but one passion to go out of its place, or to acquire an unnatural force, and presently the balance of the soul will be broken; its powers will jar among themselves, and their operations become discordant.—*Keep thy heart, therefore, with all diligence;* for all thy diligence is here required. And though thine own keeping alone will not avail, unless the assistance of a higher power concur, yet of this be well assured, that no aid from heaven is to be expected, if thou shalt neglect to exert thyself in performing the part assigned thee.

HAVING now shown the importance of exercising government over the heart, I proceed to consider more particularly in what that government consists, as it respects the thoughts, the passions, and the temper.

I begin with the thoughts, which are the prime movers of the whole human conduct. All that makes a figure on the great theatre of the world, the employments of the busy, the enterprises of the ambitious, and the exploits of the warlike, the virtues which form the happiness, and the crimes which occasion the misery of mankind, originate in that silent and secret recess of thought which is hidden from every human eye. The secrecy and silence which reign there, favour the prejudice entertained by too many, that thought is exempted from all controul. Passions, they perhaps admit, require government and restraint, because they are violent emotions, and disturb society. But with their thoughts, they plead, no one is concerned. By these, as long as they remain in their bosom, no offence can be given, and no injury committed. To enjoy unrestrained the full range of imagination, appears to them the native right and privilege of man.

Had they to do with none but their fellow-creatures, such reasoning might be specious. But they ought to remember, that, in the sight of the Supreme Being, thoughts bear the character of good or

evil

evil, as much as actions; and that they are, in especial manner, the subjects of divine jurisdiction, because they are cognizable at no other tribunal. The moral regulation of our thoughts, is the particular test of our reverence for God. If we restrain our passions from breaking forth into open disorders, while we abandon our imagination in secret to corruption, we show that virtue rests with us upon regard to men; and that however we may act a part in public with propriety, there is before our eyes no fear of that God who *searcheth the heart*, and *requireth truth in the inward parts*.

But, even abstracting from this awful consideration, the government of our thoughts must appear to be of high consequence, from their direct influence on conduct. It is plain, that thought gives the first impulse to every principle of action. Actions are, in truth, no other than thoughts ripened into consistency and substance. So certain is this, that to judge with precision of the character of any man, and to foretel with confidence what part he will act, no more were requisite, than to be rendered capable of viewing the current of thought which passes most frequently within him. Though by such a method we have no access to judge of one another, yet thus it is always in our power to judge of ourselves. Each of us, by impartially scrutinizing his indulged and favourite thoughts, may discover the whole secret of his real character. This consideration alone is sufficient to show, of what importance the government of thought is to the *keeping of the heart*.

But, supposing us convinced of its importance, a question may arise, How far it is within our power, and in what degree thoughts are subject to the command of the will? It is plain that they are not always the offspring of choice. Often they are inevitably impressed upon the mind by surrounding objects. Often they start up, as of themselves, without any principle of introduction which we are able to trace. *As the wind bloweth where it listeth, and thou canst not tell whence it cometh, nor whether it goeth*, equally rapid in its transitions, and inscrutable in its progress, is the course of thought. Moving along a train of connexions which are too delicate for our observation, it defeats all endeavours either to explore or to stop its path. Hence vain and fantastic imaginations sometimes break in upon the most settled attention, and disturb even the devout exercises of pious minds. Instances of this sort must be placed to the account of human frailty. They are misfortunes to be deplored, rather than crimes to be condemned; and our gracious Creator, who *knows our frame, and remembers*

bers we are duſt, will not be ſevere in marking every ſuch error and wandering of the mind. But, after theſe allowances are made, ſtill there remains much ſcope for the proper government of thought; and a multitude of caſes occur, in which we are no leſs accountable for what we think, than for what we do.

As, firſt, when the introduction of any train of thought depends upon ourſelves, and is our voluntary act; by turning our attention towards ſuch objects, awakening ſuch paſſions, or engaging in ſuch employments, as we know muſt give a peculiar determination to our thoughts. Next, when thoughts, by whatever accident they may have been originally ſuggeſted, are indulged with deliberation and complacency. Though the mind has been paſſive in their reception, and therefore free from blame; yet, if it be active in their continuance, the guilt becomes its own. They may have intruded at firſt, like unbidden gueſts; but if, when entered, they are made welcome, and kindly entertained, the caſe is the ſame as if they had been invited from the beginning. If we be thus accountable to God for thoughts either voluntarily introduced, or deliberately indulged, we are no leſs ſo, in the laſt place, for thoſe which find admittance into our hearts from ſupine negligence, from total relaxation of attention, from allowing our imagination to rove with entire licence, *like the eyes of the fool, towards the ends of the earth*. Our minds are, in this caſe, thrown open to folly and vanity. They are proſtituted to every evil thing which pleaſes to take poſſeſſion. The conſequences muſt all be charged to our account; and in vain we plead excuſe from human infirmity. Hence it appears, that the great object at which we are to aim in governing our thoughts, is, to take the moſt effectual meaſures for preventing the introduction of ſuch as are ſinful, and for haſtening their expulſion, if they ſhall have introduced themſelves without conſent of the will.

But when we deſcend into our breaſts, and examine how far we have ſtudied to keep this object in view, who can tell *how oft he hath offended*? In no article of religion or morals are men more culpably remiſs than in the unreſtrained indulgence they give to fancy; and that too, for moſt part, without remorſe. Since the time that Reaſon began to exert her powers, Thought, during our waking hours, has been active in every breaſt, without a moment's ſuſpenſion or pauſe. The current of ideas has been always flowing. The wheels of the ſpiritual engine have circulated with perpetual motion. Let me aſk, what has been the fruit of this inceſſant activity with the greateſt part of mankind? Of the innumerable hours that have been

employed

employed in thought, how few are marked with any permanent or useful effect? How many have either passed away in idle dreams; or have been abandoned to anxious discontented musings, to unsocial and malignant passions, or to irregular and criminal desires? Had I power to lay open that storehouse of iniquity which the hearts of too many conceal; could I draw out and read to them a list of all the imaginations they have devised, and all the passions they have indulged in secret; what a picture of men would I present to themselves! What crimes would they appear to have perpetrated in fancy, which to their most intimate companions they durst not reveal!

Even when men imagine their thoughts to be innocently employed, they too commonly suffer them to run out into extravagant imaginations, and chimerical plans of what they would wish to attain, or chuse to be, if they could frame the course of things according to their desire. Though such employments of fancy come not under the same description with those which are plainly criminal, yet wholly unblamable they seldom are. Besides the waste of time which they occasion, and the misapplication which they indicate of those intellectual powers that were given to us for much nobler purposes, such romantic speculations lead us always into the neighbourhood of forbidden regions. They place us on dangerous ground. They are for the most part connected with some one bad passion; and they always nourish a giddy and frivolous turn of thought. They unfit the mind for applying with vigour to rational pursuits, or for acquiescing in sober plans of conduct. From that ideal world in which it allows itself to dwell, it returns, to the commerce of men, unbent and relaxed, sickly and tainted, averse from discharging the duties, and sometimes disqualified even for relishing the pleasures of ordinary life. *O Jerusalem! wash thine heart from wickedness. How long shall thy vain thoughts lodge within thee**?—In order to guard against all such corruptions and abuses of thought as I have mentioned, it may be profitable to attend to the following rules:

In the first place, study to acquire the habit of attention to thought. No study is more important; for in proportion to the degree in which this habit is possessed, such commonly is the degree of intellectual improvement. It is the power of attention which in a great measure distinguishes the wise and the great from the vulgar and trifling herd of men. The latter are accustomed to think, or rather to dream, without knowing the subject of their thoughts. In their unconnected rovings, they pursue no end; they follow no track. Eve-

* *Jerem.* iv 14.

ry thing floats loose and disjointed on the surface of their mind; like leaves scattered and blown about on the face of the waters.

In order to lead your thoughts into any useful direction, your first care must be, to acquire the power of fixing them, and of restraining their irregular motions. Inure yourselves to form a plan of proper meditation; to pursue it steadily; and with severe authority to keep the door shut against intrusions of wandering fancy. Let your mind, for this purpose, become a frequent object to itself. Let your thoughts be made the subject of thought and review.—" To what is my attention at present directed? Could I disclose it without a blush to the world? Were God instantly to call me into judgment, what account could I give of it to him? Shall I be the wiser or the better for dwelling on such thoughts as now fill my mind? Are they entirely consistent with my innocence, and with my present and future peace? If they are not, to what purpose do I indulge such unprofitable or dangerous musings?"—By frequent exercise of this inward scrutiny, we might gradually bring imagination under discipline, and turn the powers of thought to their proper use as means of improvement, instead of suffering them to be only the instruments of vanity and guilt.

In the second place, in order to the government of thought, it is necessary to guard against idleness. Idleness is the great fomenter of all corruptions in the human heart. In particular, it is the parent of loose imaginations and inordinate desires. The ever active and restless power of thought, if not employed about what is good, will naturally and unavoidably engender evil. Imagine not that mere occupation, of whatever kind it be, will exempt you from the blame and danger of an idle life. Perhaps the worst species of idleness is a dissipated, though seemingly busy life, spent in the haunts of loose society, and in the chase of perpetual amusement. Hence a giddy mind, alternately elated and dejected with trifles, occupied with no recollection of the past but what is fruitless, and with no plans for the future but what are either frivolous or guilty.

As, therefore, you would govern your thoughts, or indeed as you would have any thoughts that are worthy of being governed, provide honourable employment for the native activity of your minds. Keep knowledge, virtue, and usefulness, ever in view. Let your life proceed in a train of such pursuits as are worthy of a Christian, of a rational and social Being. While these are regularly carried on as the main business of life, let amusement possess no more than its proper place in the distribution of your time. Take particular care that your amusements be of an irreproachable kind, and that all your society be

either

either improving or innocent. So shall the stream of your thoughts be made to run in a pure channel. Manly occupations and virtuous principles will expel the taint, which idleness never fails to communicate to the vacant mind.

In the third place, when criminal thoughts arise, attend to all the proper methods of speedily suppressing them. Take example from the unhappy industry which sinners discover in banishing good ones, when a natural sense of religion forces them on their conscience. How anxiously do they fly from themselves? how studiously do they drown the voice which upbraids them in the noise of company or diversion? what numerous artifices do they employ to evade the uneasiness which returns of reflection would produce?—Were we to use equal diligence in preventing the entrance of vicious suggestions, or in expelling them when entered, why should we not be equally successful in a much better cause?—As soon as you are sensible that any dangerous passion begins to ferment, instantly call in other passions, and other ideas, to your aid. Hasten to turn your thoughts into a different direction. Summon up whatever you have found to be of power for composing and harmonizing your mind. Fly for assistance to serious studies, to prayer and devotion; or even fly to business or innocent society, if solitude be in hazard of favouring the seduction. By such means you may stop the progress of the growing evil. You may apply an antidote, before the poison has had time to work its full effect.

In the forth place, it will be particularly useful to impress your minds with an habitual sense of the presence of the Almighty. When we reflect what a strong check the belief of divine omniscience is calculated to give to all criminal thoughts, we are tempted to suspect, that even by Christians this article of faith is not received with sincere conviction. For who but must confess, that if he knew a parent, a friend, or a neighbour, to have the power of looking into his heart, he durst not allow himself that unbounded scope which he now gives to his imagination and desire? Whence, then, comes it to pass, that men, without fear or concern, bring into the presence of the awful majesty of Heaven that folly and licentiousness of thought which would make them blush and tremble, if one of their own fellow-creatures could descry it? At the same time, no principle is supported by clearer evidence than the omniscience of God. All religious sects have admitted it, all societies of men, in their oaths and covenants, appeal to it. The Sovereign of the universe cannot but know what passes throughout his dominions. He who supports all nature must needs pervade and fill it. He who formed the heart is certainly conscious to what passes within it.

Never let this great article of faith escape from your view. In thinking,

thinking, as well as in acting, accustom yourselves to look up with reverence to that piercing eye of divine observation, which *never slumbers nor sleeps*. Behold a pen always writing over your head, and making up that great record of your thoughts, words, and actions, from which at last you are to be judged. Think that you are never less alone than when by yourselves; for then is He still with you whose inspection is of greater consequence than that of all mankind. Let these awful considerations not only check the dissipation of corrupt fancy, but infuse into your spirits that solemn composure which is the parent of meditation and wisdom. Let them not only expel what is evil, but introduce in its stead what is pure and holy; elevating your thoughts to divine and eternal objects, and acting as the counterpoise to those attractions of the world, which would draw your whole attention downwards to sense and vanity.

SERMON XVIII.

The same SUBJECT continued.

PROVERBS, iv. 23.

Keep thy heart with all diligence: for out of it are the issues of life.

HAVING treated, in the foregoing discourse, of the government of the thoughts, I proceed to consider the government of the passions as the next great duty included in the *keeping of the heart*.

Passions are strong emotions of the mind, occasioned by the view of apprehending good or evil. They are original parts of the constitution of our nature; and therefore to extirpate them is a mistaken aim. Religion requires no more of us than to moderate and rule them. When our blessed Lord assumed the nature, without the corruption, of man, he was subject to like passions with us. On some occasions he felt the risings of anger. He was often touched with pity. He was *grieved in spirit;* he sorrowed and he wept.

Passions, when properly directed, may be subservient to very useful ends. They rouse the dormant powers of the soul. They are even found to exalt them. They often raise a man above himself, and render him more penetrating, vigorous, and masterly, than he is in his calmer hours. Actuated by some high passion, he conceives great designs, and surmounts all difficulties in the execution. He is inspired with more lofty sentiments, and endowed with more persuasive utterance, than he possesses at any other time. Passions are the active forces of the soul. They are its highest powers brought into movement and exertion. But, like all other great powers, they are either useful or destructive, according to their direction and degree: as wind and fire are instrumental in carrying on many of the beneficent operations

rations of nature; but when they rife to undue violence, or deviate from their proper courfe, their path is marked with ruin.

It is the prefent infelicity of human nature, that thofe ftrong emotions of the mind are become too powerful for the principle which ought to regulate them. This is one of the unhappy confequences of our apoftafy from God, that the influence of reafon is weakened, and that of paffion ftrengthened within the heart. When man revolted from his Maker, his paffions rebelled againft himfelf; and, from being originally the minifters of reafon, have become the tyrants of the foul. Hence, in treating of this fubject, two things may be affumed as principles: firft, that through the prefent weaknefs of the underftanding, our paffions are often directed towards improper objects; and next, that even when their direction is juft, and their objects are innocent, they perpetually tend to run into excefs; they always hurry us towards their gratification with a blind and dangerous impetuofity. On thefe two points then turns the whole government of our paffions: firft, to afcertain the proper objects of their purfuit; and next, to reftrain them in that purfuit, when they would carry us beyond the bounds of reafon. If there be any paffion which intrudes itfelf unfeafonably into our mind, which darkens and troubles our judgment, or habitually difcompofes our temper; which unfits us for properly difcharging the duties, or difqualifies us for cheerfully enjoying the comforts of life, we may certainly conclude it to have gained a dangerous afcendant. The great object which we ought to propofe to ourfelves is, to acquire a firm and fteadfaft mind, which the infatuation of paffion fhall not feduce, nor its violence fhake; which, refting on fixed principles, fhall, in the midft of contending emotions, remain free, and mafter of itfelf; able to liften calmly to the voice of confcience, and prepared to obey its dictates without hefitation.

To obtain, if poffible, fuch command of paffion, is one of the higheft attainments of the rational nature. Arguments to fhow its importance crowd upon us from every quarter. If there be any fertile fource of mifchief to human life, it is, beyond doubt, the mifrule of paffion. It is this which poifons the enjoyment of individuals, overturns the order of fociety, and ftrews the path of life with fo many miferies, as to render it indeed the valley of tears. All thofe great fcenes of public calamity, which we behold with aftonifhment and horrour, have originated from the fource of violent paffions. Thefe have overfpread the earth with bloodfhed. Thefe have pointed the affaffin's dagger, and filled the poifoned bowl. Thefe, in every age, have furnifhed too copious materials for the orator's pathetic declamation, and for the poet's tragical fong.

When from public life we defcend to private conduct, though paffion operate not there in fuch a wide and deftructive fphere, we fhall find its influence to be no lefs baneful. I need not mention the black and fierce paſſions, ſuch as envy, jealouſy, and revenge, whoſe effects are obviouſly noxious, and whoſe agitations are immediate miſery. But take any of the licentious and ſenſual kind. Suppoſe it to have unlimited ſcope; trace it throughout its courſe; and you will find that gradually, as it riſes, it taints the ſoundneſs, and troubles the peace of his mind over whom it reigns; that in its progreſs it engages him in purſuits which are marked either with danger or with ſhame; that in the end it waſtes his fortune, deſtroys his health, or debaſes his character; and aggravates all the miſeries in which it has involved him with the concluding pangs of bitter remorſe. Through all the ſtages of this fatal courſe, how many have heretofore run? What multitudes do we daily behold purſuing it, with blind and headlong ſteps?

But, on the evils which flow from unreſtrained paſſions, it is needleſs to enlarge. Hardly are there any ſo ignorant or inconſiderate as not to admit, that where paſſion is allowed to reign, both happineſs and virtue muſt be impaired. I proceed therefore to what is of more conſequence, to ſuggeſt ſome directions which may be uſeful in aſſiſting us to preſerve the government of our paſſions.

In the firſt place, we muſt ſtudy to acquire juſt views of the comparative importance of thoſe objects that are moſt ready to attract deſire. The erroneous opinions which we form concerning happineſs and miſery, give riſe to all the miſtaken and dangerous paſſions which embroil our life. We ſuffer ourſelves to be dazzled by unreal appearances of pleaſure. We follow, with precipitancy, whitherſoever the crowd leads. We admire, without examination, what our predeceſſors have admired. We fly from every ſhadow at which we ſee others tremble. Thus, agitated by vain fears and deceitful hopes, we are hurried into eager conteſts about objects which are in themſelves of no value. By rectifying our opinions, we ſhould ſtrike at the root of the evil. If our vain imaginations were chaſtened, the tumult of our paſſions would ſubſide.

It is obſerved, that the young and the ignorant are always the moſt violent in purſuit. The knowledge which is forced upon them by longer acquaintance with the world, moderates their impetuoſity. Study then to anticipate, by reflexion, that knowledge which experience often purchaſes at too dear a price. Inure yourſelves to frequent conſideration of the emptineſs of thoſe pleaſures which excite ſo much ſtrife and commotion among mankind. Think how much more of true enjoyment is loſt by the violence of paſſion, than by the want of thoſe things which give occaſion to that paſſion. Perſuade yourſelves that the favour of God and the poſſeſſion of virtue form the chief happineſs of the rational nature. Let a contented mind, and a peaceful life, hold the next place in your eſtimation. Theſe are the concluſions

clusions which the wise and thinking part of mankind have always formed. To these conclusions, after having run the race of passion, you will probably come at the last. By forming them betimes, you would make a seasonable escape from that tempestuous region; through which none can pass without suffering misery, contracting guilt, and undergoing severe remorse.

In the second place, in order to attain the command of passion, it is requisite to acquire the power of self-denial. The self-denial of a Christian consists not in perpetual austerity of life, and universal renunciation of the innocent comforts of the world. Religion requires no such unnecessary sacrifices, nor is any such foe to present enjoyment. It consists in our being ready, on proper occasions, to abstain from pleasure, or to submit to suffering, for the sake of duty and conscience, or from a view to some higher and more extensive good. If we possess not this power, we shall be the prey of every loose inclination that chances to arise. Pampered by continual indulgence, all our passions will become mutinous and headstrong. Desire, not reason, will be the ruling principle of our conduct.

As, therefore, you would keep your passions within due bounds, you must betimes accustom them to know the reins. You must not wait till some critical occasion for the exercise of self-denial occur. In vain you will attempt to act with authority, if your first essay be made when temptation has inflamed the mind. In cooler hours, you must sometimes abridge your enjoyment even of what is innocent. In the midst of lawful pleasure you must maintain moderation, abstemiousness, and self-command. The observance of this discipline is the only method of supporting reason in its proper ascendant. For if you allow yourselves always to stretch to the utmost point of innocence and safety, beyond that point you will infallibly be hurried, when passion shall arise in its might to shake the heart.

In the third place, impress your minds deeply with this persuasion, that nothing is what it appears to be when you are under the power of passion. Be assured, that no judgment which you then form can be in the least depended upon as sound or true. The fumes which arise from a heart boiling with violent passions, never fail to darken and trouble the understanding. When the gourd withered, under the shade of which the prophet Jonah reposed, his mind, already ruffled by the disappointment of his predictions, lost, on occasion of this slight incident, all command of itself; and in the midst of his impatience, he *wished to die rather than to live.* Instead of being calmed by that expostulating voice, *Dost thou well, O Jonah! to be angry because of the gourd?* he replied with great emotion, *I do well to be angry even unto death.* But did Jonah think so when his passion had abated? Do these sentiments bear the least resemblance to that humble and devout prayer which, on another occasion, when in his calm mind, he put up to God *? No two persons can differ more from each other, than the same person differs from himself, when agitated by passion, and when master of his reason. *I do well to be angry*, is the language of every man when his mind is inflamed. Every passion justifies itself. It brings in a thousand pretences to its aid. It borrows many a false colour to hide its deformity. It possesses a sort of magic, by which it can magnify or diminish objects at pleasure, and transform the appearance of every thing within its sphere.

Let the knowledge of this imposture which passion practises, place you continually on your guard. Let the remembrance of it be ever at hand, to check the extravagant judgments which you are apt to pass in those moments of delusion. Listen to no suggestion which then arises. Form no conclusions on which you are to act. Assure yourselves that every thing is beheld through a false medium. Have patience for a little, and the illusion will vanish; the atmosphere will clear up around you, and objects return to be viewed in their native colours and just dimensions.

In the fourth place, oppose early the beginnings of passion. Avoid particularly all such objects as are apt to excite passions which you know to predominate within you. As soon as you find the tempest rising, have recourse to every proper method, either of allaying its violence, or of escaping to a calmer shore. Hasten to call up emotions of an opposite nature. Study to conquer one passion by means of some other which is of less dangerous tendency. Never account any thing small or trivial which is in hazard of introducing disorder into your heart. Never make light of any desire which you feel gaining such progress as to threaten entire dominion. Blandishing it will appear at the first. As a gentle and innocent emotion, it may steal into the heart; but as it advances, it is likely to *pierce you through with many sorrows*. What you indulged as a favourite amusement, will shortly become a serious business; and in the end may prove the burden of your life. Most of our passions flatter us in their rise. But their beginnings are treacherous; their growth is imperceptible; and the evils which they carry in their train lie concealed, until their dominion is established. What Solomon says of one of them, holds true of them all, that their *beginning is as when one letteth out water*.† It issues from a small chink, which once might have been easily stopped; but being neglected, it is soon widened by the stream; till the bank is at last totally thrown down, and the flood is at liberty to deluge the whole plain.

In the fifth place, the excess of every passion will be moderated by frequent meditation on the vanity of the world, the short continuance

* See *Jonah*, ii.   † *Prov.* xvii. 14.

of life, the approach of death, judgment, and eternity. The imaginary degree of importance which the neglect of such meditation suffers us to bestow on temporal things, is one great cause of our vehemence in desire, and our eagerness in pursuit. We attach ourselves to the objects around us, as if we could enjoy them for ever. Higher and more enlarged prospects of the destination of man would naturally cool his misplaced ardour. For what can appear so considerable in human affairs, as to discompose or agitate the mind of him to whose view eternity lies open, and all the greatness of the universe of God? How contemtible will seem to him this hurry of spirits, this turmoil of passion, about things which are so soon to end?—Where are they who once disturbed the world with the violence of their contests, and filled it with the renown of their exploits? What now remains of their designs and enterprises, of their passions and pursuits, of their triumphs and their glory? The flood of time has passed over them, and swept them away, as if they had never been. *The fashion of the world* changes continually around us. We succeed one another in the human course, like troops of pilgrims on their journey. Absurdly we spend our time in contending about the trifles of a day, while we ought to be preparing for a higher existence. Eternity is just at hand to close this introductory scene. It is fast rolling towards us, like the tide of a vast ocean, ready to swallow up all human concerns, and to leave no trace behind it, except the consequences of our good or bad deeds, which shall last for ever.—Let such reflections allay the heat of passion. Let them reduce all human things to their proper standard. From frivolous pursuits let them recal our attention to objects of real importance; to the proper business of man; to the improvement of our nature, the discharge of our duty, the rational and religious conduct of human life.

In the last place, to our own endeavours for regulating our passions, let us join earnest prayer to God. Here, if any where, divine assistance is requisite. For such is the present blindness and imperfection of human nature, that even to discover all the disorders of our heart is become difficult; much more, to rectify them, is beyond our power. To that superiour aid, then, which is promised to the pious and upright, let us look up with humble minds; beseeching the Father of mercies, that while we study to act our own part with resolution and vigilance, he would forgive our returning weakness; would strengthen our constancy in resisting the assaults of passion; and enable us by his grace so to govern our minds, that without considerable interruptions we may proceed in a course of piety and virtue.

It now remains to treat of the government of temper, as included in the *keeping of the heart*. Passions are quick and strong emotions while which by degrees subside: Temper is the disposition which remains after these emotions are past, and which forms the habitual propensity of the soul. The passions are like the stream when it is swoln by the torrent, and ruffled by the winds. The temper resembles it when running within its bed, with its natural velocity and force. The influence of temper is more silent and imperceptible than that of passion. It operates with less violence; but as its operation is constant, it produces effects no less considerable. It is evident, therefore, that it highly deserves to be considered in a religious view.

Many, indeed, are averse to behold it in this light. They place a good temper upon the same footing with a healthy constitution of body. They consider it as a natural felicity which some enjoy; but for the want of which, others are not morally culpable, nor accountable to God; and hence the opinion has sometimes prevailed, that a bad temper might be consistent with a state of grace. If this were true, it would overturn that whole doctrine, of which the gospel is so full, that regeneration, or change of nature, is the essential characteristic of a Christian. It would suppose that grace might dwell amidst malevolence and rancour, and that heaven might be enjoyed by such as are strangers to charity and love.—It will readily be admitted, that some, by the original frame of their mind, are more favourably inclined than others towards certain good dispositions and habits. But this affords no justification to those who neglect to oppose the corruptions to which they are prone. Let no man imagine that the human heart is a soil altogether unsusceptible of culture; or that the worst temper may not, through the assistance of grace, be reformed by attention and discipline. Settled depravity of temper is always owing to our own indulgence. If, in place of checking, we nourish that malignity of disposition to which we are inclined, all the consequences will be placed to our account, and every excuse from natural constitution be rejected at the tribunal of Heaven.

The proper regulation of temper affects the character of man in every relation which he bears; and includes the whole circle of religious and moral duties. This, therefore, is a subject of too great extent to be comprehended in one discourse. But it may be useful to take a general view of it; and before we conclude the doctrine of *keeping the heart*, to shew what the habitual temper of a good man ought to be, with respect to God, to his neighbour, and to himself.

FIRST, with respect to God, what he ought to cultivate is a devout temper. This imports more than the care of performing the offices of religious worship. It denotes that sensibility of heart towards the Supreme Being, which springs from a deep impression of his perfections on the soul. It stands opposed, not only to that disregard

gard of God which forms the description of the impious, but to that absence of religious affections which sometimes prevails among those who are imperfectly good. They acknowledge, perhaps, the obligations of duty. They feel some concern to *work out their salvation*. But they apply to their duty through mere constraint; and serve God without affection or complacency. More liberal and generous sentiments animate the man who is of a devout temper. God dwells upon his thoughts as a benefactor and a father, to whose voice he harkens with joy. Amidst the occurrences of life, his mind naturally opens to the admiration of his wisdom, the reverence of his power, the love of his transcendent goodness. All nature appears to his view as stamped with the imprefs of these perfections. Habitual gratitude to his Maker for mercies past, and cheerful resignation to his will in all time to come, are the native effusions of his heart.

Such a temper as this deserves to be cultivated with the utmost attention; for it contributes, in a high degree, both to our improvement and our happiness. It refines, and it exalts human nature. It softens that hardness which our hearts are ready to contract from frequent intercourse with this rugged world. It facilitates the discharge of every duty towards God and man. At the same time it is a temper peaceful and serene, elevated and rejoicing. It forms the current of our affections to flow in a placid tenour. It opens pleasing prospects to the mind. It banishes harsh and bitter passions; and places us above the reach of many of the annoyances of worldly life. When the temper is truly devout, *the peace of God which passeth understanding keepeth the heart and soul*. I proceed,

SECONDLY, to point out the proper state of our temper with respect to one another. It is evident, in the general, that if we consult either public welfare or private happiness, Christian charity ought to regulate our disposition in mutual intercourse. But as this great principle admits of several diversified appearances, let us consider some of the chief forms under which it ought to show itself in the usual tenour of life. Universal benevolence to mankind, when it rests in the abstract, is a loose indeterminate idea, rather than a principle of real effect; and too often floats as an useless speculation in the head, instead of affecting the temper and the heart.

What first presents itself to be recommended, is a peaceable temper; a disposition averse to give offence, and desirous of cultivating harmony, and amicable intercourse in society. This supposes yielding and condescending manners, unwillingness to contend with others about trifles, and, in contests that are unavoidable, proper moderation of spirit. Such a temper is the first principle of self-enjoyment. It is the basis of all order and happiness among mankind. The positive and contentious, the rude and quarrelsome, are the bane of society. They seem destined to blast the small share of comfort which nature has here allotted to man. But they cannot disturb the peace of others, more than they break their own. The hurricane rages first in their own bosom, before it is let forth upon the world. In the tempests which they raise, they are always tost; and frequently it is their lot to perish.

A peaceable temper must be supported by a candid one, or a disposition to view the conduct of others with fairness and impartiality. This stands opposed to a jealous and suspicious temper, which ascribes every action to the worst motive, and throws a black shade over every character. As you would be happy in yourselves, or in your connexions with others, guard against this malignant spirit. Study that charity *which thinketh no evil;* that temper which, without degenerating into credulity, will dispose you to be just; and which can allow you to observe an error, without imputing it as a crime. Thus you will be kept free from that continual irritation which imaginary injuries raise in a suspicious breast; and will walk among men as your brethren, not your enemies.

But to be peaceable, and to be candid, is not all that is required of a good man. He must cultivate a kind, generous, and sympathizing temper, which feels for distress, wherever it is beheld; which enters into the concerns of his friends with ardour; and to all with whom he has intercourse is gentle, obliging, and humane. How amiable appears such a disposition, when contrasted with a malicious or envious temper, which wraps itself up in its own narrow interest, looks with an evil eye on the success of others, and with an unnatural satisfaction feeds on their disappointments or miseries! How little does he know of the true happiness of life, who is a stranger to that intercourse of good offices and kind affections, which, by a pleasing charm, attach men to one another, and circulate joy from heart to heart!

You are not to imagine, that a benevolent temper finds no exercise, unless when opportunities offer of performing actions of high generosity, or of extensive utility. These may seldom occur. The condition of the greater part of mankind, in a good measure, precludes them. But in the ordinary round of human affairs, a thousand occasions daily present themselves of mitigating the vexations which others suffer, of soothing their minds, of aiding their interest, of promoting their cheerfulness or ease. Such occasions may relate to the smaller incidents of life. But let us remember, that of small incidents the system of human life is chiefly composed. The attentions which respect these, when suggested by real benignity of temper, are often more material to the happiness of those around us, than actions

which

which carry the appearance of greater dignity and splendour. No wife or good man ought to account any rules of behaviour as below his regard, which tend to cement the great brotherhood of mankind in comfortable union.

Particularly amidst that familiar intercourse which belongs to domestic life, all the virtues of temper find an ample range. It is very unfortunate, that within that circle, men too often think themselves at liberty to give unrestrained vent to the caprice of passion and humour. Whereas there, on the contrary, more than any where, it concerns them to attend to the government of their heart; to check what is violent in their tempers, and to soften what is harsh in their manners. For there the temper is formed. There, the real character displays itself. The forms of the world disguise men when abroad. But within his own family, every man is known to be what he truly is.—In all our intercourse, then, with others, particularly in that which is closest and most intimate, let us cultivate a peaceable, a candid, a gentle, and friendly temper. This is the temper to which, by repeated injunctions, our holy religion seeks to form us. This was the temper of Christ. This is the temper of Heaven.

We are now to consider, thirdly, the proper state of temper, as it respects the individual himself. The basis of all the good dispositions which belong to this head, is humility. By this I understand, not that meanness of spirit which leads a man to undervalue himself, and to sink below his rank and character; but what the scripture expresses with great propriety, when it exhorts *every man, not to think of himself more highly than he ought to think, but to think soberly**. He who adopts all the flattering suggestions of self-love, and forms claims upon the world proportioned to the imaginary opinion which he has conceived of his merit, is preparing for himself a thousand mortifications. Whereas, by checking the risings of ill-founded vanity, and retreating within those bounds which a moderate estimation of our character prescribes, we escape the miseries which always pursue an arrogant mind, and recommend ourselves to the favour both of God and man.

Hence will naturally arise a contented temper, which is one of the greatest blessings that can be enjoyed by man, and one of the most material requisites to the proper discharge of the duties of every station. For a fretful and discontented temper renders one incapable of performing aright any part in life. It is unthankful and impious towards God; and towards men, provoking and unjust. It is a gangrene which preys on the vitals, and infects the whole constitution with disease and putrifaction. Subdue pride and vanity, and you will take the most effectual method of eradicating this distemper. You will no

* *Rom.* xii. 3.

longer

longer behold the objects around you with jaundiced eyes. You will take in good part the bleſſings which Providence is pleaſed to beſtow, and the degree of favour which your fellow-creatures are diſpoſed to grant you. Viewing yourſelves, with all your imperfections and failings, in a juſt light, you will rather be ſurpriſed at your enjoying ſo many good things, than diſcontented, becauſe there are any which you want.

From a humble and contented temper will ſpring a cheerful one. This, if not in itſelf a virtue, is at leaſt the garb in which virtue ſhould be always arrayed. Piety and goodneſs ought never to be marked with that dejection which ſometimes takes riſe from ſuperſtition, but which is the proper portion only of guilt. At the ſame time, the cheerfulneſs belonging to virtue is to be carefully diſtinguiſhed from that light and giddy temper which characterizes folly, and is ſo often found among the diſſipated and vicious part of mankind. Their gaiety is owing to a total want of reflexion; and brings with it the uſual conſequences of an unthinking habit, ſhame, remorſe, and heavineſs of heart, in the end. The cheerfulneſs of a well-regulated mind ſprings from a good conſcience and the favour of heaven, and is bounded by temperance and reaſon. It makes a man happy in himſelf, and promotes the happineſs of all around him. It is the clear and calm ſunſhine of a mind illuminated by piety and virtue. It crowns all other good diſpoſitions, and comprehends the general effect which they ought to produce on the heart.

Such, on the whole, is the temper, or habitual frame of mind, in a good man: Devout towards God; towards men, peaceable, candid, affectionate, and humane; within himſelf, humble, contented, and cheerful. To the eſtabliſhment of this happy temper all the directions which I before ſuggeſted for the due regulation of the thoughts, and for the government of the paſſions, naturally conduce; in this they ought to iſſue; and when this temper is thoroughly formed within us, then may the heart be eſteemed to have been *kept with all diligence.* That we may be thus enabled to keep it, for the ſake both of preſent enjoyment, and of preparation for greater happineſs, let us earneſtly pray to Heaven. A greater bleſſing we cannot implore of the Almighty, than that he who made the human heart, and who knows its frailties, would aſſiſt us to ſubject it to that diſcipline which religion requires, which reaſon approves, but which his grace alone can enable us to maintain.

SERMON

SERMON XIX.
On the UNCHANGEABLENESS of the DIVINE NATURE.

JAMES, i. 17.

Every good and every perfect gift is from above, and cometh down from the Father of Lights, with whom is no variableness, neither shadow of turning.

THE divine nature, in some views, attracts our love; in others, commands our reverence; in all, is entitled to the highest attention from the human mind. We never elevate our thoughts, in a proper manner, towards the Supreme Being, without returning to our own sphere with sentiments more improved; and if, at any time, his greatness oppresses our thoughts, his moral perfections always afford us relief. His almighty power, his infinite wisdom and supreme goodness, are sounds familiar to our ears. In his immutability we are less accustomed to consider him; and yet it is this perfection which, perhaps, more than any other, distinguishes the divine nature from the human; gives complete energy to all its other attributes, and entitles it to the highest adoration. For, hence are derived the regular order of nature, and the stedfastness of the universe. Hence flows the unchanging tenour of those laws which, from age to age, regulate the conduct of mankind. Hence the uniformity of that government, and the certainty of those promises, which are the ground of our trust and security. Goodness could produce no more than feeble and wavering hopes, and power would command very imperfect reverence, if we were left to suspect that the plans which goodness had framed might alter, or that the power of carrying them into execution might decrease. The contemplation of God, therefore, as unchangeable in his nature and in all his perfections, must undoubtedly be fruitful both of instruction and of consolation to man. I shall, first, endeavour to illustrate, in some degree, the nature of the divine immutability; and then make application of it to our own conduct.

EVERY good and every perfect gift cometh down from the Father of Lights. The title which in the text is given to the Deity, carries an elegant allusion to the Sun, the source of light, the most universal benefactor of nature, the most regular and constant of all the great bodies with which we are acquainted in the universe. Yet even with the Sun there are certain degrees of *variableness*. He apparently rises and sets; he seems to approach nearer to us in summer, and to retire farther off in winter; his influence is varied by the seasons, and his lustre is affected by the clouds. Whereas with him who is the *Father of Lights*, of whose everlasting brightness the glory of the Sun is but a faint image, there is no *shadow of turning*, not the most distant approach to change.

In his being or essence it is plain that alteration can never take place. For as his existence is derived from no prior cause, nor dependent on any thing without himself, his nature can be influenced by no power, can be affected by no accident, can be impaired by no time. From everlasting to everlasting, he continues the same. Hence it is said, that *he only hath immortality;* that is, he possesses it in a manner incommunicable to all other beings. Eternity is described as the *high and holy place in which he dwelleth;* it is a habitation in which none but the *Father of Lights* can enter. The name which he taketh to himself is, *I am.* Of other things, some have been and others shall be; but this is he, *which is, which was, and which is to come.* All time is his; it is measured out by him in limited portions to the various orders of created beings; but his own existence fills equally every point of duration; *the first and the last, the beginning and the end, the same yesterday, to day, and for ever.*

As in his essence, so in his attributes and perfections, it is impossible there can be any change. To imperfect natures only it belongs to improve and to decay. Every alteration which they undergo in their abilities or dispositions, flows either from internal defect, or from the influence of a superior cause. But as no higher cause can bring from without any accession to the divine nature, so within itself it contains no principle of decay. For the same reason that the self-existent Being was from the beginning powerful and wise, just and good, he must continue unalterably so for ever. Hence, with much propriety, the divine perfections are described in scripture by allusions to those objects to which we ascribe the most permanent stability. *His righteousness is like the strong mountains. His mercy is in the heavens; and his faithfulness reacheth unto the clouds.* These perfections of the divine nature differ widely from the human virtues, which are their faint shadows. The justice of men is at one time severe, at another time relenting; their goodness is sometimes confined to a partial fondness for a few, sometimes runs out into a blind indulgence towards all. But goodness and justice are in the Supreme Being calm and steady principles of action, which, enlightened by perfect wisdom, and never either warped by partiality, or disturbed by passion, persevere in one regular and constant tenor. Among men, they may sometimes break forth with transient splendour, like those wandering fires which illuminate for a little the darkness of the night. But in God, they shine with that uniform brightness, which we can liken to nothing so much as to the untroubled, eternal lustre of the highest heavens.

From this follows, what is chiefly material for us to attend to, that in the course of his operations towards mankind, in his counsels and decrees, in his laws, his promises, and his threatenings, there is *no variableness nor shadow of turning* with the Almighty. *Known to him*

him *from the beginning were all his works.* In the divine idea the whole fyſtem of nature exiſted, long before the foundations of the earth were laid. When he ſaid, *Let there be light*, he only realized the great plan which, from everlaſting, he had formed in his own mind. Foreſeen by him was every revolution which the courſe of ages was to produce. Whatever the counſels of men can effect was comprehended in his decree. No new emergency can ariſe to ſurpriſe him. No agitations of anger or of ſorrow, of fear or of hope, can ſhake his mind or influence his conduct. He reſts in the eternal poſſeſſion of that ſupreme beatitude, which neither the virtues nor the crimes of men can in the leaſt affect. From a motive of overflowing goodneſs, he reared up the univerſe. As the eternal lover of righteouſneſs, he rules it. The whole fyſtem of his government is fixed; his laws are irrevocable; and, what he once loveth, *he loveth to the end.* In ſcripture, indeed, he is ſometimes ſaid to *be grieved*, and *to repent.* But ſuch expreſſions, it is obvious, are employed from accommodation to common conception; in the ſame manner as when bodily organs are, in other paſſages, aſcribed to God. The ſcripture, as a rule of life addreſſed to the multitude, muſt make uſe of the language of men. The divine nature, repreſented in its native ſublimity, would have tranſcended all human conceptions. When, upon the reformation of ſinners, God is ſaid to *repent of the evil* which he hath threatened againſt them; this intimates no more than that he ſuits his diſpenſations to the alterations which take place in the characters of men. His diſpoſition towards good and evil continues the ſame, but varies in its application as its objects vary; juſt as the laws themſelves, which are capable of no change of affection, bring rewards or puniſhments at different times to the ſame perſon, according as his behaviour alters. Immutability is indeed ſo cloſely connected with the notion of ſupreme perfection, that wherever any rational conceptions of a Deity have taken place, this attribute has been aſcribed to him. Reaſon taught the wiſe and reflecting in every age to believe, that, as what is eternal cannot die, ſo what is perfect can never vary, and that the great Governor of the univerſe could be no other than an unchangeable Being.

From the contemplation of this obvious, but fundamental truth, let us proceed to the practical improvement of it. Let us conſider what effect the ſerious conſideration of it ought to produce on our mind and behaviour.

It will be proper to begin this head of diſcourſe by removing an objection which the doctrine I have illuſtrated may appear to form againſt religious ſervices, and in particular againſt the duty of prayer. To what purpoſe, it may be urged, is homage addreſſed to a Being whoſe purpoſe is unalterably fixed; to whom *our righteouſneſs extendeth not;* whom by no arguments we can perſuade, and by no ſupplications we can mollify? The objection would have weight, if our religious addresses were designed to work any alteration on God; either by giving him information of what he did not know; or by exciting affections which he did not possess; or by inducing him to change measures which he had previously formed. But they are only crude and imperfect notions of religion which can suggest such ideas. The change which our devotions are intended to make, is upon ourselves, not upon the Almighty. Their chief efficacy is derived from the good dispositions which they raise and cherish in the human soul. By pouring out pious sentiments and desires before God, by adoring his perfection, and confessing our own unworthyness, by expressing our dependence on his aid, our gratitude for his past favours, our submission to his present will, our trust in his future mercy, we cultivate such affections as suit our place and station in the universe, and are thereby prepared for becoming objects of the divine grace. Accordingly, frequent assurances are given us in Scripture, that the prayers of sincere worshippers, preferred through the great Mediator, shall be productive of the happiest effects. *When they ask, they shall receive; when they seek, they shall find; when they knock, it shall be opened to them.* Prayer is appointed to be the channel for conveying the divine grace to mankind, because the wisdom of heaven saw it to be one of the most powerful means of improving the human heart.

When religious homage is considered in this light, as a great instrument of spiritual and moral improvement, all the objections which scepticism can form from the divine immutability, conclude with no more force against prayer, than against every other mean of improvement which reason has suggested to man. If prayer be superfluous, because God is unchangeable, we might upon similar grounds conclude, that it is needless to labour the earth, to nourish our bodies, or to cultivate our minds, because the fertility of the ground, the continuance of our life, and the degree of our understanding, depend upon an immutable Sovereign, and were from all eternity foreseen by him. Such absurd conclusions reason has ever repudiated. To every plain and sound understanding it has clearly dictated, that to explore the unknown purposes of Heaven belongs not to us; but that He who decrees the end, certainly requires the means; and that, in the diligent employment of all the means which can advance either our temporal or spiritual felicity, the chief exertions of human wisdom and human duty consist. Assuming it then for an undoubted principle, that religion is a reasonable service, and that, though with the *Father of Lights* there be no *variableness*, the homage of his creatures is nevertheless, for the wisest reasons, required by him, I proceed to shew what sentiments the contemplation of divine immutability should raise in our minds, and what duties it should chiefly enforce.   I.

I. Let it excite us to admire and adore. Filled with profound reverence, let us look up to that Supreme Being who sits from everlasting on the throne of the universe; moving all things, but remaining immoveable himself; directing every revolution of the creation, but affected by no revolutions of events or of time. He beholds the heavens and the earth *wax old as a garment, and decay like a vesture.* At their appointed periods he raises up, or he dissolves worlds. But amidst all the convulsions of changing and perishing nature, his glory and felicity remain unaltered.—The view of great and stupendous objects in the natural world strikes the mind with solemn awe. What veneration, then, ought to be inspired by the contemplation of an object so sublime as the eternal and unchangeable Ruler of the universe! The composure and stillness of thought introduced by such a meditation, has a powerful tendency both to purify and to elevate the heart. It effaces, for a time, those trivial ideas, and extinguishes those low passions, which arise from the circle of vain and passing objects around us. It opens the mind to all the sentiments of devotion; and accompanies devotion, with that profound reverence which guards it from every improper excess. When we consider the Supreme Being as employed in works of love; when we think of his condescension to the human race in sending his Son to dwell on the earth; encouraged by favours, and warmed by gratitude, we are sometimes in danger of presuming too much on his goodness, and of indulging a certain fondness of affection, which is unsuitable to our humble and dependent state. It is necessary that he should frequently appear to our minds in all that majesty with which the immutability of his nature clothes him; in order that reverence may be combined with love, and that a mixture of sacred awe may chasten the rapturous effusions of warm devotion. Servile fear, indeed, would crush the spirit of ingenuous and affectionate homage. But that reverence which springs from elevated conceptions of the divine nature, has a happy effect in checking the forwardness of imagination, restraining our affections within due bounds, and composing our thoughts at the same time that it exalts them.

When, from the adoration of the unchangeable perfection of the Almighty, we return to the view of our own state, the first sentiment which ought naturally to arise, is that of self-abasement. We are too apt to be lifted up by any little distinctions which we possess; and to fancy ourselves great, only because there are others whom we consider as less. But what is man, with all his advantages and boasted powers, before the eternal *Father of Lights?* With God there is no variableness; with man there is no stability. Virtue and vice divide the empire of his mind; and wisdom and folly alternately rule him. Hence he is changeable in his designs, fickle in his friendships, fluctuating in his whole character. His life is a series of contradictions. He is one thing to-day, and another to-morrow; sometimes obliged by experience to alter his purpose, and often led to change it through levity. Variable and unequal himself, he is surrounded with fleeting objects. He is placed as in the midst of a torrent, where all things are rolling by, and nothing keeps its place. He has hardly time to contemplate this scene of vicissitude, before he too is swept away. Thus circumstanced in himself, and in all the objects with which he is connected, let him be admonished to be humble and modest. Let the contemplation of the unchanging glory of his Creator inspire him with sentiments of due submission. Let it teach him to know his proper place; and check that vanity which is so ready to betray him into guilt.

Let the same meditation affect him with a deep sense of what he owes to the goodness of the Deity. His goodness never appears in so striking a light, as when viewed in connection with his greatness. The description which is given of him in the text, calls, in this view, for our particular attention. It presents to us the most amiable union of condescension with majesty, of the moral with the natural perfections of God, which can possibly be exhibited to the imagination of man. *From the Father of Lights, with whom there is no variableness, neither shadow of turning, cometh down every good and perfect gift.* The most independent of all Beings is represented as the most beneficent. He who is eternal and immutable, exalted above all, and incapable of receiving returns from any, is the liberal and unwearied Giver of every thing that is good.—Let such views of the divine nature not only call forth gratitude and praise, but prompt us to imitate what we adore. Let them shew us that benevolence is divine; that to stoop from our fancied grandeur, in order to assist and relieve one another, is so far from being any degradation of character, that it is our truest honour, and our nearest resemblance to *the Father of Lights.*

II. Let the consideration of the divine immutability convince us, that the method of attaining the favour of Heaven is one and invariable. Were the Almighty a capricious and inconstant Being, like man, we should be at a loss what tenour of conduct to hold. In order to conciliate his grace, we might think of applying sometimes to one supposed principle of his inclination, sometimes to another; and, bewildered

wildered amidst various attempts, would be overwhelmed with dismay. The guilty would essay to flatter him. The timid, sometimes by austere mortifications, sometimes by costly gifts, sometimes by obsequious rites, would try to appease him. Hence, in fact, have arisen all the corruptions of religious worship among men; from their forming the divine character upon their own, and ascribing to the Sovereign of the universe the mutability of human passions. God is represented by the psalmist David as saying to the wicked, *Thou thoughtest that I was altogether such an one as thyself.** This continues to be the description of all the superstitious and enthusiastic sects, which, since the days of David, have sprung up in the world.

It is our peculiar happiness, under the gospel, to have God revealed to us in his genuine character, as *without variableness or shadow of turning.* We know that at no time there is any change, either in his affections, or in the plan of his administration. One light always shines upon us from above. One clear and direct path is always pointed out to man. The Supreme Being is, and was, and ever will be, the supporter of order and virtue; the *righteous Lord loving righteousness.* The external forms of religion may vary; but under all dispensations which proceed from God, its substance is the same. It tends continually to one point, the purification of man's heart and life. This was the object of the original law of nature. This was the scope of the Mosaic institution amidst all its sacrifices and rites; and this is unquestionably the end of the gospel. So invariably constant is God to this purpose, that the dispensation of mercy in Christ Jesus, which admits of the vicarious atonement and righteousness of a Redeemer, makes no change in our obligation to fulfil the duties of a good life. The Redeemer himself hath taught us, that to the end of time the moral law continues in its full force; and that *till heaven and earth pass away, one jot or tittle shall in no wise pass from it.*† This is the only institution known to men, whose authority is unchanging and constant. Human laws rise and fall with the empires that gave them birth. Systems of philosophy vary with the progress of knowledge and light. Manners, sentiments, and opinions, alter with the course of time. But throughout all ages, and amidst all revolutions, the rule of moral and religious conduct is the same. It partakes of that immutablity of the divine nature, on which it is founded. Such as it was delivered to the first worshippers of God, it continues to be, at this day, to us; and such it shall remain to our posterity for ever.

III.

* *Psalm* l. 21.   † *Matt.* v. 18.

III. Let the contemplation of this perfection of the divine nature teach us to imitate, as far as our frailty will permit, that constancy and stedfastness which we adore. All the moral attributes of the Supreme Being, are standards of character towards which we ought to aspire. But as in all these perfections there are properties peculiar to the divine nature, our endeavours to resemble them are laid under great restrictions by the dissimilarity between our nature and the divine. With respect to that attribute which we now consider, the circumstances are evident which preclude improper imitation. To man it is frequently necessary to correct his errours, and to change his conduct. An attempt, therefore, to continue wholly invariable, would, in our situation, be no other than imprudent and criminal obstinacy. But withal, the immutable rectitude of the Deity should lead us to aspire after fixedness of principle, and uniformity in conduct, as the glory of the rational nature. Impressed with the sense of that supreme excellence which results from unchanging goodness, faithfulness, and truth, let us become ashamed of that levity which degrades the human character. Let us *ponder our paths*, act upon a well-regulated plan, and remain consistent with ourselves. Contemplating the glory of the Father of Lights, let us aim at being transformed, in some degree, *into the same image from glory to glory*. Finally,

IV. Let the divine immutability become the ground of confidence and trust to good men, amidst all the revolutions of this uncertain world. This is one of the chief improvements to be made of the subject, and therefore requires full illustration. There are three lights in which we may view the benefit redounding to us from that attribute of God which we now consider. It assures us of the constancy of Nature; of the regular administration of Providence; of the certain accomplishment of all the divine promises.

First, it gives us ground to depend on the constant and uniform course of Nature. On the unchangeableness of God rests the stability of the universe. What we call the laws of nature are no other than the decrees of the Supreme Being. It is because He is *without variableness or shadow of turning*, that those laws have continued the same since the beginning of the world; that the Sun so constantly observes his time of rising and going down; that the seasons annually return; the tides periodically ebb and flow; the earth yields its fruits at stated intervals; and the human body and mental powers advance to maturity by a regular progress. In all those motions and operations which are incessantly going on throughout nature, there is is no stop nor interruption, no change nor innovation; no deflection from their main scope. The same powerful and steady hand which gave the first impulse to the powers of nature, restrains them from ever exceeding their prescribed line. Hence arises the chief comfort of our present life. We find ourselves in a regular and orderly world. We look forward to a known succession of events. We are enabled to form plans of action. From the cause we calculate the effect; and from the past, we reason with confidence concerning the future.

Accustomed from our infancy to this constancy in Nature, we are hardly sensible of the blessing. Familiarity has the same effect here, as in many other enjoyments, to efface gratitude. But let us, for a moment, take an opposite view of things. Let us suppose, that we had any cause to dread capriciousness or change in the power who rules the course of nature; any ground to suspect that, but for one day, the Sun might not rise, nor the current of the waters hold their usual course, nor the laws of motion and vegetation proceed as we have been accustomed to behold them. What dismay would instantly fill all hearts! what horror would seem to overspread the whole face of Nature! What part could we act, or whither could we run, in the midst of convulsions, which overturned all the measures we had formed for happiness, or for safety? The present abode of man would then become, as Job describes the region of the grave, *a land of darkness, as darkness itself, and the shadow of death; without any order; and where the light is as darkness.* * With what joy ought we then to recognise an unvarying and stedfast Ruler, under whose dominion we have no such disasters to dread; but can depend on the course of nature continuing to proceed as it has ever gone on, until the period shall arrive of its final dissolution!

But though the great laws of Nature be constant like their Author, yet in the affairs of men there is much variety and change. All that regards our present possessions and enjoyments was, for wise reasons, left, in a great measure, uncertain; and from this uncertainty arises the distress of human life. Sensible of the changes to which we lie open, we look round with anxious eyes, and eagerly grasp at every object which appears to promise us security. But in vain is the whole circle of human things explored with this view. There is nothing on earth so stable as to assure us of undisturbed rest, nor so powerful as to afford us constant protection. Time, death, and

* *Job*, x. 22.

and change, triumph over all the labours of men. What we build up, they inceffantly deftroy. The public condition of nations, and the private fortunes of individuals, are alike fubject to reverfe. Life never retains long the fame form. Its whole fcenery is continually fhifting around us.—Amidft thofe endlefs viciffitudes, what can give any firm confolation, any fatisfying reft to the heart, except the dominion of a wife and righteous Sovereign, *with whom there is no variableness, nor fhadow of turning?* Though all things change, and we ourfelves be involved in the general mutability, yet as long as there is fixed and permanent goodnefs at the head of the univerfe, we are affured that the great interefts of all good men fhall be fafe. That *river* perpetually flows, *the ftreams whereof make glad the city of God.* We know that the Supreme Being loved righteoufnefs from the beginning of days, and that he will continue to love it to the laft. Under his government none of thofe revolutions happen which have place among the kingdoms of the earth; where princes die, and new fovereigns afcend the throne; new minifters and new counfels fucceed; the whole face of affairs is changed; and former plans fall into oblivion. But *the throne of the Lord is eftablifhed for ever; and the thoughts of his heart endure to all generations.* We ferve the fame God whom our fathers worfhipped, and whom our pofterity fhall adore. His unchanging dominion comprehends all events and all ages; eftablifhes a connecting principle which holds together the paft, the prefent, and the future; gives ftability to things which in themfelves are fluctuating, and extracts order from thofe which appear moft confufed. Well may the *earth rejoice, and the multitude of ifles be glad,* becaufe there reigneth over the univerfe fuch an immutable Lord.

Were you to unhinge this great article of faith; were you either to *fay with the fool,* that there is *no God,* or to fuppofe with the fuperftitious, that the God who rules is variable and capricious; you would indeed *lay the axe to the root of the tree,* and cut down, with one blow, the hope and fecurity of mankind. For you would then leave nothing in the whole compafs of nature, but a round of cafual and tranfitory being; no foundation of truft, no protection to the righteous, no ftedfaft principle to uphold and to regulate the fucceffion of exiftence. Inftead of that magnificent fpectacle which the world now exhibits, when beheld in connexion with the divine government, it would then only prefent to view a multitude of fhort-lived creatures fpringing out of the duft, wandering on the face of the earth without guide or protector, ftruggling for a few years againft the torrent of uncertainty and change; and then sinking into utter oblivion, and vanishing like visions of the night. Mysterious obscurity would involve the beginning of things; disorder would mark their progress; and the blackness of darkness would cover their final result. Whereas, when Faith enables us to discover an universal Sovereign, whose power never fails, and whose wisdom and goodness never change, the prospect clears up on every side. A ray from the great source of light seems to illuminate the whole creation. Good men discover a parent and a friend. They attain a fortress in every danger; a refuge amidst all storms, *a dwelling-place in all generations.* They are no longer *afraid of evil tidings. Their heart is fixed, trusting in the Lord.*

Though these reasonings, from the unchanging tenour of divine government, cannot but afford much comfort to good men, their satisfaction, however, becomes still more complete, when they consider the explicit promises which are given them in the word of God. The immutability of the divine purpose assures them most perfectly of those promises being fulfilled in due time, how adverse soever circumstances may at present appear to their accomplishment. *The Strength of Israel is not a man that he should lie, nor the son of man that he should repent. Hath he said it, and shall he not do it? Hath he spoken, and shall he not make it good?* Men have the command only of the present time. When that is suffered to pass, changes may befal, either in their own state, or in the situation of things around them, which shall defeat their best intentions in our behalf, and render all their promises fruitless. Hence, even setting aside the danger of human inconstancy, the confidence which we can repose on any earthly protector is extremely imperfect. Man, in his highest glory, is but a reed floating on the stream of time, and forced to follow every new direction of the current. But God is *the rock of ages.* All time is equally in his hands. Intervening accidents cannot embarrass him; nor any unforeseen obstacle retard the performance of his most distant promise. *One day is with the Lord as a thousand years, and a thousand years are as one day.* There is no vicissitude of the human state in which good men cannot take sanctuary with him as a sure and abiding friend; the safe conductor of their pilgrimage here, as well as the eternal rest of their souls hereafter. All their patrons may desert them; and all their friends may die: but *the Lord still lives, who is their rock; and the most high God, who is their Redeemer.* He hath promised that he *will not leave them when they are old, nor forsake them when their strength faileth;* and that even when *their heart shall faint; and their flesh fail, he will be the strength of their heart, and their portion for ever.* His immutability is not only the ground of trust in him during their own abode on earth, but gives them the satisfaction of looking forward to the same wise and good administration as continued to the end of time. When departing hence, and bidding adieu to life, with all its changeful scenes, they can with comfort and peace leave their family, their friends, and their dearest concerns, in the hands of that God who reigneth for ever; and whose *countenance shall always behold the upright* with the same complacency. *My days are like a shadow that declineth, and I am withered like the grass. But thou, O Lord, shalt endure for ever; and thy remembrance to all generations. The children of thy servants shall continue; and their seed shall be established before thee.**

Such are the benefits which good men may derive from meditation on God as without *variableness or shadow of turning*. It inspires them with sentiments of devout, humble, and grateful adoration. It points out to them the unvarying tenour of conduct which they ought to hold; checks their fickleness and inconstancy; and, amidst all distresses and fears, affords them comfort. The immutability of God is the surest basis on which their hopes can be built. It is indeed the pillar on which the whole universe rests.—On such serious and solemn meditations let our thoughts often dwell, in order to correct that folly and levity which are so apt to take possession of the human heart. And if our minds be overawed, and even depressed, with so high a view of the divine nature, let them be relieved by the reflection, that to this unchangeable God we are permitted to look up through a gracious Mediator, who, though possessed of divine perfection, is not unconscious of human distress and frailty.

SERMON

* *Psalm* cii. 11, 12. 28.

SERMON XX.

On the COMPASSION of CHRIST.

Preached at the Celebration of the Sacrament of the Lord's Supper.

HEBREWS, iv. 15.

We have not an high priest which cannot be touched with the feeling of our infirmities; but was in all points tempted like as we are, yet without sin.

WHEN we compare the counsels of Providence with the plans of men, we find a like difference obtain, as in the works of nature compared with those of art. The works of art may, at first view, appear the most finished and beautiful; but when the eye is assisted to pry into their contexture, the nicest workmanship is discerned to be rough and blemished. Whereas the works of nature gain by the most accurate examination; and those which on a superficial survey appear defective or rude, the more intimately they are inspected, discover the more exact construction and consummate beauty. In the same manner the systems of worldly policy, though at first they seem plausible and profound, soon betray in their progress the narrowness of the human understanding; while those dispensations of Providence, which appeared to furnish objections either against the goodness or the wisdom of Heaven, have, upon a more extensive view of their consequences, frequently afforded the most striking proofs of both.

God manifested in the flesh was to the *Jews a stumbling-block, and to the Greeks foolishness.* It contradicted every prepossession which their confined ideas of religion and philosophy led them to entertain. If a superiour Being was to interpose for the restoration of a degenerate world, they concluded that he would certainly appear in celestial majesty. But *the thoughts of God are not as the thoughts of men.* The divine wisdom saw it to be fit that the Saviour of mankind should in all things be made like unto those whom he came to save. By living as a man among men, he dispensed instruction in the most winning manner. He added to instruction the grace and the force of his own example. He accommodated that example to the most trying and difficult situations of human life; and, by suffering a painful death, he both taught men how to suffer and die; and in that nature which had offended, he offered a solemn expiation to God, for human guilt.

Besides these ends, so worthy of God, which were accomplished by the incarnation of Christ, another, of high importance, is suggested in the text. Human life is to good men, as well as to others, a state of suffering and distress. To supply them with proper consolation and encouragement during such a state, was one great purpose of the undertaking of Christ. With this view he assumed the office of their high priest, or mediator with God; and the encouragement which this office affords them, will be proportioned to their assured belief, first of his power, and next of his compassion. His power is set forth in the verse preceding the text, and the proper argument is founded upon it. *Seeing that we have a great high priest who is passed into the heavens, Jesus the Son of God, let us hold fast our proffession.* But though it be encouraging to know that our high priest is the *Son of God*, and that he is *passed into the heavens*, yet these facts alone are not sufficient to render him the full object of our confidence. For, as the apostle afterwards observes, it belongs to the character of a high priest *to be taken from among men, that he may have compassion on the ignorant, and them that are out of the way, seeing that he himself is compassed with infirmity*. In order then to satisfy us of our high priest's possessing also the qualifications of mercy and compassion, we are told that he is *touched with the feeling of our infirmities, and was in all points tempted like as we are*. The force of this consideration I purpose now to illustrate. I shall first explain the facts which are stated in the text, and then show how from these our Saviour's compassion is to be inferred, and in what manner it may be accommodated to the consolation and hope of good men amidst various exigencies of life.

The assertion in the text of Christ's being *touched with the feeling of our infirmities*, plainly implies that he had full experience both of the external distresses, and of the internal sorrows of human nature. Assuming a body such as ours, he subjected himself to all the natural consequences of corporeal frailty. He did not chuse for himself an easy and opulent condition, in order to glide through the world with the

the least molestation. He did not suit his mission to the upper ranks of mankind chiefly, by assimilating his state to theirs: but, born in meanness, and bred up to labour, he submitted to the inconveniencies of that poor and toilsome life which falls to the share of the most numerous part of the human race. Whatever is severe in the disregard of relations or the ingratitude of friends, in the scorn of the proud or the insults of the mean, in the virulence of reproach or the sharpness of pain, was undergone by Christ. Though his life was short, he familiarized himself in it with a wide compass of human woe; and there is almost no distressful situation to which we can be reduced, but what he has experienced before us. There is not the least reason to imagine that the eminence of his nature raised him above the sensations of trouble and grief. Had this been the case, he would have been a sufferer in appearance only, not in reality; there would have been no merit in his patience, or in the resignation which he expressed. On the contrary, it appears, from many circumstances, that the sensibility of his nature was tender and exquisite. He affected none of that hard indifference in which some ancient philosophers vainly gloried. He felt as a man, and he sympathized with the feelings of others. On different occasions we are informed that he was *troubled in spirit*, that *he groaned*, and that *he wept*. The relation of his agony in the garden of Gethsemane exhibits a striking picture of the sensations of innocent nature oppressed with anguish. It discovers all the conflict between the dread of suffering on the one hand, and the sense of duty on the other; the man struggling for a while with human weakness, and in the end recollected in virtue, and rising superiour to the objects of dismay which were then in his view. *Father! if it be possible, let this cup pass from me. Nevertheless, not as I will, but as thou wilt. Thy will be done.* Thus was our Saviour *touched with the feeling of our infirmities.* He was *a man of sorrows and acquainted with grief.*

It is added in the text, that he was *in all points tempted like as we are*. To be tempted is, in the language of Scripture, to undergo such trials of virtue as are accompanied with difficulty and conflict. Though our Lord was not liable to any temptations from depravity of nature, yet he was perpetually exposed to such as arise from situations the most adverse to virtue. His whole life was in this respect a course of temptation; that is, a severe trial of his constancy by every discouragement. He suffered repeated provocations both from friends and foes. His endeavours to do good were requited with the most obstinate and perverse opposition. Sometimes by the solicitations of ignorant multitudes he was tempted to accept the proffers of worldly greatness. Oftener, by the insults of multitudes, more blind and brutal, he was tempted to desert an office which exposed him to so much misery. Together with the world, the powers of darkness also combined their efforts against him. we are informed that he was *led into the wilderness*, and, amidst the horrors of a wild and dreary solitude, was *tempted of the devil*. The great adversary of mankind seems to have been permitted to exert unusual proofs of his power and malice, on purpose that the trial of our Saviour's constancy might be more complete, and his victory over him more illustrious and distinguished.

From all these circumstances, the conclusion is obvious, that our Lord knows, from personal experience, all the discouragements and temptations which virtue can suffer. Though he participated not of the corruption, yet he felt the weakness of human nature. He felt the strength of passion. He is no stranger to the disturbance and commotion, which either the attacks of the world, or the powers of darkness, are able to raise within the breast of man. One remarkable difference, indeed, takes place between our temptations and those of Christ. Though he was *tempted like as we are, yet he was without sin.* Though the conflict was the same, the issue was different. We are often foiled; He always overcame. But his disconformity to us in this respect, is far from weakening the strength of our present argument. For sin contracts and hardens the heart. Every degree of guilt, incurred by yielding to temptation, tends to debase the mind, and to weaken the generous and benevolent principles of human nature. If from our Lord's being *tempted like as we are*, we have any ground to expect his sympathy, from his being tempted, *yet without sin*, we are entitled to hope that his sympathy, unallayed and perfect, will operate with more complete energy.

From this view of the facts which are stated in the text, I proceed to show how justly we may infer our Saviour's compassion, and in what manner it is to be accommodated to the consolation of good men amidst various exigencies of life.

It has been the universal opinion of mankind, that personal experience of suffering humanizes the heart. In the school of affliction, compassion is always supposed to be most thoroughly learned; and hence, in the laws of Moses, when the Israelites are commanded not to opprefs the ftranger, this reafon is given, "for ye know the heart of a ftranger, feeing ye were ftrangers yourfelves in the land of Egypt.* The diftreffed, accordingly, fly for confolation to thofe who have been their companions in woe. They decline the profperous, and look up to them with a fufpicious eye. They confider them as ignorant of their feelings, and therefore regardlefs of their complaints. Amidft the manifold forrows of life, then, how foothing is the thought that our great Interceffor with God was a fellow-fufferer with ourfelves, while he paffed through this valley of tears.

But was it neceffary for Chrift, it may be faid, to affume our nature in order to acquire the knowledge of its infirmity and diftrefs? As a divine perfon, was he not perfectly acquainted with our frame before he defcended to the earth? Did he ftand in need of being prompted to compaffion by the experience of our forrows? Could his experimental knowledge of human weaknefs increafe the benevolence of a nature which before was perfect?—No: he fubmitted to be *touched with the feeling of our infirmities, and to be tempted like as we are;* not in order to become acquainted with our nature, but to fatisfy us that he knew it perfectly; not in order to acquire any new degree of goodnefs, but to give us the firmer confidence in the goodnefs which he poffeffed, and to convey the fenfe of it to our hearts with greater force and effect.

Diftruft is a weaknefs peculiarly incident to the miferable. They are apt to reject hope, to indulge fear, and to tinge, with the dark colour of their own minds, every object which is offered for their encouragement. The reprefentations given us of the Deity in Scripture, afford undoubtedly much ground for truft in his goodnefs. But the perfection of an Almighty Being, who dwelleth in the fecret place of eternity, *whom no man hath feen or can fee,* is overwhelming to a timid apprehenfion. The goodnefs which it promifes is a new and unknown form of goodnefs. Whatever proceeds from a nature fo far fuperiour to our own, is beheld with a degree of awe, which is ready to overpower hope. Upon this account, under the Old Teftament difpenfation, the Supreme Being is often defcribed with the attributes of a man, in order to give a fhade and foftening to his greatnefs, and to accommodate his goodnefs more to our capacity. The relentings of a friend, the pity of a parent, and the fighs of a mourner, are afcribed to the Almighty. But we eafily perceive fuch attributes to be no more than figures and allufions. The comfort

* *Exod.* xxii. 9.

comfort which they afford is not definite nor precise. They leave the mind under an anxious uncertainty, left it err in its interpretation of those allegories of mercy. In the person of Jesus Christ the object of our trust is brought nearer to ourselves; and of course adapted more effectually to our encouragement. Those well-known tender affections, which are only figuratively ascribed to the Divinity, are in our great Mediator thoroughly realized. His goodness is the goodness of human nature exalted and rendered perfect. It is that species of goodness with which we are best acquainted, compassion to the unhappy; and compassion cultivated by that discipline which we know to be the most powerful, the experience of sorrows.

For such reasons as these, "because the children are partakers of "flesh and blood, Christ himself likewise took part of the same. In "all things it behoved him to be made like unto his brethren, that he "might be a merciful" as well as a "faithful high priest." When we consider his assumption of our nature in this light, what a mild and amiable aspect does it give to the government of heaven! What attentive solicitude of goodness is shewn in carrying on the dispensation of our redemption upon a plan so perfectly calculated to banish all distrust, and to revive the most timid and dejected heart! How naturally does that inference follow which the Apostle makes in the verse immediately succeeding the text; "let us therefore come bold-"ly to the throne of grace, that we may obtain mercy, and find grace " to help in time of need!" More particularly, in consequence of the doctrine which I have illustrated, we are taught to hope,

I. THAT under all our infirmities and errors, regard will be had to human imperfection; that a merciful distinction will be made between what is weak and what is wilfully criminal in our conduct; and that such measures of obedience only will be exacted as are proportioned to our circumstances and powers. What can more encourage our religious services, than to be assured that the God whom we worship, " knows our frame, and remembers we are dust;" and that the Mediator, through whom we worship him, " is touched " with the feeling of our infirmities?" The most virtuous are the most apt to be dejected with the sense of their frailty. While vain and superficial men are easily flattered with favourable views of themselves, and fond hopes of divine acceptance, the slightest apprehension of guilt is ready to alarm the humble and delicate mind; just as on coarse bodies an impression is not easily made, while those of finer
contexture

contexture are soon hurt; and as on an exquisite polish the least speck is visible. But though religion promotes great sensibility to all feelings of a moral nature, yet it gives no countenance to excessive and superstitious fears. That humility which checks presumption, and that jealousy which inspires vigilance, are favourable to piety; while those suspicions which lead to despondency are injurious to God, hurtful to ourselves, and repugnant to that whole system of mercy which I have been illustrating.

You complain, that when you engage in the solemn exercises of devotion, your spirits are depressed by a load of cares and sorrows; that in your thoughts there is no composure, and in your affections no elevation; that after your utmost essays, you are incapable of fixing your attention steadily on God, or of sending up your prayers to him with becoming warmth and fulness of heart. This debility and wandering of mind you are apt to impute to some uncommon degree of guilt. You consider it as the symptom of incurable hardness of heart, and as a melancholy proof of your being abandoned by God.—Such fears as these in a great measure refute themselves. If you were really obdurate, you would be insensible of guilt. Your complaints of hardness of heart are an evidence of your heart being at that moment contrite and actually relenting.—Are there any circumstances of inward discomposure and perplexity of which He is unconscious, who at a critical period of his life was "heavy and sore amazed;"* who was obliged to complain that his soul was "troubled within him;" and to acknowledge, that though "the spirit was willing, yet the flesh was weak?" To a superiour nature, untouched with human frailty, you might in such situations look up with some degree of terrour. But He who remembers the struggles of his own soul, will not, surely, judge yours like a hard and unfeeling master. Acquainted with the inmost recesses of human nature, he perceives the sincerity of your intentions; he sees the combat you maintain; he knows how much of your present confusion and disorder is to be imputed, not to your inclination and will, but to an infirm, an aged or diseased body, or to a weak and wounded spirit; and therefore will be far from rejecting your attempts to serve him, on account of the infirmities which you lament. He hears the voice of those secret aspirations which you are unable to express in words, or to form into prayer. Every penitential tear which your contrition sheds, pleads your cause more powerfully with him, than all the arguments with which you could fill your mouth. II.

* Mark, iv. 33.

II. From our Saviour's experience of human misery, we may juftly hope that he will fo compaffionately regard our diftreffed eftate, as to prevent us from being loaded with unneceffary troubles. He will not wantonly add affliction to the afflicted; nor willingly crufh what he fees to be already broken. In the courfe of that high adminiftration which he now exercifes, he may indeed judge certain intermixtures of adverfity to be proper for our improvement. Thefe are trials of virtue through which all, without exception, muft pafs. Rugged was the road by which our divine Mediator himfelf went before us to glory; and by becoming our companion in diftrefs, he meant to reconcile us to our lot. He ennobled adverfity, by fharing it with us. He raifed poverty from contempt, by affuming it for his own condition. The feverity of his trials tends to lighten ours. When the general of an army lies on the fame hard ground, drinks of the fame cold ftream, carries the fame weight of armour with the loweft centinel, can any of his foldiers repine at what they endure?

Whatever afflictions our Lord may judge to be neceffary for us, of this we may reft affured, that he will deal them forth, not with harfh and imperious authority, but with the tendernefs of one, who knows from experience how deeply the human heart is wounded by every ftroke of adverfity. He will not lay more upon us than he fees we are able to bear. " Though he caufe grief, yet will he have " compaffion according to the multitude of his tender mercies. He " willl ftay his rough wind in the day of the eaft wind:"* For it is his ftate, but not his nature, which is now changed. Notwithftanding his high exaltation, he ftill retains the compaffionate fentiments of " the man of forrows." Still, we are affured by an infpired writer, " he is not afhamed to call us his brethren."† And with the heart of a brother he regards thofe few and troubled days, fuch as his own once were, which good men are doomed to pafs in this evil world.

From his compaffion, indeed, we are not to expect that fond indulgence or unfeafonable relief by which the weak pity of men frequently injures its objects. It is to the material interefts, more than to the prefent cafe, of good men, that he attends. When under the impatience of forrow we exclaim, "Hath he forgotten to be gra- " cious? hath he in anger fhut up his tender mercies?" we recollect not in whofe hands we are. His compaffion is not diminifhed when its operations are moft concealed. It continues equally to flow, though the channels by which it is conducted towards us lie too deep

* Ifaiah, xxvii. x.   † Heb. ii. 11.   for

for our obfervation. Amidft our prefent ignorance of what is good or ill for us in this life, it is fufficient for us to know, that the immediate adminiftration of univerfal government is placed in the hands of the moft attentive and compaffionate friend of mankind. How greatly does this confideration alleviate the burden of human woe! How happily does it connect with the awful difpenfations of religion the mildeft ideas of tendernefs and humanity!

III. The text leads us to hope, that amidft all the infirmities of our ftate, both under the temptations and under the diftreffes of life, our bleffed Lord will afford us a proper meafure of affiftance and fupport. *In that he hath fuffered being tempted, he is able to fuccour them who either fuffer, or are tempted;** that is, he is perfectly qualified for difcharging this beneficent office; he knows exactly where the wound bleeds, where the burden preffes, what relief will prove moft feafonable, and how it can be moft fuccefsfully applied. The manner in which it is conveyed by him to the heart we may be at a lofs to explain; but no argument can be thence drawn againft the credibility of the fact. The operations which the power of God carries on in the natural world, are no lefs myfterious than thofe which we are taught to believe that his fpirit performs in the moral world. If we can give no account of what is every day before our eyes, how a feed becomes a tree, or how the child rifes into a man, is it any wonder that we fhould be unable to explain how virtue is fupported, and conftancy ftrengthened, by God within the heart? If men by their counfels and fuggeftions can influence the minds of one another, muft not divine fuggeftion and counfel produce a much greater effect? Surely, the Father of Spirits muft, by a thoufand ways, have accefs to the fpirits which he has made, fo as to give them what determination, or impart to them what affiftance he thinks proper, without injuring their frame, or difturbing their rational powers.

Accordingly, whenever any notions of religion have taken place among mankind, this belief has in fome meafure prevailed, that, to the virtuous under diftrefs, aid was communicated from above. This fentiment is fo congruous to our natural impreffions of the divine benignity, that both among poets and philofophers of ancient times it was a favourite idea, and often occurs in their writings. But what among them was no more than loofe conjecture or feeble hope,

* *Heb.* ii. 18.

hope, has received full confirmation from the gospel of Christ. Not only is the promise of divine assistance expresly given to Christians, but their faith in that promise is strengthened by an argument which must carry conviction to every heart. If Christ had full experience of the insufficiency of human nature to overcome the difficulties wherewith it is now surrounded, will he withhold from his followers that grace without which he sees they must perish in the evil day? If in the season of his temptation and distress, an angel was sent from heaven *to strengthen him*,† shall no celestial messenger be employed by him on the like kind errand to those whom he styles his brethren? Can we believe that he who once *bore our griefs and carried our sorrows* will, from that height of glory to which he is now exalted, look down upon us here contending with the storm of adversity, labouring to follow his steps through the steep and difficult paths of virtue, exposed on every side to arrows aimed against us by the powers of darkness; and that, seeing our distress and hearing our supplications, he will remain an unconcerned spectator, without vouchsafing us either assistance to support our frailty, or protection to screen us amidst surrounding dangers? Where were then the benevolence of a divine Nature? Where, the compassion of that Mediator who was trained to mercy in the school of sorrow? Far from us be such ungrateful suspicions of the generous friend of human kind!—Let us exert ourselves as we can, and we shall be assisted. Let us pray, and we shall be heard; for there is one to present our prayers, whom *the Father heareth always*. These, will he say, are my followers on earth, passing through that thorny path of temptation and sorrow which I once trode. *Now I am no more in the world: but these are in the world. Holy Father! thine they were, and thou gavest them me. Keep them through thine own name. Sanctify them through thy truth. Keep them from the evil one; that they may be where I am, and may behold the glory which thou hast given me.**

Such is the comfort which arises to us from our Saviour's participation of the infirmities of human nature; and thus it may be applied to various situations of anxiety and distress.

WHEN we review what has been said, it is necessary that, in the first place, I guard you against a certain misimprovement which may be made of this doctrine. The amiable view which it gives of our Lord's

† *Luke*, xxii. 43.   * *John*, xvii.

Lord's clemency may flatter fome men with unwarrantable hopes, and lead them to imagine, that in his experience of human weaknefs an apology is to be found for every crime. Perfons of this character muft be taught, that his compaſſion differs widely from that undiftinguiſhing and capricious indulgence which is fometimes found among men. It is the compaſſion of an impartial mind, enlightened by wifdom, and guided by juſtice, extending to the frailties of the fincere, but not to the fins of the prefumptuous, and leaft of all to the crimes of thofe who encourage themfelves in evil from the hope that they ſhall meet with compaſſion.

A courfe of deliberate guilt admits of no apology from the weaknefs of human nature. For notwithſtanding all the infirmities incident to it, no man is under a neceſſity of being wicked. So far is our Saviour's experience of our nature from affording any ground of hope to prefumptuous offenders, that it ought to fill them with terrour. For it ſhews them how thoroughly qualified he is to difcriminate accurately the characters of men, and to mark the boundaries between frailty and perverfenefs. He who from his own feelings well knows all the workings of the human heart clearly difcerns how different their temper is from what was once his own. He perceives that vice, not virtue, is their choice; and that, inftead of refifting temptation, they refift confcience. He fees that infirmity affords them no excufe; and that the real caufe of their acting a criminal part, is not becaufe they cannot do better, but, in truth, becaufe they will not. Having forfeited every title to compaſſion, they are left in the hands of juſtice; and according *as they have fown,* they muft expect *to reap.*

BUT, in the next place, to fuch as are fincere and upright, the doctrine which I have illuſtrated affords high encouragement, and powerfully recommends the Chriſtian Religion. It places that religion in its proper point of view, as a medicinal plan, intended both for the recovery of mankind from guilt, and for their confolation under trouble. *The law was given by Mofes; but grace and truth came by Jefus Chrift.* The law was a difpenfation of mere authority. The Gofpel is a difpenfation, not of authority only, but of relief. If it difcovers new duties, and impofes new obligations, it opens alſo fources of comfort which were before unknown to the world.

A Mediator between God and his creatures was an object after which men in all nations, and under all forms of religion, had long

and

and anxiously fought. The follies of superstition have served to disclose to us, in this instance, the sentiments of nature. The whole religion of Paganism was a system of mediation and intercession. Depressed by a conscious sense of guilt, nature shrunk at the thought of adventuring on a direct approach to the Sovereign of the universe; and laboured to find out some auspicious introductor to that awful presence. With blind and trembling eagerness, the nations fled to subordinate deities, to tutelar gods, and to departed spirits, as their patrons and advocates above. Them they studied to sooth with such costly gifts, such pompous rites, or such humble supplications, as they thought might incline them to favour their cause, and to support their interest with the Supreme Divinity. While mankind were bewildered in this darkness, the Gospel not only revealed the true Mediator, who in this view may be justly called *the desire of all nations*, but placed his character and office in a light most admirably fitted, as has been shewn in this Discourse, to support the interest of virtue in the world; and to encourage the humble, without flattering the presumptuous. What plan of religion could be more suited to the circumstances of man, or more worthy of the goodness of his Creator? What more animating to the pious worshipper, in performing those solemn acts of devotion to which we are called by the service of this day?

I cannot conclude without taking notice how remarkably this dispensation of religion is calculated to promote a spirit of humanity and compassion among men, by those very means which it employs for inspiring devotion towards God. We are now drawing nigh to the Supreme Being through a Mediator, for whose compassion we pray on account of the experience which he has had of our frailty. We trust, that having been acquainted with distress, he *will not despise nor abhor the affliction of the afflicted.* The argument by which we plead for his compassion, concludes still more strongly for mutual charity, and sympathy with one another. He who, in the midst of the common sufferings of life, feels not for the distressed; he who relents not at his neighbour's griefs, nor scans his failings with the eye of a brother, must be sensible that he excludes himself from the commiseration of Christ. He makes void the argument by which he pleads for his mercy; nay, he establishes a precedent against himself. Thus the Christian religion approves itself as worthy of God, by connecting

ing devotion in strict union with charity. As in its precepts the love of God and the love of man are joined, so in its institutions the exercise of both is called forth; and to worship God through the mediation of a compassionate High Priest, necessarily supposes in the worshippers a spirit of compassion towards their own brethren.

SERMON

SERMON XXI.

On the LOVE of PRAISE.

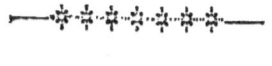

John, xii. 43.

For they loved the praise of men more than the praise of God.

THE state of man on earth is manifestly designed for the trial of his virtue. Temptations every where occur; and perpetual vigilance and attention are required. There is no passion, or principle of action in his nature, which may not, if left to itself, betray him into some criminal excess. Corruption gains entrance, not only by those passions which are apparently of dangerous tendency, such as covetousness and love of pleasure; but by means of those also which are seemingly the most fair and innocent, such as the desire of esteem and praise. Of this the text suggests a remarkable instance. When our Lord appeared in the land of Judea, the purity of his doctrine, and the evidence of his miracles, procured him a considerable number of followers, chiefly among the lower classes of men. But the Pharisees, who were the leading and fashionable sect, galled with the freedom of his reproofs, decried him as an impostor. Hence it came to pass, that though *some of the rulers believed in him, yet, because of the Pharisees, they did not confess him.* Rulers, persons who, by their rank and education, ought to have been superiour to any popular prejudice, were so far overawed by the opinions of others, as to stifle their conviction, to dissemble their faith, and to join with the prevailing party in condemning one whom in their hearts they revered: for which this reason is given, that *they loved the praise of men more than the praise of God.* Since, then, the love of praise can mislead men into such culpable and dishonest conduct, let us, with some attention, examine the nature of this passion. Let us consider how far it is an allowable principle of action; when it begins to be criminal; and upon what accounts we ought to guard against its acquiring the entire ascendant.

WE are intended by Providence to be connected with one another in society. Single unassisted individuals could make small advances towards any valuable improvement. By means of society our wants are supplied, and our lives rendered comfortable; our capacities are enlarged, and our virtuous affections called forth into proper exercise. In order to confirm our mutual connection, it was necessary that some attracting power, which had the effect of drawing men together, and strengthening the social ties, should pervade the human system. Nothing could more happily fulfil this purpose, than our being so formed as to desire the esteem, and to delight in the good opinion, of each other. Had such a propensity been wanting, and selfish principles left to occupy its place, society must have proved an unharmonious and discordant state. Instead of mutual attraction, a repulsive power would have prevailed. Among men who had no regard to the approbation of one another, all intercourse would have been jarring and offensive. For the wisest ends, therefore, the desire of praise was made an original and powerful principle in the human breast.

To a variety of good purposes it is subservient, and on many occasions co-operates with the principle of virtue. It awakens us from sloth, invigorates activity, and stimulates our efforts to excel. It has given rise to most of the splendid, and to many of the useful enterprises of men. It has animated the patriot, and fired the hero. Magnanimity, generosity, and fortitude are what all mankind admire. Hence such as were actuated by the desire of extensive fame, have been prompted to deeds which either participated of the spirit, or, at least, carried the appearance of distinguished virtue. The desire of praise is generally connected with all the finer sensibilities of human nature. It affords a ground on which exhortation, council, and reproof can work a proper effect. Whereas to be entirely destitute of this passion, betokens an ignoble mind, on which no moral impression is easily made. Where there is no desire of praise, there will be also no sense of reproach; and if that be extinguished, one of the principal guards of virtue is removed, and the path opened to many opprobrious pursuits. He whose countenance never glowed with shame, and whose heart never beat at the sound of praise, is not destined for any honourable distinction; is likely to grovel in the sordid quest of gain, or to slumber life away in the indolence of selfish pleasures.

Abstracting from the sentiments which are connected with the love of praise as a principle of action, the esteem of our fellow-creatures is an
object

object which, on account of the advantages it brings, may be lawfully pursued. It is necessary to our success in every fair and honest undertaking. Not only our private interest, but our public usefulness, depends in a great measure upon it. The sphere of our influence is contracted or enlarged in proportion to the degree in which we enjoy the good opinion of the public. Men listen with an unwilling ear to one whom they do not honour; while a respected character adds weight to example, and authority to council. To desire the esteem of others for the sake of its effects, is not only allowable, but in many cases is our duty; and to be totally indifferent to praise or censure, is so far from being a virtue, that it is a real defect in character.

But while the love of praise is admitted to be a natural, and, in so many respects, an useful principle of action, we are to observe, that it is entitled to no more than our secondary regard. It has its boundary set; by transgressing which, it is at once transformed from an innocent into a most dangerous passion. More sacred and venerable principles claim the chief direction of human conduct. All the good effects which we have ascribed to the desire of praise, are produced by it when remaining in a subordinate station. But when passing its natural line, it becomes the ruling spring of conduct; when the regard which we pay to the opinions of men, encroaches on that reverence which we owe to the voice of conscience and the sense of duty; the love of praise having then gone out of its proper place, instead of improving, corrupts; and instead of elevating, debases our nature. The proportion which this passion holds to other principles of action is what renders it either innocent or criminal. The crime with which the Jewish rulers are charged in the text, was not that they loved the praise of men; but that they loved it *more than the praise of God*.

Even in cases where there is no direct competition between our duty and our fancied honour, between the praise of men and the praise of God, the passion for applause may become criminal by occupying the place of a better principle. When vain glory usurps the throne of virtue; when ostentation produces actions which conscience ought to have dictated; such actions, however specious, have no claim to moral or religious praise. We know that good deeds, done merely *to be seen of men*, lose their reward with God. If, on occasion of some trying conjuncture, which makes us hesitate concerning our line of conduct, the first question which occurs to us be, not whether an action is right in itself, and such as a good man ought to perform, but whether it is such as will find acceptance with the world, and be favourable to our fame, the conclusion is too evident, that the desire of applause has obtained an undue ascendant. What a wise and good man ought to study, is to preserve his mind free from any such solicitude concerning praise, as may be in hazard of overcoming his sense of duty. The approbation of men he may wish to obtain, as far as is consistent with the approbation of God. But when both cannot be enjoyed together, there ought to be no suspense. He is to retire contented with the testimony of a good conscience; and to show, by the firmness of his behaviour, that, in the cause of truth and virtue, he is superior to all opinion.—Let us now proceed to consider the arguments which should support such a spirit, and guard us against the improper influence of praise or censure in the course of our duty.

In the first place, the praise of men is not an object of such value in itself as to be entitled to become the leading principle of conduct. We degrade our character when we allow it more than subordinate regard. Like other worldly goods, it is apt to dazzle us, with a false lustre; but if we would ascertain its true worth, let us reflect both on whom it is bestowed, and from whom it proceeds. Were the applause of the world always the reward of merit; were it appropriated to such alone as by real abilities, or by worthy actions, are entitled to rise above the crowd, we might justly be flattered by possessing a rare and valuable distinction. But how far is this from being the case in fact? How often have the despicable and the vile, by dexterously catching the favour of the multitude, soared upon the wings of popular applause, while the virtuous and the deserving have been either buried in obscurity, or obliged to encounter the attacks of unjust reproach? The laurels which human praise confers, are withered and blasted by the unworthiness of those who wear them. Let the man who is vain of public favour be humbled by the reflection that, in the midst of his success, he is mingled with a crowd of impostors and deceivers, of hypocrites and enthusiasts, of ignorant pretenders and superficial reasoners, who, by various arts, have attained as high a rank as himself in temporary fame.

We may easily be satisfied that applause will be often shared by the undeserving, if we allow ourselves to consider from whom it proceeds. When it is the approbation of the wise only and the good which is pursued, the love of praise may then be accounted to contain itself within just bounds, and to run in its proper channel. But the testimony of the discerning few, modest and unassuming as they commonly are, forms but a small part of the public voice. It seldom amounts to more than a whisper, which amidst the general clamour is drowned. When the love of praise has taken possession of the mind, it confines not itself to an object so limited. It grows into an appetite for indiscriminate praise. And who are they that confer this praise? A mixed multitude of men, who in their whole conduct are guided by humour and caprice, far more than by reason; who admire false appearances, and pursue false gods; who enquire superficially, and judge rashly; whose sentiments are for the most part erroneous, always changeable, and often inconsistent. Nor let any one imagine, that by looking above the crowd, and courting the praise of the fashionable and the great, he makes sure of true honour. There are a great vulgar, as well as a small. Rank often makes no difference in the understandings of men, or in their judicious distribution of praise. Luxury, pride, and vanity, have frequently as much influence in corrupting the sentiments of the great, as ignorance, bigotry, and prejudice, have in misleading the opinions of the crowd.—And is it to such judges as these that you submit the supreme direction of your conduct? Do you stoop to court their favour as your chief distinction, when an object of so much juster and higher ambition is presented to you in *the praise of God?* God is the only unerring Judge of what is excellent. His approbation alone is the substance, all other praise is but the shadow, of honour. The character which you bear in his sight is your only real one. How contemptible does it render you, to be indifferent with respect to this, and to be solicitous about a name alone, a fictitious, imaginary character, which has no existence except in the opinions of a few weak and credulous men around you? They see no farther than the outside of things. They can judge of you by actions only; and not by the comprehensive view of all your actions, but by such merely as you have had opportunity of bringing forth to public notice. But the Sovereign of the world beholds you in every light in which you can be placed. The silent virtues of a generous purpose and a pious heart attracts his notice equally with the most splendid deeds. From him you may reap the praise of good actions which you had no opportunity of performing. For he sees them in their principle; he judges of you by your intentions; he

knows

knows what you have done. You may be in his eyes a hero or a martyr, without undergoing the labours of the one, or the sufferings of the other. His infpection, therefore, opens a much wider field for praife, than what the world can afford you; and for praife, too, certainly far more illuftrious in the eye of reafon. Every real artift ftudies to approve himfelf to fuch as are knowing in his art. To their judgment he appeals. On their approbation, he refts his character, and not on the praife of the unfkilled and rude. In the higheft art of all, that of life and conduct, fhall the opinions of ignorant men come into the moft diftant competition with his approbation who is the fearcher of all hearts, and the ftandard of all perfection?—The teftimony of his praife is not indeed, as yet, openly beftowed. But though the voice of the Almighty found not in your ears, yet by confcience, his facred vicegerent, it is capable of being conveyed to your heart. The fofteft whifper of divine approbation is fweeter to the foul of a virtuous man, than the loudeft fhouts of that tumultuary applaufe which proceeds from the world.

Confider, farther, how narrow and circumfcribed in its limits that fame is which the vain-glorious man fo eagerly purfues. In order to fhew him this, I fhall not bid him reflect that it is confined to a fmall diftrict of the earth; and that when he looks a little beyond the region which he inhabits, he will find himfelf as much unknown as the moft obfcure perfon around him. I fhall not defire him to confider, that in the gulph of oblivion, where all human memorials are fwallowed up, his name and fame muft foon be inevitably loft. He may imagine that ample honours remain to gratify ambition, though his reputation extend not over the whole globe, nor laft till the end of time. But let him calmly reflect, that within the narrow boundaries of that country to which he belongs, and during that fmall portion of time which his life fills up, his reputation, great as he may fancy it to be, occupies no more than an inconfiderable corner. Let him think what multitudes of thofe among whom he dwells are totally ignorant of his name and character; how many imagine themfelves too important to regard him; how many are too much occupied with their own wants and purfuits to pay him the leaft attention; and where his reputation is in any degree fpread, how often it has been attacked, and how many rivals are daily rifing to abate it: Having attended to thefe circumftances, he will find fufficient materials for humiliation in the midft of the higheft applaufe.——From all thefe confiderations it clearly appears, that though the efteem of our fellow-creatures be

pleafing

pleasing, and the pursuit of it, in a moderate degree, be fair and lawful, yet that it affords no such object to desire, as entitles it to be a ruling principle.

In the second place, an excessive love of praise never fails to undermine the regard due to conscience, and to corrupt the heart. It turns off the eye of the mind from the ends which it ought chiefly to keep in view; and sets up a false light for its guide. Its influence is the more dangerous, as the colour which it assumes is often fair; and its garb and appearance are nearly allied to that of virtue. The love of glory, I before admitted, may give birth to actions which are both splendid and useful. At a distance they strike the eye with uncommon brightness; but on a nearer and stricter survey, their lustre is often tarnished. They are found to want that sacred and venerable dignity which characterises true virtue. Little passions and selfish interests entered into the motives of those who performed them. They were jealous of a competitor. They sought to humble a rival. They looked round for spectators to admire them. All is magnanimity, generosity, and courage, to public view. But the ignoble source whence these seeming virtues take their rise is hidden. Without, appears the hero; within, is found the man of dust and clay. Consult such as have been intimately connected with the followers of renown; and seldom or never will you find that they held them in the same esteem with those who viewed them from afar. There is nothing, except simplicity of intention, and purity of principle, that can stand the test of near approach and strict examination.

But supposing the virtue of vain-glorious men not to be always false, it certainly cannot be depended upon as firm or sure. Constancy and steadiness are to be looked for from him only whose conduct is regulated by a sense of what is right; *whose praise is not of men, but of God;* whose motive to discharge his duty is always the same. Change, as much as you please, the situation of such a man; let applause or let censure be his lot; let the public voice which this day has extolled him, to-morrow as loudly decry him; on the tenour of his behaviour these changes produce no effect. He moves in a higher sphere. As the sun in his orbit is not interrupted by the mists and storms of the atmosphere below, so, regardless of the opinions of men, *through honour and dishonour, through good report and bad report,* he pursues the path which conscience has marked out. Whereas the apparent virtues of that man whose eye is fixed on the world, are precarious and temporary. Supported only by circumstances, occasions, and particular

cular regards, they fluctuate and fall with thefe. Excited by public admiration, they difappear when it is withdrawn; like thofe exhalations which, raifed by heat from the earth, glitter in the air with momentary fplendour, and then fall back to the ground from whence they fprung.

The intemperate love of praife not only weakens the true principles of probity, by fubftituting inferiour motives in their ftead, but frequently alfo impels men to actions which are directly criminal. It obliges them to follow the current of popular opinion whitherfoever it may carry them; and hence *fhipwreck* is often made both *of faith and of a good confcience*. According as circumftances lead them to court the acclamations of the multitude, or to purfue the applaufe of the great, vices of different kinds will ftain their character. In one fituation they will make hypocritical profeffions of religion. In another they will be afhamed of their Redeemer, and of his words. They will be afraid to appear in their own form, or to utter their genuine fentiments. Their whole character will become fictitious, opinions will be affumed, fpeech and behaviour modelled, and even the countenance formed, as prevailing tafte exacts. From one who has fubmitted to fuch proftitution for the fake of praife, you can no longer expect fidelity or attachment on any trying occafion. In private life, he will be a timorous and treacherous friend. In public conduct, he will be fupple and verfatile; ready to defert the caufe which he had efpoufed, and to veer with every fhifting wind of popular favour. In fine, all becomes unfound and hollow in that heart, where, inftead of regard to the divine approbation, there reigns the fovereign defire of pleafing men.

In the third place, this paffion, when it becomes predominant, moft commonly defeats its own end, and deprives men of the honour which they are fo eager to gain. Without preferving liberty and independence, we can never command refpect. That fervility of fpirit which fubjects us to the opinions of others, and renders us tributaries to the world for the fake of applaufe, is what all mankind defpife. They look up with reverence to one who, unawed by their cenfures, acts according to his own fenfe of things, and follows the free impulfe of an honourable mind. But him who hangs totally on their judgment, they confider as their vaffal. They even enjoy a malignant pleafure in humbling his vanity, and withholding that praife which he is feen to court. By artifice and fhow he may fhine for a time in the public eye; but it is only as long as he can fupport the belief of acting from principle. When the inconfiftencies into which he falls detect his character, his reputation passes away like the pageant of a day. No man ever obtained lasting fame who did not, on several occasions, contradict the prejudices of popular opinion.

There is no course of behaviour which will at all times please all men. That which pleases most generally, and which only commands durable praise, is religion and virtue. Sincere piety towards God, kind affection to men, and fidelity in the discharge of all the duties of life; a conscience pure and undefiled; a heart firm to justice and to truth, superior to all terrours that would shake, and insensible of all pleasures that would betray it; unconquerable by the opposition of the world, and resigned to God alone; these are the qualities which render a man truly respectable and great. Such a character may, in evil times, incur unjust reproach. But the clouds which envy or prejudice has gathered around it will gradually disperse; and its brightness will come forth, in the end, as the noon-day. As soon as it is thoroughly known, it finds a witness in every breast. It forces approbation even from the most degenerate. The human heart is so formed as to be attuned, if we may use the expression, to its praise. In fact, it is this firm and inflexible virtue, this determined regard to principle beyond all opinion, which has crowned the characters of such as now stand highest in the rolls of lasting fame. The truly illustrious are they who did not court the praise of the world, but who performed the actions which deserved it. They were perhaps traduced, in their life time, by those whom they opposed. But posterity has done them ample justice; and they are the men whom the voice of ages now concurs in celebrating. *The memorial of virtue is immortal; because it is approved of God and of men. When it is present, men take example at it; and when it is gone, they desire it. It weareth a crown, and triumpheth for ever; having gotten the victory; striving for undefiled rewards.**

In the fourth place, as an immoderate passion for human praise is dangerous to virtue, and unfavourable to true honour, so it is destructive of self-enjoyment and inward peace. Regard to the praise of God prescribes a simple and consistent tenour of conduct, which in all situations is the same; which engages us in no perplexities, and requires no artful refinement. *Walking uprightly, we walk surely,* because we tread an even and open path. But he who turns aside from the straight road of duty in order to gain applause, involves himself in an intricate labyrinth. He will be often embarrassed concerning the course which he ought to hold. His mind will be always on the stretch. He will be

---

* *Wisdom of Solomon,* iv. 1, 2.

be obliged to liften with anxious attention to every whifper of the popular voice. The demands of thofe mafters whom he has fubmitted to ferve, will prove frequently contradictory and inconfiftent. He has prepared a yoke for his neck which he muft refolve to bear, how much foever it may gall him.

The toils of virtue are honourable. The mind is fupported under them by the confcioufnefs of acting a right and becoming part. But the labours to which he is doomed who is enflaved to the defire of praife, are aggravated by reflection both on the uncertainty of the recompence which he purfues, and on the debafement to which he fubmits. Confcience will, from time to time, remind him of the improper facrifices which he has made, and of the forfeiture which he has incurred, of the praife of God for the fake of praife from men. Suppofe him to receive all the rewards which the miftaken opinion of the world can beftow, its loudeft applaufe will often be unable to drown the upbraidings of an inward voice; and if a man is reduced to be afhamed of himfelf, what avails it him to be careffed by others?

But, in truth, the reward towards which he looks who propofes human praife as his ultimate object, will be always flying, like a fhadow before him. So capricious and uncertain, fo fickle and mutable is the favour of the multitude, that it proves the moft unfatisfactory of all purfuits in which men can be engaged. He who fets his heart on it, is preparing for himfelf perpetual mortifications. If the greateft and beft can feldom retain it long, we may eafily believe that from the vain and undeferving it will fuddenly efcape. There is no character but what on fome fide is vulnerable by cenfure. He who lifts himfelf up to the obfervation and notice of the world, is, of all men, the leaft likely to avoid it. For he draws upon himfelf a thoufand eyes that will narrowly infpect him in every part. Every opportunity will be watched of bringing him down to the common level. His errours will be more divulged, and his infirmities more magnified, than thofe of others. In proportion to his eagernefs for praife will be his fenfibility to reproach. Nor is it reproach alone that will wound him. He will be as much dejected by filence and neglect. He puts himfelf under the power of every one to humble him, by witholding expected praife. Even when praife is beftowed he is mortified by its being either faint or trite. He pines when his reputation ftagnates. The degree of applaufe to which he has been accuftomed grows infipid; and to be always praifed from the fame topics, becomes at laft much the fame with not being praifed at all.

All

All these chagrins and disquietudes are happily avoided by him who keeps so troublesome a passion within its due bounds; who is more desirous of being truly worthy than of being thought so; who pursues the praise of the world with manly temperance, and in subordination to the praise of God. He is neither made giddy by the intoxicating vapour of applause, nor humbled and cast down by the unmerited attacks of censure. Resting on a higher approbation, he enjoys himself in peace, whether human praise stays with him, or flies away. *With me it is a small thing to be judged of you, or of man's judgment. He that judgeth me is the Lord. My witness is in Heaven, and my record is on high.*

In the fifth and last place, the advantages which redound from the praise of men, are not such as can bear to be put in competition with those which flow from the praise of God. The former are necessarily confined within the verge of our present existence. The latter follow us beyond the grave, and extend through all eternity. Not only is the praise of men limited in its effects to this life, but also to particular situations of it. In the days of health and ease it may brighten the sunshine of prosperity. It may then sooth the ear with pleasing accents, and gratify the imagination with fancied triumphs. But when the distressful seasons of life arrive, it will be found altogether hollow and unsubstantial: And surely, the value of any possession is to be chiefly estimated by the relief which it can bring us in the time of our greatest need. When the mind is cast down with sorrow and grief, when sickness spreads its gloom around us, or death rises in awful prospect to our view, the opinions and the discourses of the world will appear trifling and insignificant. To one who is occupied with nearer and more affecting interests, the praise or the censure of the world will seem like the noise of distant voices, in which he has small concern. But then is the season when the praise of God supports and upholds the labouring soul. Brought home to the heart by the testimony of a good conscience, and by *the divine Spirit bearing witness with our spirits*, it inspires fortitude, and produces a *peace which passeth understanding*.

At present we behold an irregular and disordered state of things. Virtue is often deprived of its proper honours, and vice usurps them in its stead. The characters of men are mistaken; and ignorance and folly dispose of human applause. But the day hastens apace which shall close this scene of errours, and vindicate the rights of justice and truth.

Then

Then *shall he rendered to every man according to his works.* Envy shall no longer have the power of obscuring merit, nor popular prejudices be able to support the undeserving. Hidden worth shall be brought to light, and secret crimes revealed. Many who passed through the world in the silent obscurity of humble but steady goodness, shall be distinguished as the favourites of heaven; while the proud, the ambitious, and the vain, are left to everlasting dishonour. The great Judge hath declared, that *whosoever has been ashamed of him and of his words, of that man shall he be ashamed when he cometh in the glory of his Father, with all the holy angels.* Every departure from duty shall at the period of final distribution, terminate in ignominy. True honour and true virtue shall be seen to coincide; and when all human fame has passed away like smoke, the only praise which shall be for ever remembered is that divine testimony, *Well done, thou good and faithful servant; enter thou into the joy of thy Lord.*

These arguments clearly show the importance of preserving the love of praise under proper subordination to the principle of duty. In itself, it is an useful motive to action; but when allowed to extend its influence too far, it corrupts the whole character, and produces guilt, disgrace, and misery. To be entirely destitute of it, is a defect. To be governed by it, is depravity. The proper adjustment of the several principles of action in human nature, is a matter that deserves our highest attention. For when any one of them becomes either too weak or too strong, it endangers both our virtue and our happiness. *Keep thy heart therefore with all diligence;* pray that God would enable thee to keep it with success; *for out of the heart are the issues of life.*

END OF THE FIRST VOLUME.

www.ingramcontent.com/pod-product-compliance
Lightning Source LLC
Chambersburg PA
CBHW032101220426
43664CB00008B/1086